Center of Mass

A Lady Cop's Career on DC's
Violent Streets

Deborah R. Wolf

Preface

When I think back on my career as one of the first female Patrol Officers on the DC Metropolitan Police Department, the words "Center of Mass" come to mind.

The first reason is that the Police District I was assigned to was located right smack in the middle of Washington, DC. It was by far the smallest in the city compared to the other six Districts. At the time, it was so small because it had the highest percentage of crime. It was also the only Police District that didn't border "foreign" territories like Maryland or Virginia. When looking at the Third District on a map, those three words, "Center of Mass" only seem appropriate.

Center of Mass is also a term familiar to anyone who has learned to fire a weapon. Instructors will continually remind their students to aim for Center of Mass. It actually means to try and shoot the torso, which in all probability will eliminate the immediate threat.

My life as a Police Officer could also be correlated to the Center of Mass concept. For so long, I was surrounded by violence and insanity that after awhile it almost seemed normal. From my understanding, over 98% of Police Officers never fire their weapon in the line of duty. I wish I could say the same, but I cannot.

This is my story to the best of my recollection. Some of the dates may not be totally accurate and I changed several names because my intent is not to embarrass anyone after all these years. But everything is factual and well documented. I hope that anyone who reads this will come away with some understanding of just how difficult, yet rewarding the life of a street cop truly is.

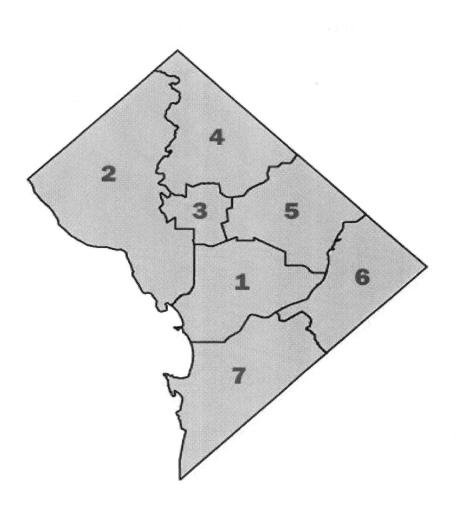

Dedication

I would like to dedicate this book to Prince William County, Virginia Police Officer Ashley Marie Guindon. Officer Guindon was shot and killed on February 27, 2016. She had just been sworn in the previous day and this was her very first tour of duty. She was also a member of the U.S. Marine Corps Reserve. Although I did not know her personally, she so reminded me of myself when I was her age. We even resembled each other in photographs, with the pulled back hair and uncertain smile.

Although my events happened long before Ashley was even born, I can't help but wonder how I was able to escape with my life and she was not. Sometimes it's just a matter of turning left at that intersection instead of right. If Rita Head had been standing to the left of the door when it popped open, she would have been the one to shoot David Leach and not me. If I hadn't taken Duke out of the cruiser, I wouldn't have had to shoot the dogs. And on and on and on. We can all "what if" our way through life but what a waste of time that would be.

Today, I choose not to dwell on the past or play the victim. I've come too far for that. Officer Guindon, I believe you would have been one hell of a cop. I wish we could have met but it wasn't meant to be. I promise though that you will never be forgotten. Ever.

1.

I graduated from Wilmington College in Wilmington, Ohio in June of 1973 with a BA in Sociology and a minor in History. Now what? Sometime before graduation, I went to Columbus to take an exam for the Department of Treasury. The only thing I recall is that we looked at photographs of everyday scenes for a certain period of time. Then the pictures were removed and we had to answer questions like "Is the man in the overcoat wearing a hat?" Or "Is the woman in the red dress carrying a purse?" Well I certainly hope so! Only a man would ask such a dumb question. I must have missed the hat and purse though because I never heard back from them. I don't even remember what kind of job I was going for in the first place.

So once again, now what? I decided I was going to get a job in Cincinnati and make that my permanent home since so many of my college friends lived around there. I picked up a copy of the Cincinnati Enquirer to look at the jobs in the classified section. This was when I first had an inkling that maybe something in law enforcement would be interesting. But back in the summer of 1973, there was only one job in Cincinnati, Ohio for women that even remotely smacked of law enforcement: Jail Matron. That was it. Take it or leave it. Now, I didn't ever want a job then, or now, that had the word 'Matron' in its title. Bye, bye, Cincinnati. I will miss your chili parlors though.

I was born in Bethesda, Maryland and spent about half my life there so it seemed only logical to return to that area and call it home.

Sometime during the summer I picked up a copy of the Washington Post and turned to the classifieds. Under job listings there was something listed for a social worker that paid $7,000 a year. That was for me! After all, I had just gotten my degree in that field and knew I could change the world at twenty-two. But wait! Next to the social work listing was a big announcement from the Metropolitan Police Department in DC saying they were recruiting Officers to join their team. I didn't give it much thought until I saw that the starting pay was $10,000. Now I'm no mathematical genius, but I knew that a $3,000 difference was huge back then.

So, without any further ado, I sent for an application and decided to become a cop in Washington, DC.

2.

This was during the age of affirmative action and the courts had recently ruled that women were to be given the same opportunities as men. This meant women would now be assigned to scout cars (DC's term for a patrol cruiser), and foot beats. Answering 911 calls and doing everything that comes with it. Before, women could only work in Youth Division or be a Jail Matron (not that word again).

From my understanding, it hadn't been all that long ago the scout cars were integrated. Now, for the most part, there had to be one White and one Black Officer assigned to each car. This probably caused a great deal of pain during the transition but by 1973, the situation was going relatively smoothly.

Then those damn courts had to really upset the applecart and allow Broads to come onboard! Really?!?! We all know that this is a man's job and these bitches need to get back behind the desks where they belong. Why, they couldn't possibly back me up when something serious went down. They're clearly not strong enough and besides I'm not working with someone who's PMSing half the time. No way! This job is dangerous enough as it is and I'm not babysitting some dame who will fall apart at the first sight of blood. Blah! Blah! Blah!

At the time I didn't know any of this because when I took the physical, I was told to lose 10 pounds before they would hire me. So it was all Atkins diet, all the time and the weight came right off.

After a few more blips, I was told to report to the recruitment office at Pennsylvania and Branch Ave SE on September 17, 1973 to be sworn in as a DC Metropolitan Police Officer.

I remember the office was in a strip mall and it was set up like a classroom with lots of desks. There were about 20 of us and we all stood, raised our right hand and promised to fairly enforce the law, support the Constitution and be a good American. Or something like that. Then after we sat down, a group of scruffy looking men came in and began slowly walking down the aisles, looking at each of us very intently. Sometimes, they would point at a recruit and say, "You come with me." No further explanation was given. It was kind of scary because I had no idea what they were doing. Of course, there was that part of me that wanted to be picked too. A tall blonde woman sitting next to me was

chosen and I was so pissed. She was obviously
special and I wasn't. Later, I found out
these people were selected to immediately go
undercover since they had no history with the
Department and weren't known by anybody. Even
decades later, I have a slight resentment I
wasn't picked and Janice Roddy was.

3.

Now that we were sworn in, I guessed
that the next thing we would do is start
classes at the Police Academy. I was ready,
or so I thought. Angie Dickenson was my role
model when she was The Policewoman on tv. I
could do this. I was young, dumb and by this
time, thin.
Just give me the address of the Academy
and I Am There! I was told it was in an area
called Blue Plains which was way the hell down
in SW. It turned out that Blue Plains was
actually a pretty name for the city's sewage
treatment plant. And just down the street was
a place that I had visited in 1962, when I was
eleven years old. It was a series of many
buildings that warehoused kids that had no
homes. It was called Junior Village and I
think a group from my parent's church in
Bethesda decided to go to appease their so
called White guilt and feel better about
themselves. Somehow, I got dragged along and
even after all this time, I remember the
experience vividly. We went into these rooms
filled with cribs overflowing with Black
babies and toddlers. They appeared to be
unkempt, loud and extremely unhappy. There
didn't seem to be anyone in charge and the
whole thing was very scary. Nobody told me
what the purpose of the trip was, but I really

didn't care. I just wanted to go home. So home we went, back to our white bread existence in all White Bethesda, Maryland. All White schools in all White neighborhoods. Segregation was never discussed and I didn't know enough to ask.

Now I was staying with my sister Jeanne, her husband and two young kids in Bladensburg, Maryland until I could get a place of my own. And that time had come. I found an efficiency apartment at 512 M St SW for $185 a month which was rather extravagant at the time. It was located in what was then called the New Southwest. What that meant was that in the late 1960's, a huge part of SW was completely destroyed in the name of urban development. There were all these grand plans, when in fact, countless numbers of people were displaced and beautiful, historic buildings torn down. The area never really recovered and even today, almost fifty years later, it still looks like shit. But I had my very own studio apartment. I was on top of the world.

4.

The $185 did not include parking because I couldn't quite fit that in the budget. So I was constantly on the move, trying to find the perfect spot, whether it was legal or not. None of it mattered because the car was registered in Pennsylvania to my parents and any and all tickets would never make it up to the Keystone state. Or so I thought. Also, DC had recently purchased several items called the Denver boot. Never heard of it, nor did I care (at the time anyway).

I was given a date and told to report
to Police headquarters at 300 Indiana Ave NW.
Was this related to the Police Academy? No
such luck. The Academy class wasn't going to
start for a couple of weeks so I was assigned
to work in an office doing filing until it
started. This was not what I signed up for but
I went through the motions and filed away.
At the end of two weeks, I reported to the
Property Division to get whatever I needed to
start the Academy. This included recruit
uniforms, Sam Browne belt with empty holster,
raincoat, boots, coats and I don't remember
what else except it was heavy, and jammed into
two large garbage bags. At the time, the 3rd
Street tunnel by the Capitol was not completed
so we were allowed to park there. I began
dragging these two bags down the street and as
I was crossing 4th Street, both bags ripped
open and most of my equipment was strewn all
over the middle of the intersection.
Just about then, a marked cruiser pulled up
and stopped. A cute, uniformed Officer jumped
out and began helping me pick up my stuff.
Since both bags were ripped, we put everything
in the trunk of his car and he drove me to the
parking area. He said his name was Dave and he
was a Crime Scene Search Officer in 1D. I
didn't really know what that meant but we
exchanged phone numbers and agreed to meet up
later.
        As I think about all the items that
were put in my possession that day, I'm
puzzled about something. I absolutely cannot
recall where and under what circumstances I
was given my badge. A Police Officer's badge
is probably the most personal piece of
property you will ever have. A badge number
is used for so many things. When a citizen is

angry at you, what is the first thing they demand? Your badge number. Every single document you write has your badge number written on it, right next to your signature. It becomes a part of you, and even years later I still use it in some capacity.

5.

I furnished my apartment with lots of secondhand furniture and even though it wouldn't ever appear in a magazine, it was mine and I felt all grown up at twenty-two. Across the street from my building was a shopping mall with a Safeway and Peoples Drug store. The neighborhood was still a bit shady and since I didn't have a service revolver yet, I carried my Police baton inside my jacket as a deterrent.

One evening, as I was returning home from Safeway, a man followed me into the building. I didn't pay him any attention until he exited the elevator on my floor and turned in the direction of my apartment. Was this guy going to try and mug me? As I continued to walk down the hall, I slowly removed the wooden baton and turned around. Now what? I waved it menacingly in his direction, secretly praying he would go away. Thank goodness he did because I had no idea what I would have done next. I had never in my life been in any kind of physical altercation. And this was what I had chosen for my life career? Little did I know how much violence would play such a significant part in my life.

My studio apartment was on the fifth floor and fairly small, but I had a balcony overlooking the Potomac River and National airport. The laundry room was downstairs and

one day I was there doing wash when a girl about my age came in with her basket. She was very friendly and we got to talking. When it came time to leave, she invited me to her apartment for a drink, which I accepted.
I stopped by later and she was there with a couple of girlfriends. The talk was easy and we all shared a little bit about ourselves. As I was talking, I mentioned I was a Police recruit about to start at the Academy. Well, these girls immediately freaked out and were doing everything they could to politely get rid of me. While this was going on, a huge Black guy walked in and my laundry room friend ran up to him and began frantically whispering in his ear. The only thing missing was that she wasn't jumping up and down, pointing at me.

That was my first personal experience with people that weren't real happy being around the Po Po. So I made my escape and never ran into any of them again.

6.

Finally the Big Day came to report to the Academy. I dressed in my Navy blue uniform pants, Navy blue long sleeve uniform shirt (with recruit patch on the left sleeve), black shoes, black belt and Navy blue "girl" clip on necktie. My hair was fairly long so it had to be pulled up enough that it didn't touch my shoulders.

After I arrived at 0630 hours, I saw that there were about sixty other young people, dressed just like me, milling nervously around the front entrance. At exactly 0700, several men came outside carrying clipboards. One of them began to loudly read off names and directed us into two groups. We were told to stand at attention and not say a word.

When the groups were formed, one of the men, a Sergeant, told us that these were the two recruit classes that were about to take place for the next eight weeks. The class I was in was 73-8. The seventy three was the year, and the eight was the eighth class held so far that year.

We were directed to the second floor where each class went to a separate classroom. We were seated alphabetically with our names taped to the front of the desk. The class was about 50/50 Black and White and about 25% women.

An older Black Sergeant entered the room and identified himself as Sgt. Smith. He said he would be one of our instructors. I always remembered him because one day he saw me with my hands in my pockets. In no uncertain terms, he told me that a Police Officer should never, ever have their hands in their pockets at Any Time. He said it was a safety issue because I could lose valuable time if I had to reach for a weapon and my hands were in my pockets. More than four decades later I can still hear him, and I cringe whenever I see an Officer on the street doing exactly that. I just want to go up and smack them, but so far I've restrained myself.

When I tell people today that I was only in the Academy for eight weeks, they can't believe it could possibly be that short amount of time. It was a bit out of the ordinary for one reason: The Christmas Detail. Every December, a large number of Officers were assigned to the Christmas Detail. These Officers directed traffic downtown, I guess to

keep all the shopping traffic from becoming
gridlocked. It seemed like every intersection
was covered in the heart of the city. And with
sixty young recruits currently in the Academy,
we were viewed as the "fresh meat" that would
immediately be assigned to the Christmas
Detail, so the veteran Officers could do real
Police work.

The Academy consisted of classroom
instruction, which included DC laws and Police
procedures. Also, PT inside the gym, and out
running a mile. When we ran the mile, the
women were put in front of the men and told we
better keep up or else. I think that pissed us
all off because every one of us ran as well,
if not better than the guys.

7.

PT in the gym was led by a big White
hulk of a guy who, as it turned out, wasn't
even a cop. He was a Police cadet, a frigging
teenager for goodness sake. And he was leading
the class as though he owned it. Which he
kinda did, because there was nothing we could
do but seethe while we were put through the
paces.

Later he did become the real Po Po, but
every time our paths crossed, I did the most
mature thing I could think of. I silently
scorned him as I stuck my nose in the air and
turned my head away. The last time I saw him,
he had gotten fat and lumpy. Karma is a bitch,
or so they say.

Aside from torturous exercises, we were
taught self-defense. This involved how to
properly hit someone with your baton
(pronounced ba' ton and not ba ton').

We were told to always aim for the shins and
not the head because there was the definite
possibility the person would try to grab the
stick in midair and use it on you. They're not
expecting to be smacked in the shins and it
was going to hurt like hell.

Also, we learned the choke hold, which
was later banned, because it was used
improperly several times and a couple of
people died. If done correctly, it's a very
practical tool that I became very proficient
at. It's really a shame that Officers are no
longer able utilize it.

So what is the choke hold and how do
you do it? If someone becomes combative and
you need to stop them in their tracks, you're
required to use the minimum amount of force
necessary to effect an arrest. If the suspect
(known as S-1 from now on), takes a fighting
stance, you can't shoot him as much as you may
want to.

In my case, as a woman, S-1 usually
ignored me and went after my partner as if I
wasn't there. This was a good thing because I
could then walk behind him without any problem
and place my right foot between his legs for
traction. In one motion, I brought my left arm
around his neck and quickly grabbed my left
wrist with my right hand. I then began pulling
backwards with the area of my arm between the
wrist and elbow against his windpipe. He would
be totally off balance and unable to escape my
grip. After a short period of time, he would
"go to sleep" and by the time he came to, the
handcuffs were on his wrists and he was
usually compliant. You just had to pay
attention and not suffocate him to death.

8

The Academy was pretty intense but very interesting, since I didn't know nothin' from nothin.' So much information was coming at us in every direction that at times it was overwhelming. But one day, an "older" Officer who was in the break room, took a group of us aside and told us our real education would come when we were out on the street. For the most part, this turned out to be completely true.

After a couple weeks, they told us we were going on a field trip to Lorton, Virginia to learn how to shoot. Lorton, at the time, was the site of a large prison where many of DC's criminals went to do their time. It was located about 25 miles south of the District, just off I-95. At the time, it was considered to be in the boondocks, and anyone who lived in the area never admitted they lived in Lorton, Virginia. It was a dirty word in the real estate market. Somebody who lived just up the road from the prison and had a sense of humor, hung a professionally made sign at the end of their driveway that read "Prison View Estate."

Just north of the prison, were hundreds of acres of untouched land. On this property was a large outdoor shooting range where we would learn to properly learn how to fire a .38 caliber Smith & Wesson six shot revolver. There were a few Colts in the mix but for the most part it was S & W. We loaded into several busses and drove Southbound on 95 to the Lorton exit. Then it was down an old country road for about a mile, past the prison walls and guard towers. I was in total awe since the only prisons I'd ever seen were in movies.

This place looked really old and it was, because it was built in 1910. It later closed in 2001 because of overcrowding and deterioration.

After the country road, we turned onto a very bumpy dirt road for another half mile. The busses parked and we got out and lined up in groups. There were several firearms instructors that announced we would be assigned our weapons. One then pointed to several cardboard boxes sitting on the ground. Inside and filled to the top were countless numbers of guns, all piled on top of each other.

We were instructed to go up to one of the boxes, pull out a revolver and read off the serial number to the instructor who recorded it next to our name. Now, I had never in my life touched, let alone picked up anything resembling a firearm. I would have been more comfortable reaching into a box filled with snakes. But what was I going to do? Refuse and then quit? No, that wasn't going to happen. So I gingerly reached into the box and gently pulled out the service revolver that was about to be assigned to me. I knew that even though my finger was as far away from the trigger as possible, I was sure the damn thing was going to magically fire and do bodily harm to someone. Of course, it wasn't even loaded but I didn't know that at the time.

At a very young age, my parents joined the Friends meeting in Yardley, Pennsylvania. They were better known as Quakers, and there is a thriving population in the area. Many people mistake them for Mennonites or Amish, but that's not the case. What Quakers are probably most known for is their stance on nonviolence. Throughout our history, when the draft has been invoked during a War, Quakers have been able to declare themselves to be Conscientious Objectors. This meant they may still have to serve, just not in any capacity that involved combat. One of the most famous CO's in recent times was Muhammed Ali. Ironic isn't it since he made a fortune beating the crap out of people?

So here I was picking a gun out of a box which I would be carrying on my side for many years. And might have to possibly use. How was that going to go over with my parents and their Quaker friends up in Bucks County, Pennsylvania?

That wasn't on my mind though. The instructors told us to holster our weapons and listen to a safety lecture. We were told to raise our hands if we had never handled a firearm before. I was hesitant because I didn't want to be looked at as a total loser. But raise my hand I did. Instead of being mocked in front of the group, the lead instructor smiled and pointed out to the rest of the class that those of us that raised our hands were just the kind of students he liked. Really?!?! Yes, because we didn't have any bad habits that had to be unlearned. We were firearms virgins, so to speak.

They taught us everything we needed to know about firing a gun. The longer they talked, the closer we were getting to actually shooting this thing.

Finally, one at a time, we lined up in a booth facing a target about 10 yards away. When my turn came, I put on ear and eye protection, and on command I opened the cylinder, inserted 6 bullets in each hole and closed the cylinder. This was it! Somebody yelled that the line was clear and to fire at will. I raised my weapon, aligned the sights as they taught me and pulled the trigger. The noise alone startled the shit out of me. I kept firing until all 6 rounds were spent, just to get it over with. I may have hit the target once, but the instructor didn't seem upset and gave me a couple of tips that I promptly forgot.

9.

It seemed like we shot forever. At different distances, from different stances, weak hand and holding it without any support from your other hand. It was all a blur and I hated every minute of it. But this was part of the deal, so I tried my best.

One day after we arrived at the range, we were told there was a special treat for all of us. I was hoping it would be that we could get back on the bus and return to the Academy. But no. We were going to do skeet shooting. A lot of the other recruits thought that was just wonderful. I'm not even sure I knew what skeet shooting was, but I soon found out. These mechanisms were set up some distance down range and a disc-like object, also known as a clay pigeon, was inserted. We were instructed on the proper way to load and unload a shotgun and then, once again, lined up so we could have "fun" and shoot clay pigeons.

I'm sure I was at the end of the line so I could see what the hell I was in for. What I was seeing were a lot of people practically being knocked over from the mighty recoil of that shotgun. There were grimaces from the pain and a various assortment of "shits" and "fucks" uttered under breath. Oh boy, I couldn't wait for my turn. I put the end of the shotgun against my right shoulder and raised it, waiting for the command "pull." These clay things arose from the ground and my job was to align them in my sights, pull the trigger and blow them to smithereens. I think the only thing I got right was that I pulled the trigger. That's when my shoulder shattered in a thousand pieces from the recoil. Well, not really but Holy Shit that hurt! I looked around and it seemed that everyone else was suffering from the same thing.

We all did this several more times, each turn worse than the last. I know I never hit anything except the dirt barrier at the end of the range.

At one point the instructors apparently took pity on us and said they were going to give us an item that would help with the pain. Oh good, drugs! One of them walked over to us carrying a big box marked Kotex. He then handed each one of us a Kotex (snarky female joke included) and told us to use that as a pad (haha) to cushion our shoulders. The macho guys at first would have none of it. Notice I said "at first." Heck, I practically ripped the thing out of the instructor's hand. My pride had gone out the window hours ago. Its unfortunate there's no photographic evidence of what had to have been a hilarious sight. Sixty Police recruits with a Kotex hanging from their shoulder. Then again, maybe it's just as well that there is not.

10.

After firing innumerable rounds from my service revolver for about a week, I passed the final test and was officially permitted to carry this Smith and Wesson six shot gun on my hip. And for all the years thereafter, I have always hated shooting. I don't like anything to do with guns. I'm not interested in debating the second amendment or becoming involved in any political protests. I'm familiar with all the arguments people make for their right to bear arms. I'm just not interested in the debate.

Do I currently have any weapons? Yes I do. I legally bought a S & W snub nose five shot .38 revolver at a sporting goods store on E Street NW in 1974 for $95. Then, a few years ago I purchased a Beretta .22 automatic and more recently, a 9mm Ruger. I also possess the HR218 carry permit which allows me to legally carry any of these weapons in all fifty states and the U.S. territories.

Do I arm myself every time I leave my home? No, not always. Most of the time I forget. And carrying a handgun is a total drag, especially when the weather is warm. It's uncomfortable and it's not always that easy to conceal. To me a gun is a tool, albeit a deadly one. Nothing more, nothing less. I would have been dead years ago if I didn't have one when I needed it most. But those stories are left for later in this journey.

After qualifying at the range, there was still one more thing to do. The gas house! Among the equipment we had initially been given was a gas mask, used primarily for mass demonstrations of which there are many in Washington, DC.

We were marched up a hill to a small building. One at a time we entered the front door holding our mask in our hands. The room

inside was filled with tear gas and once
inside we were instructed to put on our masks.
I think we had to wait several seconds first,
but by that time my entire body was on fire.
My eyes had burned off, I couldn't breathe and
of course I couldn't get the damn mask on. I
finally did but the gas had already permeated
the inside before I got it on so the situation
became worse. We couldn't leave the house
until we got the okay, but by then it was too
late. The damage was done and I hoped I would
never have to experience that again.
Unfortunately I did though. Years later, on
the street my partner accidentally sprayed me
full on in the face instead of the prisoner we
were trying to arrest. I never forgave that
SOB.

11.

     Back to the Academy for more classroom
instruction and PT. I actually was becoming
physically fit, even though I was still
smoking half a pack of cigarettes a day.
The Christmas Detail was getting closer so
there was another important thing we had to
learn: directing traffic. In the parking lot
there was an intersection with working traffic
lights on each corner. We were taught the ins
and outs of safely getting vehicular traffic
through an intersection. Left turns, keeping
the area clear, directing pedestrians, correct
hand signals, etc. The only cool thing about
it was I got to blow my whistle. I never did
get the hang of any of it though. Even after
years on the street I was so pathetic at
directing traffic, I wasn't allowed to do it
for fear I'd be inadvertently signaling cars

to run into each other. Is it any wonder I was never assigned to Traffic Division?

We were almost to the end, but there was one more hurdle. It was a three day assignment with an FTO (Field Training Officer). This involved walking a foot beat with an experienced Officer somewhere in Southeast DC to get a taste of what was to become the real deal.

My FTO was Brad Bowman who was not in the least bit happy about being stuck with a young, dumb, female recruit. But stuck with me he was.

We were picked up by a 7D scout car which was supposed to drive us to our beat at the very end of South Capitol Street, at the Maryland line. On the way, they received a call to respond to a domestic dispute. Could this be my very first Police call? We went to the address of the building and walked up the stairs to the apartment in question. The 7D Officers stood on both sides of the door and struck it loudly with their batons while at the same time yelling "Police." It was duly noted that the pronunciation was always "Po-Leese." Heavy emphasis on the "Leese." That's just the way they do it in DC, cops and civilians alike.

There was no answer so I waited for them to kick in the door like in the movies. But they just shrugged and we left. This not making for an interesting story to tell friends and family.

So it was back to the scout car and our foot beat. The area we were assigned to was primarily blocks of small businesses with low cost housing added to the mix. I was really excited, although my uniform had recruit/janitor written all over it. I was the semi Po Po at this point but I didn't care.

One of the first things Brad told me was that there were probably snipers up on the roofs that hated cops and had me in their sights at this very moment. It didn't occur to ask why he wasn't in their sights too. I dutifully scanned the nearby roofs and when I told him I didn't see anyone, he assured me that they were well hidden. It also didn't occur to me to ask why we didn't request assistance to root out these sniper nests that wanted to kill cops. Little did I know this was just the beginning of what would become a common practice of harassing female Officers so they (we) would quit.

Brad also told me every car that passed us could very well have a shooter inside who was more than willing to execute me. Once again, it was just me and not him. Since he was usually walking on the outside of the sidewalk, this would have been a pretty difficult shot to make without hitting him too, but what did I know at the time?

12.

The way people viewed us on the street was a real eye opener. They looked at Brad with distrust and hostility, not only because he was the Po Po but because he was White in an all-Black neighborhood. I was a different story altogether. They didn't know what to make of me because they had never seen a female Police Officer pounding a beat. I found out later the consensus was that I was a School Crossing Guard. There certainly was an air of curiosity. I almost felt like people were going to approach and just touch me like a zoo animal.

A common thread that became apparent almost immediately was that when someone did need Police assistance, I was totally ignored and any conversation was directed toward the male Officer. It was very off-putting because there were times I felt I had some bits of wisdom to add to the mix but they were having none of it. It didn't help that the male Officers were frequently ignoring me too. After a couple of days of walking with Brad Bowman, I was put on a foot beat by myself: the South-side of the 1500-1700 blocks of L St NW. Couldn't cross the street to the North-side, for whatever reason. This was in the heart of downtown, just around the corner from the Washington Post.

After walking back and forth for awhile, a Sergeant that was detailed to oversee me stopped by. He announced he had found the perfect parking garage for us to have sex in, and for me to get in his cruiser at once. I somehow was able to talk my way out of his proposition, but he was persistent. For the rest of my time on L St, I made sure to step inside a building whenever I saw his cruiser approaching.

After the three days of OJT (on the job training), I returned to the Academy relatively unscathed. We had final instructions and then one day Sgt. Smith entered the classroom with what he called a "wish list." This was when we could make a request as to what Police District we would be assigned to.

DC has 7 Police Districts. Roughly, this is how they were laid out:

First District: Most of downtown, Capitol Hill and the "new" Southwest. My apartment was in the First District.

Second District: Everything West of Connecticut Ave NW. This included part of downtown, Georgetown and everything north to the Maryland line. A vast area with lots of money and embassies.

Third District: The smallest area, East of Connecticut Ave. 3D had Adams Morgan, a richly diverse area with a large Latino population. U Street, once known as Black Broadway and where the riots started five years before, at 14th Street NW. Ah yes, 14th Street. I'll get into that at length, later.

Proudly Posing in my Recruit Uniform

Graduation Day at the Police Academy with my
Father. I was young, dumb and thin.

13.

Fourth District: Mount Pleasant
(another major Latino area bordering Adams
Morgan), a large area with lots of row houses,
small commercial businesses and some industry.
Borders Rock Creek Park to the West and
continues north to the Maryland line. I lived
way up in 4D for about five years after I
married Frank.

Fifth District: Part of Capitol Hill
and lower income housing the closer you got to
the Anacostia River. Also included RFK

stadium, home of the Washington Redskins at the time and DC General Hospital.

Sixth District: East of the Anacostia River and the area that I know the least about. North of Minnesota Ave SE and borders Prince Georges county, Maryland. Primarily Black and lower income.

Seventh District: South of Minnesota Ave SE and I was never very familiar with this District either. St. Elizabeth's Hospital is there where the mentally ill were treated. And of course, the Police Academy is in 7D.
So if this is not 100% accurate, it's pretty close. Good enough for government work anyway.

14.

I knew nothing about Police Districts so I raised my hand and asked which one had the most action. I was told that 3D was the most active and highest crime District in the city at the time. So that went to the top of my wish list.

After some time, Sgt. Smith returned with our assignments. And I was assigned to the Third District! Yipee! The young, dumb, thin White girl from the suburbs was about to begin the journey of a lifetime.

There was a graduation ceremony in the Academy auditorium which my parents attended from Pennsylvania, along with my sister Jeanne. I think we even shook hands with the current Chief, Jerry Wilson. Class pictures were taken along with pictures taken with the family. I looked so happy and innocent, not knowing what was in store down the road.

After graduation, I took all my equipment and drove to 3D to check in and get a locker. 3D is located at 1620 V St NW, in the middle of the block, surrounded by old row houses. When I arrived, I couldn't find a place to park so I went around to the back of the station and found an empty space. Over the space was a sign that said "Inspector Jefferson." Not knowing who or what an Inspector Jefferson was, I pulled in and parked. I gathered all my stuff and dragged it inside the front door where I was met by the Desk Sergeant. He directed me downstairs to a locker room and told me to choose any one that didn't have a lock on it. While I was making my decision, a Blonde woman quickly came in, holding several bottles of liquor. When she saw me, she handed me the bottles, told me to hide them in my coat and follow her. She then walked away and I was right behind her, trying not to drop any or make any noise.

        We went upstairs to a second floor office and she told me to put the bottles on a desk in front of a big, overweight White guy, later identified as Sgt. B. B. Bryant. He seemed quite happy with the loot in front of him, so if he was happy, I was happy. The woman was Officer Joyce Hennessy and it turned out I was in the Vice office. They both thanked me and I left, never finding out what that was all about.

        I did quickly find out who Inspector Jefferson was however. He was the Head of the entire Third District and I, a lowly dumb ass rookie was parked in his reserved spot. I got the hell out of there before he ever found out whose car it was.

        A very interesting beginning indeed.

The patrol division of 3D was made up of three sections: A, B and C. There were three because each section covered an eight hour period of the day. Yes, that equaled twenty four hours. Each section was divided in half, one section going out on the street an hour before the other. That way there was never a shift change where every unit was at the station at the same time. There was always coverage on the street.

Bear with me. I know this may be boring but I have to explain it anyway. Each section did every shift for two weeks and then switched to another shift. For example, if I was working midnights, I'd do two weeks of that and then do two weeks of evenings and then two weeks of day work. To help remember, I used the acronym NED (nights, evenings, days). A lot of us marked calendars a whole year in advance because it was impossible to plan anything otherwise.

So I was assigned to C section and this is where I would stay for the next six years. There were a couple of other rookies put in C section too but the one that I latched onto was another female named Susan Castle. She was a petite brunette, about my age and a whole lot more street smart than I was. We hit it off immediately, both realizing that we were in very unfriendly territory.

From my understanding, it wasn't that long ago the Scout cars were almost exclusively segregated. The White Officers rode while the Black Officers walked. I'm not sure exactly when this changed but it was probably in the mid to late 60s. When I arrived in 1973, each car had to have one

White (male) and one Black (male) assigned to it.

Then affirmative action came along and ta da, here we were. And believe me, we were not welcomed with open arms. Many of the men made their feelings perfectly clear from the get go that they wanted nothing to do with us. We were too weak and we couldn't possibly back our partner up. We just didn't have what it took to be a good street cop.

And surprisingly, the wives were even worse. They just knew what would happen during those long, dark lonely nights when we were sitting twelve inches from their men in that scout car. Some of them even went so far as to carry picket signs downtown at Police Headquarters.

16.

The uniforms we wore back then were totally impractical and uncomfortable. The jacket was too tight and if that wasn't bad enough, there was a strap that went over your left shoulder and was attached at both ends to your Sam Browne belt which carried all the essentials (gun, handcuffs, pepper spray, keys, extra ammo, flashlight, baton and knife). This stuff weighed a ton and maneuverability was just short of nonexistent. Can't forget the hat and necktie either. They couldn't decide whether we should wear the men's style hats or the type the Crossing Guards wore. And was it going to be the long, men's clip-on tie or the crossover tie? There must have been endless meetings about this important decision because it seemed like every other week a memo came out telling us to wear one thing and then a couple weeks later

we had to switch back. I was so confused I
didn't bother wearing a hat most of the time.
The only good thing about those coats was that
they were so tight I could hide Tampax down
the front when it was that time of month with
no fear of it falling out. God forbid I pull
one out of my bag and tell my partner to drive
me to the station to take care of business.
After a while I didn't care but at the time
female Officers didn't have periods. Added to
this most unbecoming uniform were the
fashionable "shit kickers" we were required to
wear. They had to be black and polished to a
dazzling sheen. For many years I wore men's
combat boots (insert joke here), usually with
a steel toe just in case. They weren't
designed for the many foot beats we had to
walk, but what were you going to do? In full
gear, especially in the winter we all
resembled the Michelin man.

17.

It was now my first day on the street
as a rookie cop. I put on most of my uniform
at home, being careful to cover it up with a
civilian coat so nobody would know who I was.
Then it was off to 3D, which was halfway
across town from my apartment in Southwest.
At the time, there was a big, empty lot at the
corner of 17th and U St NW where we could park
our POVs (privately owned vehicles).
In the locker room, I completed putting on my
uniform and nervously went upstairs to
rollcall. This was in a room about the size of
a classroom. All along the perimeter were
desks and then rows of desks toward the front.
Facing the desks were a couple of tables with

a podium in the middle and behind that, a
blackboard.

Being a Sociology major, I was well
aware of territorial instincts in human
beings. I figured the more Seniority you had,
the further back you sat in that room. So amid
all the stares, some hostile and some just
curious, I sat down in the second row.
We were all given sheets of paper, later
referred to as Hot Sheets. These contained
lists of all the stolen vehicles in the last
twenty-four hours, and descriptions of wanted
criminals. Also, at the top was the Color Code
of the day. Whenever you called downtown for
information, usually a criminal record, you
had to give the person on the other end of the
line the color code so they would supposedly
know that you were the real Po Po. The color
changed every twenty four hours but frequently
if I didn't happen to have the right color,
they'd give me the info anyway.

So back to rollcall. At the exact time
it began, you better be in your seat. There
was no coming in late because if you were, you
could be fined $35 which was a significant sum
in those days. Plus you would receive a PD750
in your personnel jacket, which was a written
dereliction that stayed there for 2 years. Is
it any wonder I am still obsessively time
oriented even today?

18.

A Sergeant with a clipboard began
handing out assignments, starting with Scout
85 through 104, and then the two Police
Wagons. Each scout car was assigned to a
certain area of 3D and for the most part
stayed in that area unless given a call by the

dispatcher to respond elsewhere. For example, Scout 85, 88 and 89 worked the Adams Morgan area. Scout 101, 102, 103 and 104 worked the South end of 3D, bordering L St NW. At any given time, there were vehicles at the NE Shop, for maintenance and repairs. The NE shop was of course located in Northeast, off Florida Ave near Gallaudet University. If the scout car of two assigned partners was in the Shop, they were either given an extra car if one was available or they walked a foot beat.

I was supposed to be put with an FTO until I could be certified to patrol alone, but that wasn't always the case. And when that happened, I was usually stuck with an angry, White male that wanted nothing to do with me. And believe me, that was a long eight hours. One guy absolutely refused to work with me and when he was given an ultimatum, he promptly resigned, moved to Pennsylvania and became a mailman.

Another Officer, who went on to become a Captain, would not talk to me under any circumstances. At the time, radio transmissions could have been in Chinese for all I could understand. Everyone was talking real fast in some kind of code. Do you think it might have been helpful if they had covered this in the Academy?

While I was riding with this Officer, Mitch Connolly, and holding a big cup of coffee, we apparently got some kind of serious call because Mitch immediately stomped on the gas. I was totally unprepared for this and the entire cup of hot coffee went all over me. We traveled at a high rate of speed with red lights and siren (Code 1).

I still had no idea what the deal was but when Mitch abruptly stopped, jumped out and began running, I jumped out and began running too. There was no way I was going to be discovered sitting in that scout car with a dumbfounded look on my face. I figured the best thing to do was follow my partner even though he was doing everything he could to get rid of me. Afterwards, there was no apology for the coffee incident. I knew damn well that he had done it on purpose but there was nothing I could do about it. So I spent the rest of the shift soaked in what had quickly become cold, disgusting coffee.

After a while, I found there to be a pattern to all this. For the most part, the White male Officers were openly hostile. This included some of the Officials, but not so much. I think they had been read the riot act and kept their feelings more to themselves. There was always an undercurrent of tension and until one of us had been truly street tested, it would continue.

19.

Looking back, it seemed that the Black male Officers were a hell of a lot more helpful than the Whites. This was probably because it wasn't all that long ago they were feeling the effects of blatant discrimination and racism themselves. Many of them identified with exactly what we were going through. Of course, I grew up on the other side of segregation. Born and raised in Bethesda, Maryland, I grew up in an all-White environment. Grades K through 12 were 100% White and here I was assigned to an area that was almost all Black.

When I was entering the 6th grade at a new school in Kensington, Maryland, my Mother took me into the main office to register. The Principal came out and told me I had a choice: I could either choose beloved Mrs. Hobby who had been there for about a hundred years. Or I could choose the new teacher. This is where she leaned down and whispered, "He's a Negro, you know."

It came out like "Neeeeegro." I remember thinking "Oh, okay. I'm going to pick the Negro." I also remember her looking at me in astonishment, as though I was crazy. My Mother never batted an eyelash.

So, Mr. Darius Edward Brown became my 6th grade teacher. What I didn't know was that because of his color, he had to commute every day from the District. There were no people of color living anywhere in this neighborhood. Mr. Brown was very large and kind of scary. But I think we all liked him until he started doing something that was a complete no no. If somebody misbehaved, he made you hold your hands out so he could hit your knuckles with a ruler. This definitely did not go over well, especially in 1962. A Negro man hitting White children in the classroom. It stopped immediately and the rest of the school year was uneventful.

20.

For me, being plunked down in the middle of the Third District was like entering an alien planet. It had only been five years since the riots in 1968 started at 14th and U St NW, after Dr. King was murdered.

I quickly discovered that I could barely understand what anyone was saying on the street. It was like a whole new language to me, lots of street slang and what Frank would later call, rappin' and slappin.'

One time I was working with Tyrone Poole and some guy was arguing with him about something. The guy then turned toward me and said something unintelligible. I just pretended I understood what he said but when I realized Tyrone was becoming very angry, I couldn't help but ask what was going on. He told me the man had just said something terrible about my Mother. Well, that was good enough for me so I locked him up for Disorderly Conduct. Nobody was going to talk about my Mother like that and get away with it.

A charge of Disorderly Conduct was the biggest joke in town. For a mere $10 fine you could curse out the Po Po, swing at the Po Po and do all kinds of obnoxious things. When in doubt, make it Disorderly Conduct. It was quite the bargain and everyone involved would be back on the street in no time.

Periodically, at roll call a Sergeant would yell at us to stop making so many Disorderly arrests. But it was kind of halfhearted because a lot of them were making these lockups too. Sometimes it was all kind of a game. To give some idea of how many people were booked in a year at 3D, the number was about 10,000. That was a hell of a lot of people coming through, considering this the smallest Police District in the whole city.

21.

My first Christmas Eve, I was walking a foot beat with Reggie Waters who later became an Assistant Chief. He was a tall, handsome

Black man who had quite a way with all the ladies. He was very nice to me and taught me a lot about being a good street cop.

Our beat was along U St NW and being that it was December, it was very cold so I bundled up to the nth degree. At the time, there were three movie theaters within a three block radius. One of the theaters was showing "The Exorcist", which was hugely popular at the time. There were reports of people screaming, getting sick, and running out of the building. Sounded like my kind of movie. Plus, Reggie and I were freezing to death. He suggested we go inside to get warm and check out the movie. I was certainly all for that so inside we went. We stood just inside the doors to the auditorium.

After about half an hour, I began to get very warm. Our uniforms were not made to easily be taken off. This was no jacket with a zipper in the front. These coats were like straightjackets. And I was getting warmer and warmer. No, make that burning hot! Suddenly I felt all the signs coming on that I was about to pass out! This Could Not Happen Under Any Circumstances! I would never hear the end of it and I would have considered it a huge blow to what I was trying to accomplish. "Oh, the little girl fainted." Not!

So I leaned down, pretending to tie my shoes, making sure my head was such that the blood was going to my brain. I stayed that way as long as I could without drawing attention. Fortunately, Reggie was fully engrossed in the movie and not paying me any mind. I think I did this a couple of times and thank goodness, never did end up on the floor.

After the movie, we went back outside and Reggie received a radio call. We were to be picked up by a scout car and driven to the scene of a homicide. This was my First Homicide! December 24, 1973 at 1424 Harvard St NW. Nobody forgets their first run to respond to a murder.

When we arrived, we were told there was a body in a rear room. The guy had been shot in the back and was lying on the floor. And now the "fun" part. I was told to stay in the room with him to guard the body. I did as they told and just stood in there next to this dead guy.

What I didn't know at first was that I was being set up. They all thought I would freak out and go running away into the night. But what they didn't know was that I had seen a couple of Detectives peeking through the outside window to watch my reaction.

So I leaned down over the guy and began fingering the bullet hole in the dude's back, acting like it was the most fascinating thing I had ever seen. I would have rolled the body over and feigned a sex act if it wouldn't have contaminated the crime scene. This White girl wasn't going to have any of their bullshit. They must have been very disappointed because when I exited the room, nobody said a word. I guess I must have passed their stupid test. For whatever reason, when I had that uniform on, nothing seemed to faze me. Of course, there were countless Oh Shit moments but they were always after the fact. That is probably why I am alive today.

That, and a little bit of luck.

22.

One morning after working the midnight shift I was invited to join the guys at a bar called Caffney's, way up on Colorado Ave NW. Apparently Caffney's was only open to cops at this time of day because I don't think any DC bars could legally be open at 8:00 am. And who was going to bust a bar full of cops?

So off we went in a caravan to Upper Northwest to drink. There must have been about ten of us, Officers and Sergeants alike. The place was a real dive but the beer was flowing by the time I arrived, so who cared? It was pretty warm inside so I took my jacket off, exposing my uniform shirt. Sgt. Popielarcheck (known as Pop) immediately came over and told me I couldn't drink in uniform. Beneath my shirt I had on a thermal underwear top so I removed the uniform shirt to appease him.

At the time, I could pound down some beers and I knew this was another kind of test. To see if I could keep up with the Big Boys. Not a problem. I made sure to match everyone drink for drink. I even bought a couple of rounds with money I could ill afford. Test passed.

Sometimes after a shift, we would go to our cars in the vacant lot at 17th and U St NW and drink copious amounts of beer. At times it got so raucous, that surrounding neighbors who were trying to sleep complained to the Watch Commander.

One night at roll call, Lieutenant McCatheran came in and announced very simply, "The oasis is now closed." This was when singer Maria Muldaur had a number one single called "Midnight at the Oasis" so we needed no further explanation.

We just moved to another location. And I never missed an opportunity to drink with the guys. It seemed to help acceptance wise, but I still had not been truly tested on the street.

My first real arrest, not counting the Disorderly was when Tyrone and I responded to Peoples Drug Store to lock up a shoplifter at Thomas Circle. Not very exciting but Tyrone made me do all the paperwork from start to finish. Let me tell you, this ain't nothing like you see on TV. There was the arrest report (PD 163), the statement from the Peoples security guard, evidence recorded, prisoner booked, attempt to get him released on personal recognizance (PR), etc. The whole sequence of events is very time consuming and this was a pretty cut and dry offense. Not real complicated. I don't believe he made PR, so the next morning I had to go to the courthouse downtown and paper the case. This process is also very time consuming because there are a whole lot of other cops doing the same thing. And there are only a certain number of Assistant US Attorneys to paper or no paper these cases.

The first appearance in court, we received comp time and then any other appearance on that particular case was overtime pay. Some Officers tried to make as many cases as possible, so they could get that overtime. It kinda became a second job of sorts. That was never my thing because I liked to have some kind of life outside the job. Plus, I didn't have a family to support at the time.

23.

Peoples Drug store at Thomas Circle was a true local landmark. It was open 24/7 and everyone from prostitutes, Johns, drug addicts, drunks and all the rest patronized it. I tried to stay out of it as much as possible because inevitably I'd get involved in something stupid.

But the Police were frequently called to throw people out, break up fights and lock up shoplifters. All the dispatcher had to say was "Peoples" and we all knew there was some kind of bullshit going on there. I quickly discovered that the majority of stuff that happened on the street involved people that were drunk and/or high. As far as I know, that is still true today.

When I was still new and in Social Worker mode, I would try to reason with these people. Try to come to an amicable solution so everyone was happy and satisfied. My partners must have been silently laughing their asses off at my naivety.

It wasn't long before I realized that sometimes the only reasonable solution was to put my face mere inches from theirs and loudly say, "Shut the fuck up right now or you're going to jail!"

Now, that didn't always work but that's when the all-purpose $10 charge of Disorderly Conduct came in handy.

24.

None of the female Officers had really gotten into anything of a violent nature yet. The verdict was still out. Drinking after shift change was one thing but the real test was yet to come and it happened that I was first.

Reggie and I were assigned to a midnight footbeat in the Adams/Morgan area. We walked along Columbia Rd and 18th St NW where all the bars and restaurants were, and still are. This was when we still used callboxes, along with "portable" radios which was similar to lugging around a brick for eight hours. Of course, there was all the rest of the equipment we had to carry. Looking back, I should have just pulled a wagon behind me.

At rollcall, when assignments were given to the footbeat Officers, we were also told, "On the half" or "On the Hour." This meant if we were given "On the half," we had to walk to the callbox on our beat and use the telephone inside, to call the station and check in on the half hour. To open the callbox, we carried a large brass key that fit into the lock. Callboxes are long gone now but I have two of my own, along with several keys. Some Officers today don't even know what a callbox is but then again, they don't know what a rotary phone is either.

Not surprisingly, there was a way of getting around having to be at the callbox at a particular time. Sometimes it was just plain inconvenient. So I always made certain I was on good terms with the person who marked us down on the large entry book kept at the station. And he took care of us so we weren't necessarily tied down to the callbox.
After all the businesses shut down at 0200 hours except the 7-11, things were pretty dead. Reggie and I wrote a lot of parking tickets and rattled some doorknobs but for the most part were just waiting for checkoff at 0700.

At about 0400 hours, we were walking North on 19th St next to Adams Elementary School, when we both heard a noise coming from the entrance.

Reggie quickly and quietly climbed the stairs toward the front door. I was right behind him, having no idea what we were about to encounter.

At the top, we observed a Black male attempting to jimmy the door open with a screw driver. As we approached, he must have heard us because he turned around, screwdriver still in his hand. Reggie told him to stop and that he was under arrest. That's when he came at Reggie with the screwdriver and all hell broke loose.

I had never been in a fight in my life, but instincts must have kicked in because I jumped right in the middle of the melee. Batons were swinging, fists were flying for what seemed like forever. But he was finally restrained and handcuffed. Reggie called for a transport unit to take this guy back to 3D and he and I walked back to do the paperwork. When I walked into the lobby of 3D and into the light, I discovered I was covered in blood. Thankfully it wasn't mine or Reggie's. By this time, everyone knew I had been in my first fight. First female in a fight? Did I backup my partner? Did I hold my own? Did I pass the Big Test?

It didn't hurt that I had blood all over my uniform shirt, but really my fate lay in whatever Reggie told them. Talk about an anxious moment. One Officer came right out and asked him in front of me. "How'd she do?'

And Reggie looked him directly in the eye and responded, "She did fine."

25.

A defining moment indeed. I don't think I ever wore that shirt again. It was my Red

Badge of Courage and I wasn't going to mess it up with a little bleach.

The next test was which one of us was going to be the first female to be permanently assigned to a scout car? This was a very big deal because it had never been done before. For years, women had been assigned to Youth Division (I guess we could be trusted with kids) or as Jail Matrons (there's that word again). Basically, women were only put in positions to support their male counterparts. I'm sure that today there are still many men that agree with that policy.

But we were here to stay and as much kicking and screaming that was going on, it wasn't going to make a difference. The annoying part was that they could make their vocal arguments right in front of us. And get away with it. Comments involving words like bitch and motherfucker were freely used with no repercussions. There was simply nowhere to complain and nobody was going to do anything anyway. Human Resource Departments were light years away.

I can't begin to guess how many times I went home after a shift and sat down and cried. Sometimes it was just that bad. One time an Officer called me at home and asked me out to dinner and then "we can fuck afterwards." He was so persistent, with the same "romantic" offer that I finally got pissed off and went to the Lieutenant. His response was to call the guy in and halfheartedly tell him to "cut it out." That was a pretty extreme response in those days.

My recruit class had been on the street for about two months now and it was also getting time for us to be certified to patrol alone. Another big deal and kind of a scary thought. But of course this was never verbalized.

The Washington Post expressed an interest in doing a story on the first female chosen to be assigned to a scout car. This was becoming an even bigger deal and I really wanted it to be me.

The bad news was that one of the other females was having an affair with the Lieutenant that was making the decision. Just my luck! Even though I liked her, I didn't like that smug look she had on her face. One evening, a bunch of us were gathered behind a school, waiting for the next call to be dispatched. That's when the dispatcher ordered Susan and I to see the Lieutenant in his office. I think we knew what was coming, so we both responded quickly to the station.

In his office, Lt. Franklin gave this setup talk about the historical significance of this decision and blah, blah, blah. Susan looked especially confident and I just stood there feeling like a total loser.

That's when I then saw him look at me and say, "Debbie, I'm choosing you to be assigned to Scout 88 with Reggie Waters." I wasn't sure if I heard him right but yes, it was me. And I bet he never "got any" from Susan ever again.

The relationship you have with your partner is very unique. You're spending at least eight hours in extremely close quarters with someone that you may have to depend on with your life. And vice versa. You spend more time with this person than with your spouse or significant other. In some ways, you probably know them better. Would curiosity sometimes arise regarding those dark, quiet nights when you're parked in an alley sitting twelve inches apart? I can only speak for myself, but I can honestly say that nothing of a sexual nature ever happened. Also, the straitjacket of a uniform would have made anything virtually impossible. Just kidding, but true. Usually we just talked or if it was really quiet, parked somewhere relatively safe and "hoodled." I have no idea where this term came from but it meant "resting one's eyes." Since 3D was so small, it was sometimes difficult to find the proper hoodle spot. At times we would park next to another scout car.

There was an elementary school on 11th St that several of us would park behind. On occasion, a transistor radio appeared and we would listen to the latest in disco. The Police radio was also being monitored in case anyone got a call.

This particular school was next to rows of low-cost housing. After we had been going there for some time, a citizen started calling 911 saying a cop had just been shot at our location. Needless to say, an Officer Down call gets the biggest response of any call known to mankind. But nobody was shot and someone had to immediately get on the air and tell the cavalry to 10-22 (disregard). Someone in those apartments was screwing with us. This went on for quite some time and we never did find out who it was.

Working with Reggie on a regular basis in the same area, every shift was a real education. You got to know the beat so well, pretty much everything about everything. Every business, every fire hydrant, all the regulars (good and bad), who and what belonged where. The list went on and on. You kinda got a feel for the area every time you went on the street. Weather conditions? Day and time of

the week? Time of the year? Holiday? All of
this was factored in. It was always a learning
experience and you had to try to keep an open
mind which wasn't always easy.

When it was hot, all hell could easily
break loose as it frequently did. There wasn't
a whole lot of central air conditioning where
I worked and people were frickin' hot. At
first I was surprised to see little kids
playing in the streets at 3:00 in the morning.
Then I realized that their homes were nothing
more than unbearable ovens.

And when it was hot and at the end of
the month, violence went up because the
welfare money was gone and everyone's nerves
were completely frayed. Then the next day, the
first of the month, the Eagle had flown. This
meant the checks had been delivered and now
people were killing each other over this
"newfound wealth." An endless cycle, every
year.

26.

The most common call we received was
for a "domestic." It seemed sometimes like
that's all we handled. Domestics came in all
shapes and sizes but once again, alcohol was
almost always involved. I learned quickly that
you can't reason with a drunk so don't even
try.

Domestics also have the potential to be
one of the most dangerous calls a Police
Officer can receive. You've got two or more
people that want to kill each other. So one
calls 911, complaining about the other.
Frequently, some kind of violence has already
occurred. Usually the man has struck his
woman, but not always.

Despite the fact I got so sick of these calls, my partner and I could never let our guard down. That was when you got hurt, or worse. First, you try to separate them. And never let either one of them out of your sight. I made that mistake once and it almost cost me dearly.

I had responded with Tyrone Poole to a domestic somewhere on 17th St NW. Man and woman ready to go at it--again. Tyrone and I were standing in the living room with the man. I guess I wasn't paying attention like I should have, because the lady slipped into the kitchen unnoticed. I should have been right behind her but I wasn't.

Suddenly, she came running out of the kitchen, holding a butcher knife over her head. And making a beeline toward the object of her hatred. She was going by me so fast that without thinking, I stuck my foot out. She immediately tripped and went down like a ton of bricks, cutting herself in the process. They didn't teach us that little trick in the Academy and I never had the opportunity to do it again. But hey, whatever works.

In those days, after a Domestic dispute was somewhat resolved, the offending person was ordered to take a walk around the block to "cool off." The other person was advised that if they wanted to take this further, they could go downtown and try to get a warrant. Unless there were visible signs of physical damage, then nothing really was done. It just wasn't taken that seriously. And there was so much other stuff going on. Fortunately, times have changed and there are many more resources available to handle domestic violence. The walk around the block has become a thing of the past.

There were some people that seemed to call 911 every day for some BS drunken complaint. A couple on 12th St were so bad that all the dispatcher had to say was their name and everyone knew where to go. It was the same old thing. Drinking to a stupor, arguing and then slugging it out. And calling 911. Over and over.

Finally, somebody came up with the perfect solution and the problem was solved. The cord to their telephone was mysteriously yanked from the wall and as far as I know, we never received another call. No cell phones in those days.

Another call that we received not infrequently was for the Unwanted Guest. A group of people gather together in someone's apartment and get rip roaring drunk. Then after several hours, the host/hostess want them to leave and they refuse. Usually half the people have passed out and the other half are incoherent and combative. This call almost always ended with a trip to jail with someone arrested for Disorderly Conduct.

Even today, I try to imagine inviting friends over and having to call the Police because they refuse to leave. Hasn't happened yet.

Most of the time I was put with a partner but not always. Whenever we acknowledged a call from the dispatcher, we would respond "10-4" and they would know there were two Officers assigned to that scout car. If an Officer responded "10-99," the dispatcher knew the Officer was alone. Then when two Officers were required for a run, two 10-99 Officers would be sent. Or one 10-4 unit. In a perfect world, if you were 10-99 and arrived on the scene first, you would wait for the other Officer before handling the situation. This wasn't always possible, especially if the situation called for immediate action.

It was only a matter of time before I was put in a Scout car by myself and I have to admit that I was pretty anxious. Was I really ready? Who the hell knew, but I wasn't going to back out now. I would guess that anyone is a bit nervous the first time they're put out alone, but I was totally focused on not showing any emotions other than I was a badass. Inside, I was probably shaking like hell. I learned very quickly that you can never show any emotion that can be perceived as weakness. Ever. With your coworkers or the public. I was fortunate that this came easily to me but I paid a high price down the road.

Where all of this came from, I have no idea. Previous to this life on the street, I was just a fun-loving, weed-smoking, hard-drinking girl from Bethesda, Maryland. I was not confrontational or an "in your face" type of person. And here I was now, basically kicking ass and taking names later. Who was this person? I didn't spend one second thinking about it. I was too busy on this crazy adventure, hanging on for dear life, so to speak.

27.

There were some areas of 3D I liked better than others. The area I liked the least was Adams/Morgan. It had a large Latino population and there were very few Spanish-speaking Officers at the time. So sometimes, you had to put yourself on a waiting list for the next available Hispanic Officer. And if the person was all hysterical about their situation, it was maddening to not be able to communicate. For all I knew, they could be telling me that somebody was behind me with a gun pointed at my head and I'd be going "Si, Si, gracias."

The worst case of a language problem actually happened years later when I was in K-9. I was driving down 17th St one night when a hysterical Latino woman flagged me down in the middle of the street. She was screaming and waving her arms and I couldn't understand a friggin' thing she was saying. Since my car was blocking traffic, I motioned that I was going to pull over to the curb so we could continue this one sided conversation safely.

Now here's the good part: For whatever reason, she went to the backdoor of the K-9 cruiser and opened it. My dog Duke looked at her with this WTF look and then at me with the same look. She then started to get into the car! Now these vehicles were not made to transport people. In the back was a large cage, meant for dogs! But here was this lady maneuvering her way into a cage that was clearly not intended for human cargo. I started yelling "NO, NO, NO!" I think everyone should know what that means but she continued to push her dumb ass completely into the cage. By this time Duke was all the way on the other side, against the door with a "Now what?" look on his face. When she pushed up against him, that was all Duke could take and he proceeded to bite her. I had already jumped out of the cruiser and was dragging her sorry ass out of the cage before she got nailed some more.

This was the kind of situation you did not want to put out over the air. Mainly, because all the busybody Officers would come by the scene to gawk and/or put their two cents in. Also, people on the outside, including the media, monitored Police scanners and would have loved to hear about this one. So I advised the dispatcher that I had a situation that needed an ambulance, a Sergeant and that I would call landline with the details. Even this brought a few rubberneckers but not quite as many.

Afterwards, I found out she was trying to tell me she had just been robbed but for the life of me, I will never understand why she got in the back of my K-9 cruiser. It took a lot of creative writing to get out of that one.

28.

I generally rode in a scout car but for various reasons, I sometimes walked a foot beat.

There was one Officer in our section that kind of caught my attention. He was very funny and always nice to me. Not one of the several classless jerks who constantly seemed to be in the vicinity. One day, we were assigned a foot beat together in the Southern part of 3D. I remember thinking "This should be interesting."

His name was Frank Weinsheimer and he was about my height, balding and had a great mustache. We hit it off immediately, or so I thought. But for the next eight hours I had to listen to him talk about his fiancée, Sue Belton. It was Sue this and Sue that. He even wanted me to give him advice from a female perspective. I couldn't wait until the shift ended so I could get away from him. He was a

nice enough guy but I wasn't going to be his
Dear Abby.

Another time I had a midnight foot beat
with a guy named Paul. He was like a hippie
from the 60s, all peace, love and the rest of
it. Why he chose to become a cop was beyond
me. And his hair was always a tad too long for
the Officials, who seemed to pick on him a
lot. His passion was rock and roll and when he
would dance through the Precinct playing air
guitar, it was all a bit too much for the
tight asses in their white shirts (This is a
reference to Officials that were ranked
Lieutenant and above who wore white shirts.
Sergeants and Officers wore blue shirts).
Paul lasted several years but then resigned to
pursue some kind of career in music. I would
love to know where he is now. Probably a mogul
in the entertainment industry.

When we had our midnight foot beat
together, the weather was really crummy and
neither one of us felt like walking around for
eight hours. The good news was that Paul and
his wife just happened to have an apartment
right in the middle of our beat on 15th St. So
we meandered over there where I took over the
couch and Paul got in bed in full uniform with
his wife for the rest of the night. Our source
up at the station, Frank Bowe, took care of us
on our marks. On the half. On the hour.
Zzzzzzzzzz.

29.

The day shift was my least favorite
because it was usually the most boring. Lots
of office thefts and alarms going off when a
business owner or employee accidentally
tripped it when they opened up. At 9:00 am,

you could always count on a bank alarm going off. It used to be that the manager would quickly call 911 and tell the operator it was an accident, and the Police didn't need to respond. Of course, S-1 caught on to that, so we had to respond regardless of any call made downtown.

Even more than domestic disputes, I hated answering burglar alarms. Back then there was no penalty for false alarms, as there is now. All these companies were collecting untold sums of money, with no incentive to repair their alarms. And we were doing all the work for them! Plus, even though we knew they were probably false, you still couldn't let your guard down.

There was a church on N St NW where the alarm went off seventy-three nights in a row. Finally, someone got the Pastor's phone number and from then on, whenever it went off at 2 or 3:00 in the morning, one of us would call him up and innocently report a possible break in. And surprise, surprise: the alarm was magically fixed.

If a storm came, especially with high winds, you could count on every alarm in the city to go off. And these aren't just the fly by night companies either. Even the Big Boys were at fault. The dirty little secret is that at least 98% of burglar alarms are false. This takes away from Police resources that could be better spent doing real Police work.

One of my favorite alarm stories was when a residential alarm went off in the middle of the night somewhere in Adams/Morgan. It was actually a loud speaker attached to the second floor that was screeching loudly nonstop.

When I arrived, it seemed like the whole neighborhood was in front of the house. And they were not happy! The alarm was not on any kind of timer and it didn't appear it was going to shut off in the near future. Nobody had a key to the house or a contact number to call the owners.

This was another situation they didn't teach us in the Academy but luckily I came up with a solution. As the neighbors gathered around me, I announced I was going to leave the block and be gone for about half an hour. Wink. Wink. And I did just that. When I returned about an hour later, the neighborhood was totally silent. I then observed wires dangling from the offending house and the speaker lying in their front yard. Problem solved. Sometimes you just have to think outside the box.

30.

Another big test came in June, 1974 while I was still in my rookie year.

I was working with Kenny Garrett on the evening shift in a scout car. Kenny was an excellent Officer who, over the years seemed to get into more situations than most people. And this particular evening was no exception. Kenny was driving West in the 1500 block of U St NW and as we passed 1532 U St, we observed a commotion out front. Upon seeing a marked unit, we were flagged down and directed to stop. I instantly saw a Black male covered in blood, laying across the front steps. People were yelling that the person who did it was on the second floor. Kenny and I ran inside but he turned around and instructed me to go back, call for an ambulance and tend to the injured victim. So that's what I did.

While I was outside, a Sergeant's cruiser pulled up and stopped. Inside, was Sgt. Conrad Morton, who jumped out and asked me what was going on? As I attempted to brief him, he pulled out a shotgun from the car and began to run up the stairs into the building. I ran behind him, still trying to give him information.

About five feet into the foyer, were stairs leading to the second floor. At the top of the stairs it was kind of dark, but I could see Kenny standing there with his gun at his side.

Sgt. Morton immediately raised the shotgun and aimed it toward Kenny. Holy Shit, he was going to shoot my partner! He was standing right next to me so I began yelling, "Don't shoot! It's Garrett! Don't shoot! It's Garrett!" He apparently didn't hear me because he was so focused on his mission to shoot Kenny Garrett that the next thing I saw and heard was a tremendous Boom! Oh my God! Sgt. Morton just shot a Police Officer! It crossed my mind that he was going to shoot me next. He seemed to come to his senses and realize he had just screwed up royally. Luckily he didn't kill Kenny, but he hit him in the legs and that was bad enough.

So in his effort to do damage control, he tried to blame it on me. He knew that as a rookie, I could be fired without any due process. His reasoning was that all he saw at the top of the stairs was a Black man holding a gun and he felt his life was in imminent danger. Yes, there was a Black man at the top of the stairs holding a gun, but it was my partner. Morton claimed I never told him that and if I had, this would have never happened. He did everything in his power to deflect responsibility. He never really learned anything out of the incident because he was always taking that damn shotgun out and arbitrarily pointing it at people. After awhile, we just automatically took cover. As "punishment", he was promoted over the years until he retired as a Captain.

To put the finishing touches on this bizarre story, it turned out that our victim had been stabbed several times. When Kenny continued upstairs, he immediately handcuffed S-1 and placed him under arrest. Apparently the guy questioned Kenny's manhood and told him if he wasn't in handcuffs, he'd kick his ass. So what did Kenny do? He removed the handcuffs and was ready to go toe to toe. Somehow a knife came into the equation and Kenny probably realized he had just made a bad decision, so he pulled out his gun and rearrested S-1. Then he went to the top of the stairs, still holding his weapon at his side and the rest is history.

Back then, there were no portable radios in the scout cars. There was only the Motorola, which was firmly bolted down between the two bucket seats. If you were in a jam somewhere away from the radio, which happened all the time, you were up shit's creek. The only portable radios were the "bricks" assigned to the foot beat Officers.

In the U St situation, if I had had a portable radio with me, I could have followed Garrett up the stairs and called for an ambulance at the same time. This was really a case where I shouldn't have left Kenny alone with S-1, but I was still new and didn't know any better. I was learning something valuable every day, and that was, never leave your partner until a situation is under control. Another time, I received a call for an MO who needed to be taken to St. Elizabeth's Hospital. MO stood for Mental Observation and was used for people who were acting crazy. "Oh he's a real MO." Or "She's acting MO." The call was at 16th and Corcoran St, and my partner was Chuck somebody, a skinny White guy who later transferred to the Charles County, Maryland Sheriff's Department.

We went upstairs to an apartment where we were greeted by a woman who told us her adult son needed to be transported back to St. Elizabeth's Hospital, because he was acting erratically and she could no longer control him. Then a tall, young man with crazy looking eyes entered the room. He seemed pretty calm but you could tell this guy wasn't right. We told him we were going to give him a ride back to St. E's but he didn't seem to hear us. All his attention then focused on me and he began to relate a story about having witnessed a DC Officer being shot to death right in front of the building a few years earlier. He went into great detail about the incident, a suspicious auto investigation that went bad. I wasn't familiar with any such shooting and figured this guy was crazier than I initially thought.

He then got even more serious and told me that all guns were bad and he wanted me to give him mine so no more people could get hurt. I looked over at Chuck who was laughing his ass off. This moron thought it was funny! I turned back toward Mr. MO who was now approaching me with his hand out. "I want you to give me your gun now so that nobody else gets hurt."

I had no portable radio of course, and my idiot partner was not taking any of this seriously. Yeah, I was going to turn my gun over to a certifiable lunatic with the hopes he was not going to use it against me.
I did the only thing I could think of. I asked the lady where her telephone was and ran into the room so I could call 911, to request backup.

Luckily, everything was resolved without incident but I did wonder if a DC Officer had actually been shot and killed in front of his building. When I did a little research, I discovered that in 1967 DC Officer Gilbert Silvia had indeed been killed exactly as this man described. Sad, but interesting.

31.

There was another Officer that I just couldn't help but like. His name was Robert Bowers and he was so shamelessly flirty all the time, it was funny. He had the opposite sex on his mind 24/7. I forget how many marriages he went through. Just couldn't keep it in his pants.

One such incident cost him $1,000 at the Trial Board. It seemed he couldn't finish his tour of duty without getting "a little" from one of the ladies of the night. Almost every DC prostitute walked the streets in 3D, so he had a lot to choose from. He picked up one of the girls and drove down to the Washington monument where she gave him great pleasure in the front of the Police cruiser. I'm really not sure what happened next but he probably "forgot" to pay her and she became very unhappy. Her pimp was probably very unhappy too, so it wasn't long before Robert was called to the Internal Affairs office, where he was cited for any number of infractions. When he went before the Trial Board, they were not impressed and fined him $1,000. He took it all in great stride and frequently joked about his thousand dollar blow job. No hard feelings (pun intended). When I was still fairly new, I was assigned to work with the infamous Officer Robert Bowers in a scout car. I was driving and after a while we received a call to respond Code 1 to an apartment building in the 1200 block of 11th St NW. Code 1 assignments only go out for the serious runs, because that's when you utilized your red lights and siren to get there quickly and safely (hopefully, at least).

This was also the first time I had driven Code 1 so I was really excited. I got to go through red lights (after looking both ways) and generally getting to do the cool stuff I had seen on TV and in the movies. After I screeched to a stop in front of the building, I turned toward Robert and saw he had a puzzled look on his face. Then he jumped out of the car, ran over to my side and opened the door for me like we were on a friggin' date. I asked him what the hell he was doing and he replied that he always opened the door for a lady. I didn't know whether to smack him or fall on the ground laughing. So I told him if he ever did that again I would hurt him. We went on to become great friends but he just couldn't stay out of trouble with the ladies, so he was eventually transferred to the Second District. I'd love to know what happened to him.

Ah, the infamous 14th St NW. Even today, when some people ask me what part of the city I worked in, all I have to say is "14th St back when it was fun." And they know exactly what I'm talking about.

I had never seen a real prostitute in my life, and here I was assigned to DC's red light district. What a learning experience that was, and my eyes probably couldn't have gotten wider those first few months. There were so many girls out there, they were practically walking into each other. On some corners there were at least five or six vying for customers. And believe me, every corner was covered. The busiest area went from L St to R St, along 14th St and all the side streets nearby. One of the favorite routes was to go North on 14th St, turn right on Q St to 13th St. Then right on 13th St, around Logan Circle to P St, and back to 14th St.

It was busy every night, but it was total insanity on weekends. Frequently it was like rush hour on a Friday afternoon.

There wasn't a lot we could legally do except rigidly enforce all the traffic regulations. I wrote so many tickets I had writer's cramp. Of course, all these single men said the same thing. They were either just passing through or they wanted to see what 14th St looked like since they had heard something about it. Nobody would ever admit they were there to get laid. Even if they did, there was nothing we could do about it. One of our unwritten rules was that the girls could not run into the street to solicit men who were stopped at an intersection. But they did it anyway if they thought they could get away with it. If it was really getting out of hand, we would herd them around by driving the scout car on the sidewalk.

Being that people tend to be territorial, these girls were no different. Everybody had their own corner and nobody better infringe on that. If someone did, they would be physically assaulted either by another ho or by their pimp who was always hovering nearby.

I'll never forget the one time a couple of White guys from Fredericksburg, Virginia decided to bring their women to 14th St to make a few bucks. They dropped them off on the corner and sat back, waiting for all the money that was going to come their way. Let's just say that it ended as quickly as it started and we never saw this group again.

I have a good friend that was walking to work in the middle of the day. She was waiting to cross the street at Thomas Circle when one of the girls approached and told her this was HER corner and to get the hell out of there. These gals did not play. Period! When I was still really new, an Officer came over the air requesting a female Officer to respond to search a prisoner. I had never done an actual search, so I was pretty nervous that I wouldn't do it right. When we arrived, there was the meanest, toughest looking woman I had ever seen in my life. She looked at me with pure hatred and I was supposed to act tough back which didn't come naturally. But I pretended that I had many years on the street and searched her without shaking too much, I guess.

For the rest of my career, she was always out there on the corner. A hardcore, drug addicted prostitute that lived a terrible life and probably died an early, horrendous death. That was the story of most, if not all of them. When the AIDS epidemic struck in the early 80s, it was just one more blow to these poor women. I didn't feel bad for them at the time but now I just feel a great deal of empathy for that miserable way of life.

33.

The girls were all dressed pretty much the same. Hot, hot, hot pants, the shorter the better. High, high, heels, either shoes or boots. Really tight tops. Long, overly teased wigs. Way too much makeup. The majority were Black but there were a few of my White regulars.

They were out there every night without fail. Hot, cold, rain or shine. Holidays, oh yes, but maybe not quite as many.
One winter night after we had just gotten about six inches of snow, there they were out on their corners. One of the more ambitious girls was actually shoveling snow at 13th and Q St NW. Still in her hot pants but her boots were high and gave her a little more warmth and traction.

For a little while, there was a Black midget prostitute out "on the stroll." The joke among the Officers was she specialized in blow jobs and charged half price. She had it "easy" because she didn't have to lean down in the car windows to make her deals, which made her kind of hard to spot.

One morning when I was driving to court after the midnight shift, I spotted one of the girls a bit out of her area. She was still wearing her "uniform" but what struck me was that she was walking her daughter to elementary school. She was protectively holding her daughter's hand and you could tell they had a special bond. After that, I would regularly inquire about her daughter when I would pass by. Her face would light up and sometimes she would show me pictures. But the conversation had to be brief or she would get in trouble for talking to the Po Po.

There was this one seventeen year old guy who was actually pimping several girls on the strip. He was a real arrogant jerk who liked to remind us he was a juvenile. Plus, his mother was on the school board and defended him every chance she got. Since he was a minor, there was really nothing substantial we could do to him because mommy pulled out all the stops for her baby.
He pissed off so many people that someone began a countdown to his eighteenth birthday so he could then be charged as an adult. Some Officers didn't even know their kid's birthday, but everyone knew his.
And then his big day came.....and we waited. It didn't take long either. He screwed up royally and there wasn't a darn thing mommy could do. This dude went to the Big Boy jail. Probably again and again. After that, we kinda lost interest. There were so many other things on the radar.

34.

Sometimes, on the 3 to 11:00 shift it would be like a relay race. All hell would be breaking loose, yet you couldn't tell the victim of a crime to sit tight so you could go up to the precinct to find your relief. You'd have to wait for that so called "split second" when you would tear up to 3D, give the relief

Officers a brief synopsis of what was going on out there, and check off with the Sergeant as fast as you could. Kind of like passing a baton in track and field without missing a beat.

That last half hour on the street, especially on midnights, you would pray nothing big time would happen on your beat.

One morning, about 0630 hours I was just driving around, waiting to be called in for shift change. I was going around Logan Circle when a frantic Black man flagged me down. Oh Shit! I pulled over and he began yelling there was a dead body lying in the middle of Columbia St. Shit! Shit! Shit! I started to tell him to wait about thirty minutes and then call it in so the day work shift could handle it. After all, the guy was dead wasn't he?
But noooooo, he wanted me to go there right then. So I had him get into the scout car and we went over to the 1500 block of Columbia St NW. I was hoping maybe he was wrong and we wouldn't find anything.

But damn, there it was. A dead body in the middle of the street and I was stuck there until the Homicide detectives arrived. Which was going to be awhile because I'm sure they had to have breakfast first, read the paper and drive through rush hour traffic to get there.

It turned out the victim was a transvestite prostitute who was lured into an alley and then beaten in the head with a brick. He/she then stumbled into the street and died. Don't know whatever happened to the case. It wasn't really on anyone's priority list. Probably wasn't even mentioned in the

Washington Post. Another poor soul who met their demise in the gutter, so to speak.

When I finally got home that morning, my neighbor Mrs. Walters greeted me in the driveway and insisted I look at her new rose bushes. It was this contrast that made everything seem crazy. It was only a couple of hours before, I was helping the Medical Examiner's assistant carry the bloody body to his van.

And then I was transported to the suburbs of Fairfax County, Virginia, commenting on Mrs. Walter's beautiful rose bushes. It wasn't until many years later I realized this might have been a bit strange. And she had no idea, because I would have never brought it up.

35.

14th St just never let up. After dark, there was illicit sex going on everywhere. Usually, it was a girl jumping into a John's car and performing oral sex somewhere around the corner. As quickly as possible, so she could return to her corner and do it all over again. Most of the time they used condoms and after the sun came up, the alleys would be littered with these disgusting things.

Cleveland Elementary School at 8th and S St NW was one of the more depressing depositories of ghetto garbage. Every morning, neighborhood residents would descend on the grounds to clean up the used condoms and dirty needles before the children arrived.

I don't know how the good people around Logan Circle ever had any peace, particularly on the weekends. There was no loitering statute in place so our hands were tied. If there had been, we would have had a lot more leverage with the girls.

The noise, the filth and the traffic were crazy. And then when the bars and clubs closed for the night, it got crazier. In addition to all this going on, we were responding to 911 calls. There were actually a couple of nights when there were so many shootings, we didn't have enough manpower to immediately handle them. It didn't happen often but it did happen.

The fighting, shootings, robberies, burglaries and the like became so commonplace, we didn't have much time to go over the circumstances with other Officers afterwards. There wasn't time, because there was another felony in progress just around the corner. Usually, around 0400, things started to slow down. I guess S-1 was tired by then. I know I was.

I always heard that the most pathetic girls turned tricks with the garbage collectors for $5.00 at the end of the night but I can't confirm that. Wouldn't surprise me though.

One day while working the 3-11:00 pm shift, I received a call for some kind of assault in the middle of the 900 block M St NW. It seemed that this old guy was in his apartment sleeping. His pregnant girlfriend took a ten dollar bill from his wallet and walked to the Safeway around the corner to buy snacks. While she was gone, he woke up and discovered her absence. Not happy with that and the fact she took some money, he got pretty angry. So he did something that certainly wouldn't have crossed my mind. He picked up an ax that just happened to be in the apartment and went outside. As she approached the building, he raised the ax overhead and decapitated her right in the middle of the street.

When I arrived, there was a huge crowd surrounding her. Lots of parents with their kids. Some were even pushing them forward so they could get a better look. I guess that was their free entertainment for the moment. There was so much blood flowing in the street that I radioed the dispatcher to send a fire truck so they could hose it down the gutter. Next thing I knew, a Sergeant came over the air telling me to respond to his location when I was back in service. He told me that I had made an inappropriate transmission over the air and I should have made the request landline. Hello! Cell phones hadn't been invented yet folks. Was I supposed to leave the scene and search out a pay phone because I might have upset someone who was monitoring my transmission?

The good news was that the blood was washed away and the body was quickly transported to the Medical Examiner's Office. The crowd then dispersed since there was nothing more to see. Just another day in paradise.

36.

That part of 9th St was particularly depressing. There was just nothing there except liquor and mom & pop stores, storefront churches and slum housing. The whole area had a "given up" quality to it. When the Safeway on 11th St finally surrendered and left, there was no place within a reasonable distance to buy real food. The little corner markets only sold crappy snacks, cigarettes and beer. There were a few playgrounds, one donated by the Kennedy's at 7th and O St NW but they were too unsafe and dirty for the most part. Kids really didn't have much of a chance around there. Who could blame them if their only role models were the local pimps and drug dealers? They seemed to be the only ones that had all the material things these kids could only dream about.

Also, in the 9th St area were most of the transvestite prostitutes. They too, had their own corners and when we'd interrupt transactions with the Johns, it was kinda funny. The guys would always swear they thought they were dealing with a woman. Yeah, right. A lot of these he/shes were so obviously males, a blind person could tell the difference. Not many women are over 6' tall, have hair on their knuckles and prominent Adam's apples. And their high pitched voices and mannerisms were more of a caricature than anything else. They all had prissy street names that they insisted on being called at all times.

When one of them would get arrested and transported to 3D, getting them to tell you their birth name for the paperwork was next to impossible. They were so enmeshed in their femininity, it was torturous to have to admit they were actually a man. A couple times I had to take one of them aside so they could whisper their real name so nobody could hear. Then I would solemnly promise I wouldn't tell anyone. It wasn't that we were doing this to harass them, it was merely part of the booking process and everyone was treated the same way. Gotta come up with that legal name.

In the summer, they'd all be on their corners in their skin tight bathing suits. Of course my first summer out there, I was checking for "the bulge." Let's just say that many of them were very good at concealing that thing.

Frequently there would be fights among the "girls." More like cat fights. They'd be swinging their purses, pulling off wigs and scratching each other. A lot more drama than over on 14th St.

37.

One night I was dispatched over to the 9th St area to transport an arrest to 3D. It seemed there was an altercation over a business transaction which resulted in a physical assault. I was there to transport the John and when I arrived on the scene, I immediately noticed that I knew the guy from somewhere. So I asked him his name and when he told me, it was an immediate "Oh Shit" moment. He was the son-in-law of my parent's oldest and dearest friends, Henry and Molly Samson. Mr. Samson was a retired FBI agent and although he was a nice man, he was an unrepentant racist. They had three children and when their oldest daughter, Allison married a Black man, he must have gone all apoplectic.

And now, here was this guy under arrest for getting in a fight with a transvestite prostitute he was trying to buy sex from. Awkward to say the least.

All the way to the station, he repeatedly explained this was all a misunderstanding. He swore he had become tired so he pulled into a parking lot to rest his eyes for a moment. Then, out of the blue this person attacked him for no reason. Soliciting for sex? From a man? Totally out of the question. I just kept on driving. Usually they admit they were soliciting for sex, but a man? How could that be? Of course they thought this was a woman! How dare I insinuate otherwise? Frequently, the dude's dick hanging below his hot pants was a pretty good clue. I think the word that's used today is the "down low." Whatever.

When we got to 3D, he called his wife Allison and told her the same concocted story. He asked her to come to 3D with bail money so he could get out. I didn't make my escape fast enough because the next thing I knew I was staring face to face with Allison Samson. She had two questions for me. Where could she get bail money in the middle of the night? And what exactly happened?

The first question was easy. At least a lot easier than the second question. Shit, do I parrot dumbass's story or do I tell her the truth? I thought about it for a minute and then told her the truth, consequences be damned. I wasn't sure what to expect but her expression didn't look overly surprised. Oh, so it wasn't his first time getting caught. I got the hell out of there and never saw either one of them again. As a footnote though, he sued the Police Department for false arrest, swore he was brutally beaten while he was in handcuffs and won $10,000 in an out of court settlement. I heard he died shortly afterwards from cancer. Ain't Karma a bitch?

38.

As my first summer on the street in 1974 was approaching, a court ruling came down that was about to change everything. All the undercover Officers that dealt with the girls on the strip were men. They were out there to make arrests when they were illegally solicited for sex. A Judge ruled this was not entirely fair, because the Johns out there were also committing crimes and needed to be dealt with accordingly. So, all the female 3D Officers were rounded up and put on a special detail to lock up the Johns.

This had never been done before, anywhere. If you watch episodes of Cops on TV, you'll see they now have it down to a science. But in 1974, we made it up as we went along. We initially gathered at the 3D-1 substation on New York Ave NW for orientation. Someone from the P&P (Prostitution & Perversion) unit stood before a blackboard and talked about sex acts and their street slang names. Also, what prices we could expect to be offered. I was so dumb, I was writing all this down like I was taking a college class or something. Wish I still had that notebook.

A reporter from the Evening Star, Toni House was allowed to sit in and follow us around, as long as she kept out of the way. It turned out that every news agency, both local and national got wind of what we were about to do so we got a lot of attention. Another thing we learned in this class was we could not dress provocatively like the girls on the strip. No hot pants, no tight tops, no hooker shoes.

We were not allowed to solicit the men. They had to approach us and say two specific things before we could arrest them.
1) They had to tell us what sex act they wanted to engage in and
2) How much they were willing to pay.

Otherwise it was entrapment. That they never had anything like that on their minds. For example, if I said "I'll give you a blowjob for $20," that was entrapment. They considered the typical hooker outfit entrapment. Once we got going, whenever we made an arrest a picture was taken standing next to the John showing just how we were dressed. This was admitted as evidence as further proof we weren't entrapping these suckers.

I'm always asked what I wore out on the street that infamous summer. Kind of a boring answer but we all basically wore cut off shorts, tee shirt and comfortable shoes. I think I probably wore sneakers. We were allowed to carry our off duty guns but we had no radios and no backup other than our female partner. In other words, nobody really knew what the hell they were doing. It's a miracle nobody was seriously hurt or worse.

My partner was this Black girl I went through the Police Academy with. Her name was Fanny Parker but she wanted us to call her Kay. She was petite and dark-skinned and we got along just fine. One thing I remember was she was thirty-two years old and a Grandmother! She was married to a taxi driver named Charles who would bring her to work in his cab and then pick her up at 3D-1 afterwards.

When I learned of my new assignment, I remember thinking "How do I tell my Mother?" "Hi mom. Just so you know. I'm going to be a hooker on 14th St all summer." No wonder this poor woman had a major stroke when she was sixty-four.

39

I would be remiss if I didn't mention a little bit about the P & P unit. The first part of the 'P' stood for Prostitution which is pretty self-explanatory. The second part of the 'P' stood for Perversion. This actually referred to homosexual prostitution. Today, it's strange to think that this particular word was used in describing a gay activity, whether it was illegal or not. But nobody gave it any thought one way or the other. It was simply "P & P." I don't know when they got around to changing the name, but it wouldn't have been soon enough.

After we took our little refresher class at 3D-1, it was time to put the show on the road. Word was put out to the girls that if we saw them tipping off a potential John, it was off to jail with that catch all charge of Disorderly Conduct. Also, they were not to get too physically close to us. After all, there was room for everybody.

I figured the whole experiment would be a failure. How could I compete with the girls without my hot pants and hooker shoes? Boy, was I wrong.

Even though we had gotten a lot of media coverage, I was still surprised at the attention we received. It seemed like every horny man within a fifty mile radius wanted to check out the circus on 14th St.

Kay and I picked a corner and waited. It didn't take long before the first car pulled up and stopped. It was a White guy with Virginia tags. He wasn't the least bit interested in me. He wanted some of that Black thang. It took nothing for him to say the magic words and that's when we realized we were in trouble. We had no transport unit or backup available and no way of calling for one because we didn't have a radio. Kay and I tried to place him under arrest but he simply drove away. Well, this wasn't working. The only thing we could do was try to get a marked unit to hide nearby and signal him when he was needed. That didn't always work either because sometimes he was given a call by the dispatcher and had to leave. More than once, we would give the signal and nobody would be there. Then, all hell would break loose. Most of these men were from the suburbs and had families. The last thing they needed was to be arrested for Soliciting Prostitution, especially if they were White trying to get some of that Black pussy. Unlike with the transvestites, they obviously couldn't claim ignorance. "Oh, I didn't know she was a Negro." Sidebar: That was still the word used back then. When appropriate, all our lookouts and reports were for Negro males and Negro females. Don't know when that switched over. So when we announced to the guy he was under arrest, it was like his whole life flashed in front of him and it didn't have a happy ending either.

We couldn't let them keep driving off, so we'd try to get them to exit their vehicle and walk over to us. Then when we would break the bad news, we were on more of a level playing field. That usually meant when the fight was on, we had a little bit more control. And resist they did. If they weren't running down the street in an effort to escape, they would fight us to get away. I have never been in so many fights in my life, before or since. If we were lucky, a scout car

Officer would drive by and assist us, but not always.

One night I was trying to arrest a guy who was in his car. I was standing by his window and when he said the words I needed to hear, I told him he was under arrest. He promptly put the car in drive and tried to pull away. This one wasn't getting away, so I dove through the window and attempted to pull his keys out of the ignition. I was actually laying across him with my legs hanging out the window while he was accelerating down 13th St toward Logan Circle. Poor Kay was left in the dust with no way to call for help.

Meanwhile, the melee was continuing in the front seat of the car. I was doing everything I could to get this guy to stop. And then he did. Very suddenly he began screaming in pain. It seemed that during our altercation, his arm got broken. I still don't know how that happened but at the time I didn't really care. I was just glad it wasn't me that got hurt. He was placed under arrest but the whole process took a bit longer since he had to go to DC General Hospital first to have a cast put on. I wonder what he told his wife about that one. Must have been a doozy.

40.

Kay and I made a lot of arrests that summer, but we were lightweights compared to one Officer. Her name was Mary Ellen Johnson and she was this short, little White girl with high teased hair. She really didn't have much in the looks department but men of all shapes and colors practically came to blows trying to solicit her. I was getting ready to put out a "Take a number" machine. She was married to another Officer and years later "accidentally" shot him in the back while cleaning her gun. And about thirty-five years after this detail, we ran into each other at a 3D reunion and she was furious at me for something I allegedly did to her in 1979. Talk about holding a grudge!

But back to the summer of '74. Somebody in the media nicknamed us the Flatfoot Floozies and it stuck. I had been called a lot worse so I thought it was kind of funny. One night, one of the girls arrested a guy who turned out to be an FBI agent. And he wasn't on duty either. That was the end of his career.

Another time a car pulled up to Kay and me and as the man began his spiel, I noticed there were three little kids in the back seat. I couldn't help but ask why he had the children in the car. It was probably an odd question coming from a "ho" but he seemed oblivious. He told us he always came here with his kids. He saw nothing wrong with leaving them there while he took care of business. Nice. Kay and I exchanged looks because we both knew this dude was going to jail one way or the other. We were able to entice him out of his car and it took nothing for him to tell us what he wanted and how much he would pay. Luckily, there was a scout car nearby to transport him but there was no way the kids could avoid seeing any of this. Plus, they had to be taken to Youth Division, where a responsible relative had to come and pick them up.

Every night was different, but every night was the same. The whole atmosphere was like a carnival, or was it a zoo? We were making so many cases you'd think with all the publicity, the men would back off, knowing they might be soliciting a cop. Not the case. One of my favorites was the pickup truck that pulled alongside me in an alley off Logan Circle. There were two White guys inside and the driver said to me, "I saw this thing on TV where the girl cops are pretending to be ho's down here. Well, I knows a ho when I sees a ho, and you be's a ho." Then he went on to say the magic words and promptly went to jail. I really didn't know whether to be flattered or offended.

Another time, two Frenchmen who spoke no English stood in front of Kay, waving $5 bills and grabbing their crotches. Since they couldn't understand us, we had a debate right there on the street about whether these actions constituted the magic words. Hmmmm. Ok, yes they did. Being that they didn't understand a word of English, how could we convey that they were under arrest? I came up with the brilliant idea of pointing at them both and then saying "Bastille" over and over. I'll never forget the look on their faces when they realized they were truly fucked, just not the way they hoped. A scout car then came by and they were led away to the Bastille. Frequently you had to make it up as you went along.

During the summer, Frank Weinsheimer seemed to be hanging around in his scout car more often. His beat was over on 9th St but he also got a lot of calls in the 14th St area. I'd be talking to some John on the street and all of a sudden he'd just take off for no apparent reason. This happened a couple of times before I noticed scout 103 lurking nearby, scaring off my potential customers. I was not happy so I marched up to the car and told Frank he was messing up my cases. He sheepishly told me he wanted to make sure I was ok. Not impressed in the least, I told him in no uncertain terms to back off. But don't go too far because I might need him for a transport.

My Soon to be Husband, Frank Weinsheimer

Frank and his partner R.C.White in scout 103.
R.C. is currently the Chief of Police in
Denver Colorado.

41.

As I recall, none of us got much sleep
or down time. We were on the street all night
and in court papering cases or testifying in
trials most of the day. It makes me tired just
thinking about it. But we were all young and
had lots of energy.

Another time, a van stopped next to us.
On the side, in big letters was the name of a
church in Woodbridge, Virginia. It was the
friggin' church bus! And it was being driven
by the Pastor! There just wasn't any shame
anywhere. I think that was another instance
when Kay and I gave each other "the look."

This guy was definitely going to jail, and so he did.

Depending on their attitude, we would sometimes telephone the wives to give them an update on their husband's whereabouts. Kind of like a public service. And I guarantee I called the Pastor's wife.

Some of these guys broke down like babies when they realized what was in store for them. Sometimes I would ask how they would like it if this shit was going on in their neighborhood every night. But they were usually too distraught to think about anything but their immediate, messed up future.

By the time these cases were ready for trial, almost every man accepted a plea deal and it never went any further in the judicial system. Every once in awhile, someone would demand to have their day in court. If they were found guilty and sentenced significantly more than the plea they had previously rejected, some would try to go back and accept the plea after all. Nope. It doesn't work that way folks. Once you say no to the offer made to you, that's it. It ain't offered again so you better think long and hard before you decide to go to trial.

That's why I chuckle when I see these politicians on TV who have gotten in trouble, getting all indignant in front of the cameras. Inevitably, they huff and puff about how this will all be resolved in a court of law. Then you never hear any more about it because they've quietly pled guilty to a lesser charge.

I discovered that in the judicial system, the last thing anyone wants is a trial. If every arrest went to trial, there would probably be a back log of several

hundred years. It's just not possible. And
people can scream and yell about how unfair
that is, but once again it's just not
possible. I guess some time is better than no
time.

Unless a case involves another Officer
who has been hurt or worse, you just can't
take any of this personally. If you do, it
will eat at you until you're a total mess.
Hell, I eventually became a total mess anyway,
but that was not for several years down the
road.

With all my wisdom based on hindsight
today, I would call working the street as a
Police Officer similar to Chinese water
torture. All those little drips over the years
take their toll. I don't think anyone gets out
completely unscathed but if that had been
suggested back then, I would have merely
scoffed and written that person off as weak.
Little did I know. Drip. Drip. Drip.

42.

Finally, the hooker detail came to an
end and I think we were all fairly worn out by
then. At least I was. Of course there had to
be a big party to celebrate. I think at the
time, there was always a reason to celebrate
something. Or nothing. The old saying that if
a day of the week ended in "y," then it was
time to drink.

The get together was at somebody's
apartment and we were all supposed to bring
someone. So I asked Frank. And he said yes.
We really hit it off from the beginning. He
was so damn funny and treated me with a lot of
respect. I was won over. We just started doing
things together and eventually became a

couple. But it had to be kept quiet at work because we didn't know how the Officials would react. Would they try to transfer one of us to another District? Neither one of us wanted that. Being that our Police beats were next to each other, we went on a lot of calls together which would have added to the stickiness of the situation. All we could do was stay totally professional and not give each other unwanted attention while on patrol.

At one point we even had a sit down and agreed that unless one of us got involved in something really serious, the other would not come to the scene unless it was to provide emergency backup. It took three years to pass after that conversation, but the time did come when we were both truly tested.

A month after the end of the detail, I was back in uniform and working day work with Tyrone Poole. It was toward the end of September in 1974 and things were kind of quiet. 3D and 2D shared the same radio frequency at the time, so we could each hear what was going on in the other's District. I had always considered 2D to be the area where nothing happened. Boy that ended September 24, 1974.

Tyrone was driving around on Connecticut Ave NW about 1130 hours when the call came out that strikes every Police Officer like a bolt of lightning, no matter where they work. A Second District Officer, Gail Cobb was walking a foot beat on L St NW, when a lookout was broadcast for a subject wanted in a bank robbery. She saw someone matching the description walk into a parking garage, so she followed him. Apparently she tried to place him under arrest, but he was able to disarm and shoot her at close range.

He then made his escape through the crowded downtown sidewalks.

A citizen called 911 and because traffic was total gridlock, an ambulance was not able to get anywhere close to the location. Since time was of the essence, she was placed in a Police cruiser and transported to the George Washington Hospital Emergency Room. But it was too late. Officer Cobb was already dead and her killer was on the loose. A lookout was broadcast and that's when all other 911 calls were basically ignored. At least the bullshit ones.

We happened to be just a couple of blocks from the shooting and I was so upset, I could barely contain myself. I asked Tyrone to stop by the Mayflower Hotel so I could use the bathroom. That was really a ploy so I could use the pay phone and call my sister Jeanne. When she answered, I completely lost it, being sure nobody could see me. I cried for several minutes but then had to pull myself together and get back to the business of searching for a cop killer.

Gail Cobb was the first and only female DC Officer killed in the line of duty (so far).

43.

Officer Cobb's killer was on the loose for a couple of days but if memory serves correctly, he turned himself in with his attorney. What happened to the case? He probably served a couple of years and then was released. The DC Judicial system doesn't exactly put the fear of God in anyone, even cop killers.

A while ago, several S-1's from DC decided to go to Virginia and ended up killing a State Trooper in Dale City. I'm sure they probably thought this wasn't really a big deal. A few years inside and they'd be right back out again, just like they do in DC. Right? Not exactly. Let's just say that this time, the wheels of justice turned quickly and one or two of them received the death penalty. Which was implemented in no time. God, I love the Commonwealth of Virginia.

Officer Cobb's funeral was a few days later in a church located on East Capitol St SE. I don't think I had ever been to a funeral in my life, let alone a line of duty service so I had no idea what to expect. Everyone wore their dress uniforms and the Department allowed as many Officers to attend as possible. The streets were still covered, but just barely.

When we arrived, there was a viewing going on inside but there were so many people, we couldn't even get close. So we basically took over several blocks of East Capitol St and fell into formation in front of the church. There was a loud speaker system broadcasting the service and I did my best to stand there and not show any emotion. But it was so damn sad and after a while, tears were streaming down my face. Had to just give into it.

Terrible things were said about Gail Cobb for years afterwards. Mainly how incompetent she was and should have never been released from the Academy. Should have been fired except she was Black and a female. On and on. I didn't know her but I do know she gave her life in the performance of her duties. And I have never heard of a male

Officer being trashed the way she was. It was kind of the "I told you so" attitude about female Officers. Even today, over forty years later I met a retired 2D Officer who insisted on giving me the inside scoop on Gail Cobb. For Christ's sake, give it a rest already!

All line of duty deaths are horrendous, but the one I never got over involved Alexandria, Virginia K-9 Officer, Andy Chelchowski. In 1989, he and his partner, Corporal Charles Hill responded to a hostage situation. In the aftermath, Corporal Hill was shot in the head and killed. Andy was shot in the legs and made a full recovery. Or so everyone thought.

I knew Andy because we both participated in Police dog competitions against each other. We both belonged to the United States Police Canine Association and I also knew him from the meetings and social events. Andy was a skinny guy with a stuttering problem. But he was really nice and funny as hell. He had a Black German Shepherd named Vader and was quite the competitor during the regional dog trials every year. Everyone liked Andy.

After he was shot, nobody knew he was suffering from terrible depression. The last time I saw him was in Gaithersburg, Maryland just months before his death. He seemed like the old Andy, but I'm sure he had lots of practice covering his emotions concerning why Charlie died and he didn't.

Months later he went across the street from his house, into some woods and shot himself in the head. Four years after the incident. Four years of living hell and he just couldn't take it anymore. His name deserves to be on the National Law Enforcement

Memorial as much as anyone else's. But it's
not.

I went to Andy's funeral in Olde Towne
Alexandria and a lot of K-9 handlers from all
across the area were also in attendance. They
stood out in the street with their dogs
sitting next to them. In the middle of the
service, the bagpipes started playing and it
was at this time, every Police dog out front
began to mournfully howl. It was the saddest
thing I had ever experienced. Even thinking
about it all these years later makes me tear
up. He was such a good man and I will never
forget him. RIP Andy

44.

DC had just gotten Home Rule when I
came on, which meant the city could govern
itself with their own elected Officials. Which
really was complete Bullshit, even today.
But DC did have its first elected mayor and
his name was Walter Washington. He was an
older Black man who offended nobody. He and
his wife lived in a historic house in an area
called La Droit Park, over by Howard
University. The exact address was 408 T St NW
and anyone who worked in 3D in the 70s and 80s
will never, ever forget that address.
Because he was our city's mayor, somebody
decided there needed to be a 24/7 security
detail at his house.

So an old, decrepit, unmarked cruiser
was parked directly in front of 408 T St NW.
The idea was that if we ever had an emergency,
we could fire that Bad Boy up and whisk the
mayor away to safety. The only problem was the
damn thing didn't even run half the time. I

guess we'd have to push the vehicle with the mayor to safety.

Each Officer was assigned the "Mayor's Detail" maybe once a week for about four hours. It was sooooo boring and everyone hated it, especially on midnights. Countless Officers were written up for sleeping behind the wheel of the cruiser.

In the summer, it was unbearably hot but I was somewhat lucky because Frank would bring me some kind of orange, slushy drink from Hot Shoppes Jr at Georgia Ave and V St NW. Boy, I loved those things. In the winter we froze our asses off because even if the car started, the heater was always broken.

Luckily, nobody ever tried to attack Mayor Washington at his home, or anywhere else. His wife, Benita was a real bitch. Let's just say she had a slight drinking problem. She was known to fall more than once trying to navigate the front steps after some kind of event. And she would never speak to us. Just stuck her nose up in the air and pretend we weren't there.

One time, Frank had the detail and Benita came home from a trip in a cab. When the hacker started to take her bags up the stairs, she stopped him. She then pointed toward Frank and said, "The boy will take care of that." Frank told her in no uncertain terms he was no "boy" and he wasn't taking her bags anywhere. I think she was so intoxicated she didn't even remember the incident, so nothing came of it.

Out of complete boredom, Officers began carving on the steering wheel. After a while it was completely unrecognizable and finally the inevitable happened. Somebody went to relieve the detail, and the steering wheel was

gone! Nobody owned up to it and an
investigation went nowhere. I always wondered
what happened to that damn steering wheel.

45

Another detail that we received
periodically was a hospital detail. S-1 would
be admitted for some medical reason and of
course somebody had to guard his sorry ass so
he couldn't escape. A chair would be
positioned outside his door and we would just
sit there for several hours until our relief
arrived. Sometimes they would be in the ICU
and unconscious (that was a good thing). The
escape factor diminished significantly when
they were out like a light.

One guy accidentally set himself on
fire during a burglary so there was a really
long detail at the Washington Hospital Center.
After being in there, I can tell you one
thing. I don't ever want to get burned. What a
horrible, painful recovery. And then he went
ahead and died anyway.

One time I went to pick up my partner
Clarence Black from a detail at the Hospital
Center. He told me he had just checked his
lottery ticket in the Washington Post and that
he had won $2,500. Wow, how cool was that? I
suggested we stop by the nearest liquor store
and cash it in. His face dropped and he said
the ticket was under the front seat of his
car. Ok, we'll stop by the Precinct parking
lot and pick it up. His face dropped even
further when he told me his wife had driven
the car that day and it was parked in a garage
downtown. Far away from 3D. Now what? You
weren't allowed to leave your District without
a good reason and $2,500 seemed like a good

enough reason to us. And what if someone broke in the car and stole it before we got there? So, red lights and siren it was. I was driving like we were responding to a shooting or something. If people only knew, as they were doing everything possible to get out of our way. Hey, this was a lot of money we were talking about. I don't know what would have happened if we'd had an accident. Something really, really bad.

We arrived safely though and Clarence retrieved his winning ticket. We then went to a liquor store where he redeemed the cash. I just knew he would share at least a little bit with me for being his so called partner in crime (that's probably a poor choice of words). He did say he wanted to give me something but it would have to wait until tomorrow. Ok, I could wait.

The next day when we met at work, he told he to close my eyes and put my hands out. Two hands, that's a good sign. When I did as he said, he put something in my hands alright. A fucking potted plant! I never forgave him! Ever!

Another Officer, Barry Roberts had the detail at the Hospital Center with S-1, who was there for a gunshot wound. While Barry was outside in the hall, a Doctor approached with a bullet that had been removed from S-1 in surgery. It was in some kind of container and Barry was supposed to safeguard it because it was a critical piece of evidence. There were several family members inside S-1's room and after awhile, one of them called for Barry to come inside immediately because there was a problem. He then did what any dumbass Police Officer would do: he set the container down holding the bullet and rushed into the room.

You know by now how this story is going to
end. Yes, the bullet magically disappeared and
gee, nobody saw a thing. So much for that
case. I think Barry had to write a very large
check to the Trial Board for that mishap.

46.

Since I was the first female assigned
to a scout car, the Washington Post expressed
an interest in doing a story on me and my
partner at the time, Reggie Waters. I was kind
of excited and apprehensive at the same time.
We were supposed to go about our duties as if
nobody was recording our every move. Yeah,
right.

The Post sent a young female
reporter/photographer named Linda Wheeler. She
was just a few years older than me and very
personable. But this was right after Watergate
when the Washington Post had just brought down
the President of the United States. We would
be easy pickings compared to that. Reggie and
I went out on the street in scout 88 with
Linda in the backseat. We were careful about
everything we said and did in front of her.
One day we were patrolling in a transport car
which meant that there were no handles on the
backseat doors. Linda was sitting in the back
as usual, and for whatever reason she was
getting on my last nerve.

We received a call to go Code 1
somewhere and Reggie really floored it. The
siren was wailing, the radio was blasting and
Linda tried to ask us what was going on over
the din but we ignored her.

When we screeched to a stop at the
scene, Reggie and I both jumped out of the
scout car and began running toward an

apartment building in the 1400 block of N St NW.

Poor Linda was stuck in the back of the vehicle, unable to get out. We heard later that she was pounding on the windows trying to get someone to open the door, but everybody thought she was a prisoner and wouldn't get involved.

I guess she eventually forgave us because she wrote a real nice article with pictures that didn't make me look fat. Speaking of her pictures, while she was on this assignment, Reggie and I got into a big fight with a guy at 13th and V St who didn't want to be arrested. Linda got some good action photos although my ass looked pretty big in one of them.

When the series of photos were included in the story, I couldn't help but notice that a black bar had been added in front of S-1's face so he couldn't be recognized. What the hell was that all about? Who was this slime ball that the Washington Post felt was so important it was necessary to cover his face? I called Linda and she told me he was some low level Post employee and her editor felt that for whatever reason, they had to hide his face. WTF?

One of the most influential newspapers in the world and they were covering for some insignificant asshole. I've never seen it done before or after in the Post. Not impressed. We got our licks on him, at least on the street because I'm sure it went nowhere after that. Probably another one of those $10 Disorderlys.

47

Reggie was a real piece of work when it came to the ladies. He was married and had a mistress on the side. Her name was Barbara and she was another female Officer. One of his many problems was he got both her and his wife pregnant at the same time.

We were working together one day when he announced we had to make a detour over to the Hospital Center. It seemed that both women had just given birth and their rooms were next door to each other on the maternity ward. Neither one knew about the other so Reggie had to go back and forth from room to room. Discreetly of course. I just sat in the visitor's lounge, quietly laughing my ass off. If these ladies only knew.

It seemed like all the male Officers had something on the side. It really was epidemic. I knew all the girlfriends and wives. That's one reason it was so funny that the wives picketed headquarters. Their husbands were the true dogs and for the most part it wasn't with the female Officers. It was predominantly with women they met on the street.

Frank had one partner, Bill Greeley, who had two completely separate families. Two sets of apartments, two sets of children and two women, neither of which he was married to. I don't know how he did it on a cop's salary. On the midnight shift, there were actually groupies that would drive up and down 14th St following the better looking Officers. There's no doubt that when things got quiet, certain sexual favors were exchanged. One Officer, David Royster was a special favorite. He took whatever he could get, whenever he could get it. Nice guy but he eventually got fired for some sexual misdeeds.

Remember, we didn't have portable radios in the scout cars. I had one partner whose main squeeze, Lydia Ryan lived in an apartment on 17th St NW. We would park the scout car in front of the building and John would go inside to take care of business. I would remain in the car and if we got a call, I would hit the siren and John would come running out, literally zipping his pants up at the same time.

It really must be true about the lure of a uniform because even the most unattractive guys seemed to have something going on. It was all I could do to keep everyone's name straight. I just kept my mouth shut and looked the other way, but what an education!

Sometimes there would be a social gathering involving the wives. The husbands would be all attentive and I'd just sit back watching in amusement. Really honey, if you only knew what I knew.

48.

Then the holiday season came around in 1974 starting with Thanksgiving. It wasn't exactly the Norman Rockwell scene everyone is familiar with.

We actually got a call for some kind of domestic dispute on Thanksgiving Day and when we arrived, the dining room table had been overturned and there was the turkey and fixings all over the floor. Along with all the broken dishes and glasses. Everyone was drunk and fighting, children were crying, dogs were barking. Not an uncommon day in the Third

District but couldn't we have a cease fire at least on Thanksgiving, for God's sake? Nah, that wasn't going to happen so we called the Wagon and all the adults went to jail and were charged with---ta da--- Disorderly Conduct.

My first Christmas Eve assigned to a scout car, I was 10-99 (alone) and observed a car run a red light at 17th and R St NW. By this time, it was about 0100 hours and officially Christmas Day. I pulled him over in front of the McDonalds at 17th and Corcoran St and walked up to the driver's side window. When I asked for his license and registration, he looked me right in the eye and announced that nobody had to obey any traffic regulations on Christmas. Then he added real nasty like, "And you don't know that Officer?!?!"

Oh, this was going to be fun. I went back to the scout car and wrote the ticket, making sure to add his comments on the back in case this went to court. I walked back to his vehicle, ticket in hand and when I tried to hand it to him, he immediately swung the door open and jumped out. Before I could react, he threw me to the sidewalk and began beating the shit out of me. My lifeline, my radio was bolted to the middle console in my scout car, about twenty five feet away.

Luckily, Frank had monitored my tag request and arrived on the scene to back me up. He was driving the Wagon and when he saw what was going on, he jumped into the fray. Then a couple of other Officers arrived and joined in on the "fun." When it was over, I was pretty bruised and battered but nothing serious. What I was pissed most about was that this guy had broken my brand new Timex watch!

Oh yeah, I was also pissed that the
second Officer that arrived on the scene,
Robert Tally, decided his job should be to
direct traffic. There was no friggin' traffic
and Frank and I still didn't have this guy
under control. So it took the assistance of
Officers Three, Four and Five to get S-1 in
handcuffs. No thanks to Tally, who was
certifiably a nut case.

A simple $10 red light ticket turned
into this dumbbell spending his Christmas at
DC General Hospital with a headful of
stitches.

That's why there is no such thing as a
"routine" traffic stop. Along with the
domestic disputes, traffic stops are one of
the most dangerous encounters a Police Officer
can have. When you approach a vehicle, you
better have your shit together or you may get
hurt. There are textbook ways to handle a
traffic stop starting with the positioning of
your cruiser. The way to approach the vehicle,
where to stand, what to say. All this can make
the difference between life and death. And
even doing everything correctly is no
guarantee the whole thing is not going to go
bad.

Just YouTube "Police shootings traffic
stops" and there are any number of them that
will make you sick. I had one several years
later that I will never forget, but I'll get
to that in the next chapter.

49.

Here's a traffic stop I will never
forget:

Clarence Black and I were working the 3
to 11 shift in scout 98 when we received a

call for an armed robbery that had just occurred at the Safeway at 17th and Corcoran St NW. Also added was that there were shots fired and the Safeway manager was last seen on foot chasing them down an alley. I was driving the scout car South on 17th from U St when we were dispatched.

As I was approaching New Hampshire Ave, a car ran the red light in front of me. To this day, I will never understand why I did what I did next.

Even though this was a red light violation, my primary purpose was to respond as quickly as possible to this armed robbery. But noooo, I just had to pull this guy over. This was 100% the wrong thing to do. But pull him over I did.

The vehicle stopped just before 16th St and I exited the scout car and began to walk up to the driver's window. Another mistake was that Clarence remained in the car. If you're with a partner, you both better get out and approach the vehicle, one on each side. Anyway, as I was getting closer, another car drove up alongside me in the next lane and stopped. Usually it was some tourist asking directions which pissed me off because it was distracting and possibly dangerous. Get a friggin' map and leave me alone!

But this was different. When I turned around, there was a very anxious looking young man that immediately blurted out, "Officer, I don't think you know it but the people in that car were just involved in a shooting behind the Safeway." Then he drove off before I could say anything.

I discreetly went back to the scout car and relayed this information to Clarence. We then returned to S-1's car, guns drawn and arrested the occupants without incident. Inside, were three guns and all the loot from the robbery. If that man had not stopped me, this incident could have ended very badly. I will go my grave always wishing I had been able to thank him for possibly saving my life. And I will always wonder what it was that made me stop this car in the first place.

Clarence and I then went on to receive an award as the Traffic Officers of the Month for the city. The Safeway manager wasn't struck by gunfire and the culprits were caught and put away on a plea bargain. Ultimately, it turned out to have a good ending but.....

50.

I was very fortunate that I was never badly injured on the street, physically that is. What actually happened to me was on a much different level and I paid a high price down the road.

Frank and I eventually moved in together in Hyattsville, Maryland around the beginning of 1975. We drove into 3D together, along with his partner RC White who lived nearby. As an aside, my partner's last name at the time was "Black" and Frank's partner's last name was "White." Go figure.

RC was a great guy who was destined to go on to bigger and better things within law enforcement. As I write this, he is currently the Chief of Police in Denver, Colorado. But back then, all three of us were lowly peons who "pushed" a scout car in the Nation's Capital.

One morning during roll call, a Sergeant was giving us the daily rundown including a lookout for a bank robber wanted in Arlington, Virginia. Included in the lookout was a vehicle with an "R" tag, which meant it was a rental car. I dutifully wrote down the information in my notebook and didn't think much more about it.

After the shift ended, RC, Frank and I got in Frank's car and proceeded to go home, by way of Michigan Ave NE. We were just making small talk when suddenly the car wanted in the bank robbery passed us. I started yelling," That's the car! That's the car!"

They had no idea what I was talking about and neither remembered the lookout from roll call. I was persistent though and Frank continued to drive just behind him in the next lane. The obvious problem was what in the hell were we supposed to do? This was a couple of decades before cell phones and Frank wasn't about to ram the guy with his own car.

It wasn't long before we both crossed over into Prince Georges County, Maryland. Still no feasible plan in sight and I wasn't completely sure they fully believed me in the first place. I knew I was right and there was no way this particular S-1 was going to get away.

We were about a mile into Maryland when we stopped at a red light. S-1 was still in front of us and it was then I saw our salvation. Across the intersection and facing us, also stopped at the light was a Prince Georges County Police cruiser.

I immediately jumped out of Frank's car and ran across the street to the Officer's vehicle. I guess Frank and RC didn't want to be seen as nonparticipants so they ran behind me.

I quickly identified myself and pointed to the wanted car, asking him to pull it over so an arrest could be made for bank robbery. Well, he just looked at me and did absolutely nothing. I repeated myself and he completely ignored me. He then turned to Frank and RC and asked, "Does she know what she's talking about?" Like I'm a total imbecile. No, it really was because I was a female that had no business being a cop. It wasn't until Frank and RC assured him that I did indeed know what I was talking about, that he took action. S-1 was placed under arrest and yes, he was the right suspect.

We all went to a Police substation nearby and proper protocol was to call the FBI. Two agents arrived and said they would take over from this point. Really?!?! No "Thanks for a good job." Nothing. They just took the guy and left. And took 100% of the credit for doing 0% of the work. It's unfortunate but the FBI had a reputation for stealing cases out from under other jurisdictions.

So the three of us just left and went home. One more example of a total lack of respect for the female Police Officer. So what! It was because of me that an armed bank robber went to jail. Toot! Toot!

51.

Frank and I still lived together and things were going well except I knew at some point, our commanding Officers were going to have to make a decision about us continuing to work together. We didn't actually work in the same scout car, but our beats were so close together that we frequently responded to the same calls. We were both under a microscope which we were well aware of.

102

When Frank broke his leg making an arrest, I didn't respond to the scene. When Frank had his front teeth knocked out after a prisoner swung a loose handcuff into his mouth, I stayed away. The prisoner who bit his hand all the way to the bone in front of the Washington Hilton, again a no show. I was well aware of what was going on with Frank, but we had made a pact which I was determined to uphold. Sometimes it wasn't easy though.

One time I responded to the Raleigh House, a place where hookers plied their trade, for an armed robbery. The Raleigh House was on 13th St, just North of Logan Circle and when we arrived, the girls were streaming out the front door yelling that the guy was heading around the circle toward P St. We immediately began driving where they were pointing and spotted a Black male quickly walking in a very suspicious manner. We didn't have a physical description at that point but as we were pulling alongside him, I heard Frank forcefully interrupt the dispatcher. All he said was, "He's got a gun."

At this point, we were right next to the guy who apparently also heard Frank. He was about three feet from me and began reaching into his waistband. I have never exited a vehicle as fast as I did that day. Clarence and I were on top of him so quickly he never had a chance. During the ensuing melee, his sunglasses fell off and got broken. But we were able to restrain him, make the arrest for armed robbery and take a fully loaded .45 automatic off the street. Thanks for the heads up, Frank!

Back at 3D in the cellblock, S-1 was very upset and angry. Not because he was being charged with a serious felony. No, he was pissed off because I had stepped on his sunglasses and broke them. He even made a written complaint with a Sergeant, demanding I replace them at my own expense. Like that was going to happen. The mindset of some criminals never ceased to amaze me. I don't think broken glasses would be at the top of my list of things to be upset about. Just a wild guess, but I think it might be the 25+ years I'd be facing in prison.

52.

It always made me chuckle when "the girls" demonstrated their crime fighting skills. It wasn't uncommon for some of the men to drive to the strip carrying a firearm. Some of them were there only to rob the women. But most of them felt they needed protection themselves and really were not a true danger to anyone. Except it was illegal for them to be packing. And the girls frowned upon it under any circumstances.

Sometimes we would be flagged down and they would give us such an accurate description of the vehicle and suspect, it rivaled anything the dispatcher voiced over the air. And nine times out of ten, there was the dumbbell still in the vicinity, usually with some Saturday night special piece of crap under his seat.

One night I was waved over on 14th St and given information of a good old boy with North Carolina tags displaying a handgun. It took all of sixty seconds to find him and place him under arrest. This guy immediately started crying hysterically and saying he would only speak to an Officer that was a member of the Masonic Temple. He wouldn't give us any information unless we found a fellow Mason. I really didn't need to ask him many questions but his histrionics were getting on my last nerve. Hmmm, an Officer in 3D who was a Mason? That would be Frank so I got on the radio and requested he respond to the 3D cellblock.

When he arrived and the two of them did the secret handshake, the dude calmed right down and allowed me to process him without further incident. As long as Frank stayed in the room. The poor guy was from some small town in North Carolina and this was his first time in the big city. He was kinda like Barney Fife in civilian clothes.

Another time, an Inspector Walters called me up to the station. I had no idea who he was except that he far outranked me. He wanted his thirteen year old son and two friends to ride along with me. There is a Ride Along program in the Department that's only for adults, but what was I going to say? "No" didn't seem like a viable option.

As we were leaving to go out on the street, Inspector Walters parting words were, "Don't let anything happen to these boys." You know what direction this story is going before I write another word.

I drove over to 14th St and of course the boy's eyes were bugging out of their heads because the girls were out in full force. I just drove around for awhile so they could enjoy the whole experience. So far, so good. But then as I was driving North on 14th St at Rhode Island Avenue, one of the ladies ran into the middle of the street right in front of my car. She was pointing and yelling, "That guy has a gun!" There was only one car in the

block ahead of me and I knew that had to be
it.

In the backseat I had this "precious
cargo" and I had been ordered not to get
involved in anything. Now what? Oh screw it,
this guy was not going to get away. I told the
boys to get as far down on the floor as they
could and No Peeking!

I called for backup and put on the red
lights and siren. He pulled over right away
and the barrel of a Smith and Wesson in his
face made a very good first impression. He was
placed under arrest and when I walked back to
the scout car, there were three sets of eyes
peering over the front seat. When I finished
for the day, I took them back to 3D to the
Inspector. He was furious with me for
endangering his little angels but I had been
put into an absolute No Win situation. If I
had to do it over again, would I have done it
differently? Hell no, that was one more gun
taken off the street. But please don't give me
anymore thirteen year old ride alongs.

53.

Ride alongs were not uncommon in 3D and
I certainly had my share. Basically, all you
had to do was sign your life away and get into
the scout car.

My sister Jeanne rode along once and
even my Mother rode with me. Oh Lord, that was
an experience when dear old Mom came along.
I was showing her the sights when a call came
out for a protest that was starting to get out
of control over by the Russian Embassy in the
1100 block of 16th St NW. Oh good, let's show
Mom the Po Po in action, so of course I drove
to the scene.

As soon as I stopped on L St, just east of 16th, I realized this probably wasn't a good idea. The mob was becoming more and more angry and it looked like the Police were directing them on L St, right toward me. And Mom! Oh Shit, this was not good! My mind was going a mile a minute as the crowd got closer. Just then the answer came to me.

Across the street there was an alley running behind the Embassy. At the entrance to the alley was a Uniformed Secret Service Officer whose job was to protect the building and its occupants. He also was not allowed to leave his post. I pointed him out to Mom and told her to run across the street as fast as she could and hide behind him. He could see what I was doing and made sure she was safe until the incident was over.

I happened to be a K-9 handler at the time so I took Duke out of the car and his mere presence was able to convince about a hundred unruly demonstrators that maybe they needed to turn around. It's amazing what one dog can do that a small army of Officers cannot.

Another time I had a vacationing Honolulu Police Officer ride with me. Everything was going well until we went to a domestic dispute in the 1400 block of Chapin St. There wasn't anything particularly memorable about it and it seemed to be handled without any further incident. Or so I thought. As we were leaving after the "Don't make us come back" speech, I heard the Honolulu Officer angrily blurt out, "And don't make me kick your fucking ass either!" WTF!
The fight was immediately on, punches were thrown and people went to jail. He was taken back to the station and told to never, ever

try to ride along again with the Metropolitan Police Department.

Another night, these two drop dead gorgeous Swedish Police Officers signed up to ride along. I'm sure I volunteered for that assignment because the next thing I knew, they were in the backseat of my scout car. I adjusted my rear view mirror so I could have them in my sightline at all times. I don't remember exactly the date of this ride along, but I do recall that it was extremely cold. It wasn't long before I noticed something terribly wrong. There was the most horrific odor coming from somewhere so I rolled down my window and stuck my head out. Nothing out of the ordinary. These guys were pretty interesting but I couldn't figure out where that damn smell was coming from. Whenever I would get out of the car it went away. I may be a bit slow or maybe I was just in denial about it's true source.

Finally I couldn't take it anymore. Let the truth be known: These two gorgeous Swedes stunk to high heaven! Only God knew when they last bathed. So here it was freezing outside and I had all the windows down trying not to throw up. I think I made up some excuse to get rid of them.

We also had Reserve Officers, who had no arrest powers or carried guns. Most of the ones I knew were very nice but then there were the Wannabes.

One of the worse got assigned to ride with me for a shift. He thought he knew everything and his intent was to take charge since I was just a lowly female. That not going to happen because I told him not to touch the radio or speak to me. Obviously that made him very unhappy but I didn't care.

We got a call for a loud party and I thought I had taken care of it with my "Don't make me......" Oh, you know the rest. I was almost to the elevator when the dipshit Reserve idiot turned back and yelled, "And don't make ME fucking come back either motherfuckers!" Just reread the paragraph about the Honolulu Officer because it was the same thing. The fight was immediately on, punches were thrown and people went to jail. I think I was able to get this guy banned for life from ever riding along again. At least with me.

54.

Ah yes, odors. One of the worse calls a Police Officer can receive is the "Unconscious person" or "Investigate the strange odor." The first is for a dead body, with or without decomposition. The dispatcher can't technically use the word "dead" because only medically qualified personnel can declare someone as deceased. But we all knew it meant permanently unconscious. Especially if there were major body parts out of place, or missing completely.

"Investigate the strange odor," especially in the summer meant the person was truly dead, usually rotting and smelling so bad that entire buildings were self-evacuating.

One of the worse was in the 1400 block of R St, on a good old hot July day. As I pulled up and stopped, I observed entire families running outside, choking and gagging. It was times like this that I questioned why I didn't take that damn social work job in the first place. But nooooo, I had to go for the extra three grand.

I did throw the Hail Mary pass though. Before I exited the Scout car I got on the radio and requested leave from my Sergeant. He of course had been monitoring the air and knew just why I was asking. "That's a negative Officer. Continue on to your assignment." The assignment in question was on the top floor, in the rear of the building. And there was no elevator!

I really didn't need the apartment number because all I had to do was follow the smell. I entered the apartment and there she was. She was an elderly woman that died sitting on the toilet and then fell over on her head with her legs sticking straight up in the air. She had obviously been there for a little while. I had no idea how long but I did know that the hotter it was, the faster the decomposition. Just leave a raw piece of meat on a hot sidewalk and you'll get the idea.

I got on the radio again and asked for an Official and Homicide detectives. It seemed appropriate to spread the joy. Oh yeah, I called Frank to please bring cigars. That supposedly helps kill the odor a bit. He responded that he would get the cigars but I would have to meet him out front on R St. There was no way he was coming upstairs. I guess love only went so far. So, armed with cheap cigars for everyone, we all did what needed to be done as quickly as possible and got the hell out of there.

Then there was the "unconscious" homeless guy we found in a vacant building. This man had been there so long, he was covered in maggots. And they were jumping on us when we turned him over! Someone told me later that they are only interested in rotting flesh and not fresh, human living bodies. Was

that supposed to be of any comfort? These
friggin' things were inside my uniform shirt,
jumping around and I'm supposed to be
thinking, "Oh, no problem." While incessantly
scratching, we did what we could to get rid of
him and into the Medical Examiner's wagon.
Then we rushed over to Howard University
Hospital to take showers using some special
medicinal soap. Afterwards we shook our
uniforms out hoping to get every last little
bugger out. And then back on the street
answering 911 calls. I'm actually scratching
now just thinking about it.

On all these Police shows on TV and
movies, they are always putting out miles and
miles of yellow crime scene tape. Never once
did I see anyone use crime scene tape in my
career. It just wasn't in our bag of tricks.
If a crowd formed at a scene, we just told
them to get the hell back and if anyone
crossed that invisible line, they were dealt
with accordingly.

On some of the shows on the
Investigative ID channel, they're hanging
yellow tape out in the middle of nowhere, even
if there's not a soul within a ten mile
radius. Really?!?!

And another thing we never did but
probably should have. We never wore gloves
when handling people, either dead or alive. At
some point, every one of us got up to our
elbows in blood and other bodily fluids. I
almost think we would have been made fun of if
we had worn protective gloves. It just wasn't
something anyone thought about. There
certainly were no gloves in any of the scout
cars. Gloves at the time were for cold
weather. And I tried to wear them as little as
possible anyway, in the event I had to use my

firearm. Even when the AIDS epidemic struck in the early 80s, nobody wore gloves. It's amazing that any of us are still alive

55.

There was a retirement home on 11th St, called Garfield Terrace that we were all familiar with. When someone apparently dies of natural causes, the Po Po still have to respond. But if the person has been actively under a doctor's care, then there's no need for a big investigation.

I got "the call" one day to respond to an apartment at Garfield Terrace. And there she was, lying in bed, obviously deceased. No signs of trauma or foul play. She was old and just died. I called for the Medical Examiner's wagon and was informed they were really busy and I would be put on their list. That meant it would be several hours, and I couldn't leave the scene until she was taken away. I noticed she had been watching one of my favorite soap operas, Search for Tomorrow. I looked around for a chair but there wasn't one so I sat down next to her on the bed and watched the rest of Search. Then, As the World Turns and General Hospital and whatever came after that. I'm sure she would have been okay with that and I was actually sorry when the Techs arrived to interrupt us.

The Roosevelt Hotel on 16th St was another one where the seniors were dying right and left. It wasn't a hotel anymore but they still called it that and anytime we were dispatched there, it was always for the same thing. To expedite the process, I always wanted to call for the wagon before I arrived,

112

but we weren't allowed to do that. I had to
make visual contact first and then call.
I was sitting at a red light one day on U St
at 16th, minding my own business when I
observed an elderly Roosevelt resident
shuffling across the street. When she saw me,
she started to walk over to my car. I had no
idea what she wanted but before I could say
anything, she wacked my arm as hard as she
could with her cane. Then she cackled, "Elbows
in, Officer."

My elbow had been resting on the
driver's side door while I was waiting for the
light to turn green and this old woman just
assaulted me with her cane! What was I
supposed to do? Lock her sorry old ass up? No,
I just drove off, rubbing my poor, bruised
arm. "Elbows in, Officer" my ass!

We got another "Unconscious Person" run
on Swann St one night. It was in a row house
and all the electricity was out. Clarence and
I entered with our flashlights and observed
all these buckets and pots filled with some
kind of mysterious liquids. We went upstairs
and saw the same thing. We finally found the
body lying on a bed. The bed was completely
surrounded by these weird containers, holding
God knows what. And the whole place being
pitch dark merely added to the creepiness.

This was a situation where we called
for assistance and then went back outside and
waited in the car. I never did ascertain what
that was all about, but then I wasn't really
interested. You just did what you had to do
and then went on to the next call.

I always kinda felt sorry for Medical
Examiner's Techs. Their job was to transport
dead bodies all day or night. Sometimes, to

make things interesting they would punk one of the rookie cops.

If a body was located on an upper floor and was particularly ripe, they would ask the rookie to assist them. The body would be put on a gurney and the rookie would be instructed to take the lead. As they were going down the stairs, gravity would take over and the head would sometimes "explode" all over the rookie. Thank The Lord it never happened to me because I know I would have fallen for it hook, line and stinker. Er, I mean sinker.

56.

About once a year the Sergeant would come into roll call and say these five simple words, "The DAR is in town."

The Daughters of the American Revolution is a group that was founded in 1890 by women who could prove some kind of ancestral lineage to the American Revolution. I think the average age of each member today is about a hundred and fifty. And when they came to town for their annual convention at DAR Constitution Hall, they all stayed at the Mayflower Hotel on Connecticut Avenue NW. I guess all the excitement must be too much for these old gals because inevitably there was always a death or two at the Mayflower. So the code word DAR in roll call meant some "lucky" Officer was going to get the Unconscious Person call sometime during their convention.

The Mayflower reminded me of the time I was in the lobby when some White guy in a suit fell out right in front of me. He seemed to be in cardiac arrest and was flopping around, foaming at the mouth. People made a circle around him and someone told me to give him mouth to mouth. Screw that! You give him mouth to mouth! My lips were not going to touch his slimy lips! We had no first aid kits or any of those masks they now have. Maybe you're beginning to see a pattern here. We had NO equipment!

When I came on in 1973, we had no body armor whatsoever. The Department would periodically request it from the DC City Council to no avail. That is one reason so many Officers were killed in the line of duty in the 1970's. The cheap ass city refused to come up with the money to protect its Police Officers.

It came to a point where Frank and I went out and bought our own bulletproof vests. Nice! We were dying to know if they worked, so we took his and put it on top of one of those really thick phonebooks to stop the bullet. I think it was something we saw on TV. He fired a .38 round pointblank into the vest. It made quite an indentation but did not penetrate the material.

It was a couple more years before the city relented and body armor became standard issue. Then the next controversy came and that involved the ammunition we carried. It seemed that what we had was not sufficient enough to effectively bring somebody down. It just wasn't strong enough or so they said. I knew nothing about ammo but when we were told it wouldn't do what it was supposed to on the street, it seemed obvious that something had to change.

The answer apparently were hollow points, which would spread upon impact and cause more internal injuries. They also didn't ricochet like regular bullets. It seemed like a no brainer, but wait! City Council would not approve them because they felt hollow points were too dangerous! WTF! You just can't make this stuff up. We certainly didn't want to hurt anybody! Especially the people that were trying to kill us. That too, took a while but eventually we were permitted to carry the horrendous hollow points in our revolvers.

57.

Frank and I were still getting along famously. We both had good, solid reputations at work so finally the time came.
We were having dinner one night in our apartment in Hyattsville when I popped the question. Yes, it was me. And he agreed it was a good idea. I had already met his Mother but not his Father. This was in February of 1975 and Frank made arrangements for him and me to meet in a week.
Unfortunately, just days before we were supposed to get together, Frank Senior dropped dead of a heart attack in a restaurant.
We went ahead and got married on July 12, 1975 in a Quaker ceremony in Adelphi, Maryland. After our honeymoon in New Orleans, we moved into Frank's Father's house on Chillum Pl NE. It was a tiny duplex on a quiet street but it was a house all the same.
Surprisingly, the Officials left us alone and didn't try to separate us. We still had that iron clad pact though just in case. We lived in an all-Black neighborhood and everyone was really nice except of course, our next door neighbors. Isn't that frequently the case?
They were this trashy family with lots of unruly kids. The adult male, Joe, hogged a

lot of the hard to come by parking spaces with
all these junky vehicles. He supposedly bought
them, fixed them up and sold them. It was very
shady but we didn't want any trouble.
After a couple of years, things started going
downhill. Joe was outside banging on those
cars morning, noon and night. And it was
getting more and more difficult to find a
place to park. Some of the neighbors came to
Frank and asked if he could do anything.
On day he wrote down all the tag numbers and
ran them through the computer when he got to
work. It turned out that half the cars were
"hot" or not properly registered.
When we got home, Frank called 4D headquarters
and asked one of his buddies if he would
handle it.

A little while later we heard a
commotion out front so we peeked through the
front curtains and there was Joe being led
away in handcuffs. His wife (or girlfriend),
Alicia came out behind him and started yelling
and pointing toward our side of the house, "I
know those damn MF honkies are behind this.
I'm gonna get yo ass for this!" And other
assorted greetings. At least the Chillum Pl
parking situation was resolved. Frank and I
knew this wouldn't be the end of it though.
The gloves were apparently off.

                           58.

      One day, the neighbors got a German
Shepherd that they called Sparkle after some
movie of the same name. That alone should have
been enough reason to take the dog away from
them. But they had a twelve year old daughter,
Diane who promised to take care of Sparkle.
And she did. For awhile.

After a bit, a wire was strung between two trees in their backyard and Sparkle was attached to the wire and left there all day. Frank and I would periodically check to make sure she wasn't tangled up and had enough water, but we were not pleased.

Sparkle soon discovered she could jump over the fence and into our yard. She couldn't jump back because the wire was too tight at that point and she was stuck. So Frank would yell for Diane to come over and get Sparkle, which she did. This happened a few times but soon it became apparent that there had to be another solution to this problem.

One evening we decided to go out for dinner so after we got ready, Frank made one last trip to check on Sparkle. There she was, again in our yard so Frank yelled for Diane to come and retrieve her. This time Diane did not answer so Frank called her name several more times with negative results.

We couldn't just leave Sparkle in our yard, tightly attached to a wire which was on the neighbor's property. Frank went back out with the intention of picking up Sparkle and putting her over the fence. He had lots of experience with German Shepherds since he had been a dog handler in the Air Force when he served in Viet Nam.

I was still in the house when I heard a gunshot. Oh Shit! I ran outside and there was Frank standing next to Sparkle who was obviously dead. It seemed that Sparkle was acting okay until Frank apparently got too close and she attacked him. I knew I had to call 911 and also request an Official from 3D to respond. This was going to get very ugly! Frank and I were very upset because we both love dogs and this was really the neighbor's fault for not properly taking care of their dog.

Diane then appeared and began screaming and wailing, which attracted any neighbors that weren't already on the scene. 4D Officers, 4D Officials and 3D Officials responded and began asking a lot of questions. It was pretty chaotic but that was nothing compared to when Alicia appeared. She already hated us for what she thought we did to her old man. But now Frank had murdered her daughter's beloved dog! The noise level with her raging at us went up significantly. It got so bad a 4D Officer threatened her with Disorderly Conduct if she didn't calm down. So here we had this "Unconscious Dog" laying in our yard and the Medical Examiner's Office doesn't respond to this kind of situation. What was going to happen to poor Sparkle's body?

Frank had had about enough of Alicia by that time so he went over to Sparkle, picked her up and dropped her over the fence into Alicia's yard. Alicia went even more ballistic and with brute strength, picked Sparkle up and threw her corpse back into our yard.

It became something like a crazy ass tennis match except instead of a ball, they were using a dead German Shepherd. Back and forth, Sparkle went between our yards. Finally an Official put a stop to the insanity and ordered Sparkle to remain in our yard.

Everyone was told to return to their homes and when it got dark, Frank and I wrapped Sparkle in garbage bags and deposited her in a dumpster at a local Hechingers.

59

I believe our drinking was getting
heavier at this point. Frank was waiting for
the Trial Board to meet and the stress of the
unknown was driving him crazy. He was
convinced he would lose his job over the
Sparkle incident and I found myself
continually reassuring him that everything
would turn out okay. But he wouldn't listen
and we began to argue and drink a lot, which
of course made the situation worse.

When he was finally cleared, the
arguing slowed down but not the drinking. The
fact that maybe we were starting to develop a
problem never occurred to either of us. When
we would come home from a particularly crazy
shift at work, we thought it was the only way
to relax and wind down. You'd drink the same
way we did if you worked the kind of job we
did.

Life did seem to be finally getting
back to normal though (whatever that meant).
3D and 14th St were still in full swing and
would remain that way for many more years.
Half the time I was patrolling alone and half
the time with a partner. I really got into
traffic enforcement and wrote countless
numbers of tickets for moving violations, in
addition to all the parking infractions. Then
I decided to get into DWI arrests and became
quite proficient. It was kind of like shooting
fish in a barrel though, since the majority of
Johns needed that liquid courage to pick up
one of the girls. At one point, I even won an
award for making the most DWI arrests in 3D
for the month.

I took a class to become certified in
administering the breathalyzer so when an

Officer would make an arrest, I would respond to the station and test them. If it was a slow shift and a drunk driver was brought in, sometimes the Officers would take a look at him/her and try to guess their BAC (blood alcohol content). Soon, money would appear, along with their guess and whoever was closest won the pot.

"I think he's a .20."

"No, no. He's a .17."

The poor drunk had no idea what was going on, but dutifully blew into the plastic tube as instructed.

I got called in one evening and when I entered the station, someone took me aside and said, "You're not going to believe who's in there?"

"Okay, I give up, who is it?"

As I entered the cellblock area, I could hear a familiar voice on the prisoner's telephone. He was trying to explain away the reason he was locked up for DWI. On the other end, I could hear a woman screaming obscenities through the line. They were going back and forth until there was a distinct click. She had just slammed the phone down after a final obscenity.

When I entered the small room where all the commotion was, I immediately recognized a pitiful looking man with one wrist handcuffed to the wall.

It was a well-known Hall of Fame Washington Redskin and he was drunk as hell. His face was beet red; he was just a total mess. He had been stopped on L St, driving drunk with a female companion at his side. The phone call he had just made was to his wife, who was having none of it. This was his third DWI arrest so he had had plenty of practice.

He seemed very happy to see me and began to laugh loudly. When I invited him to partake in the breathalyzer test, he laughed some more and then simply said, "No thank you." I tried several more times and he always said the same thing, "No thank you." Then he passed out.

I went to court to testify against him but he and his lawyers settled on a plea deal for reckless driving. When he saw me, he shook my hand and thanked me for being nice to him. Actually, I don't think he had a clue as to who I was but it was a nice gesture.

60.

The Christmas Eve/morning shift in 1977 had another Washington Post reporter ride along with me so he could record what occurred in the ghetto on the birthday of Jesus Christ. His name was John Feinstein and he was a nice enough young fellow, so off we went in Scout 98 to see what we could see. As a sidebar, John went on to become a well-known sports reporter and author of several books. But back then, he was just a snot nosed reporter trying to make a name for himself.

The girls were still out in full force even though it was Christmas Eve. The traffic may have lessened a bit, but probably not by much.

While I was patrolling in the 1400 block of P St NW, I observed a van full of young White males in front of me. Of course they were only in the area for one reason. I was in the mood to mess with them (and give John something to write about), so I pulled them over. When the driver couldn't produce a valid registration, I told him he was going to get a ticket.

There must have been at least six guys in the van and they were very unhappy, but I didn't care. I returned to the Scout car and radioed in the tag. As I was waiting for the return, all the doors to the van opened and the boys jumped out and ran over to my car. Oh, shit! I had already been beaten up on Christmas Eve three years ago by one guy. Now there were six of them!

They immediately surrounded my car as I was picking up the radio mic to call for assistance. John was definitely on his own in this one. For all they knew, he was a plainclothes Officer.

What happened next was one for the books. Instead of attacking us, they began to sing Christmas carols. They all had beautiful voices because it turned out they were in the college choir where they went to school. They must have sung at least three or four carols and when they were finished, they just stood there expectantly. Even John was staring at me with that, "Now what are you going to do?" look. Was I going to be the Scrooge or what?

I exited the Scout car, looked at each of them and said, "Merry Christmas. Now get the hell out of here. If I see you again tonight, you're all going to jail." It didn't happen often, but every once in a while I gave someone a break.

Which reminds me of the time I stopped a carload of teenagers who were speeding up 18th St. When I walked up to the car, I saw a case of Budweiser on the backseat. These kids were obviously underage and there was no way I could let them keep the beer and continue on their way. Unfortunately, I was on my way to a

call and really didn't have the time to deal
with it.

Then the lightbulb went off and I made
them get out of the car, along with the case
of Bud. I told them to open and dump out every
one of those twenty four cans of beer into the
gutter. I sorta felt sorry for them because
I'm sure they pooled every last dime they had
to buy that beer. But not enough to let them
go. If I'd done that and they had gotten in an
accident or something, full liability would
have fallen right on my shoulders. At any
rate, they'd have a great story to tell their
friends. The one about the female bitch cop
that made them throw all their beer down the
drain. Cheers!

61.

The year was drawing to a close and I
was all ready for 1978 to come around. '77 had
been a pretty eventful year, what with Sparkle
and the Trial Board.

What I didn't know was that the year
was going to end with a Big Bang, so to speak.
On December 29, 1977 I was working 10-99 in
scout 98 on the midnight shift when I received
a call to respond to 1340 Q St NW for some
type of disturbance. Since I was alone,
another Officer, Rita Head was dispatched too.
I arrived first and as I pulled up in front of
the building, a man and woman came running out
the front door.

The woman excitedly told me that she
and her boyfriend were sleeping, when they
heard a noise. As they were waking up, they
observed their neighbor from next door
standing over them with a gun pointed toward

their heads. The lady said she screamed and he ran away to his own room.

As she was telling me he lived in a back room on the second floor, Rita arrived on the scene. Now Rita was one tough broad and that's the appropriate word. She was a big Black woman that was about as street smart as they came. Nobody messed with Rita Head! We used to have to go to the Police and Fire Clinic for annual weigh ins, and Rita would get up on that scale with a Super Big Gulp in one hand and a bag of potato chips in the other. Enough said.

We walked upstairs and I knocked on the guy's door, at the same time yelling, "Po-leese. Open up." His response was, "Fuck you!" We went through this a couple of times with the same results. I then noticed his door was not completely shut so I decided to kick it open.

I stood on the left side of the door and Rita stood on the right, both of us with guns drawn. It didn't take much effort and the door popped right open. As soon as I peered inside, I saw an older Black man standing about five feet away, pointing a gun toward my head. As soon as he saw me he fired and I fired back.

I immediately took cover in the hallway, having no idea if I had hit him or not. Luckily for me, he missed.

Not having a clue where he was in the room, I very carefully poked my head into the doorway, fully expecting him to shoot at me again.

Inside the room to the right was a dresser and a bed. I could see him crouched between them and thought he was waiting for a chance to fire again. But then I noticed a gun lying on the floor, about three feet away from him. That seemed very odd so I quickly ran into the room and kicked it away. Rita entered the room too and we both grabbed him and threw him on the bed onto his back. That's when I realized I had shot him. Right in the middle of the throat! There was blood everywhere and Rita gathered anything she could find to stop the bleeding. She told me to help her but I remember saying, "This guy just tried to kill me. YOU give him first aid."

I knew I had to call for help but I didn't want to be that Officer who was always screaming unintelligibly on the radio when the shit hit the fan. I actually had prepared for this moment. I picked up the portable radio and made myself count to ten before keying the mic. I knew Frank would be listening so I made sure that as I was reporting my involvement in a shooting, I added I was unhurt. Was that pact we had made a while ago really so ironclad? It turned out that it was.

After I called for additional assistance, all hell broke loose. Paramedics, Officers, Officials and Detectives all crammed into that little room. It seemed like everyone was talking at once, most of it directed toward me. But all I could focus on was the TV blasting away. He had been watching an old Perry Mason rerun and all I could think of was that he would never know who did it. I didn't know it at the time but I think this a textbook example of dissociation. Mentally thinking about anything but the madness and horror directly in front of you.

62

Recently, in roll call we had had an
in-service lecture on how to preserve your
service revolver as evidence if you're
involved in a shooting. We were specifically
told not to turn it over to anyone but a
Mobile Crime Technician, so that as few people
as possible handled it. This was also referred
to as the Chain of Custody. The fewer, the
better for any type of evidence, in any kind
of case. That way there is a smaller chance of
it being mishandled.

So when the 3D Detectives arrived on
the scene, the first thing one of them said
was, "Let me see your service weapon" and then
stuck his hand out to give it to him. That was
NOT going to happen and I told him so. I
wasn't even going to remove it from my holster
until Mobile Crime came. This guy decided he
wanted to argue with me but I would have none
of it and told him so. An Official overheard
our rising voices and told him to leave me
alone. I really didn't need this added
stressor.

Per our agreement, Frank stayed about
two blocks away. Officers that had been on the
scene would go and find him and update him on
the situation and how they thought I was
doing.

Finally, some Homicide Detectives and
Mobile Crime Techs arrived, at which time I
turned my gun over as requested. One of the
Detectives, Robert Sharkey, took me outside
and put me in his cruiser so we could go
downtown, after he took care of some loose
ends.

As I was sitting there, I heard
somebody come over the radio and tell the

dispatcher that the guy had just died. I think by that time I was just numb because I don't recall having any kind of reaction. I was twenty six years old, I had only been on the Department for four years and I had just killed somebody. It was completely surreal. So I sat there quietly in Sergeant Sharkey's cruiser, waiting to go downtown to Police Headquarters to make a statement.

At the time of the incident, Rita had been living with the local bootlegger, Dick Sutton over off 9th St. This certainly called for a drink, so as we were pulling away in the cruiser, I saw Rita and yelled out the window, "Go see Dick!" And she knew exactly what I meant.

In the early 1970's, the Homicide Office actually had a bar to help people calm down if they were too anxiety ridden while they were talking to Detectives. I saw it with my own eyes when Kenny Garrett and I were there after Sgt. Morton shot him in 1974. In 1977, I wasn't sure if it was still there and I sure as hell didn't want to spend the rest of the night making statements without a belt or two. Good thing too because apparently the full service bar was long gone.

I was put in an interrogation room and left to sit and wait. Rita and the two witnesses also arrived and we were all separated from each other. We could hear what was going on around us though. I heard Rita ask if she could use the restroom and after waiting a couple minutes, I asked if I could use it too.

When I went out into the hallway, I saw John Feinstein waiting for me. He acted like we were long lost friends but of course all he wanted was a front page story. I was polite but then said, "No thank you" and ran into the restroom. Good try though, John.

Besides, Rita had what I wanted right there in the Ladies Room. And she didn't disappoint either. She had brought in a couple of cans of Sprite, emptied them out and filled them with Dick Sutton's vodka. As we were partaking in this delicious diversion, the female witness came in and asked if she could join us.

"Oh sure, the more the merrier."

For the rest of the night, the three of us would speak to the Detectives for a while and then ask to use the bathroom. By the time we were finished, we were pretty shit faced but nobody noticed or cared.

I then returned to 3D to have my Police powers officially revoked, pending the outcome of a Grand Jury. They already had my gun but I had to turn over my badge and sign a bunch of papers. It wasn't until then that I saw Frank for the first time. We knew we were under the microscope, so we just acted like this wasn't the monumental event it really was.

Plus, we already had made plans to go to Pennsylvania to spend New Year's Eve with my parents. Our suitcases were in the car so we left directly from 3D and hit the road.

Along the way, we were listening to the local DC radio station WMAL, and when the 6:00 am news came on, my shooting was the lead story. It was as though they were reporting about someone else, not me. The severity of what happened had not sunk in and would not for a very long time.

63

My parents had no idea as to what had occurred that night. All they knew was we were coming for a planned visit that included a New Year's Eve party at a neighbor's house. The closer we got, the more I realized I could not bring myself to tell them what I had done. Maybe it was the Quaker thing, but I was experiencing all kinds of emotions. I think the main ones were guilt and shame, even though I hadn't done anything wrong. It was all very confusing so I did what any chickenshit spouse would do. I made Frank tell them. When we arrived, I quickly made an excuse about not feeling well and ran upstairs to the guest bedroom where I hid/slept for several hours.

Finally, Frank dragged me downstairs and I don't think either of them knew what to say. So we did what many families are prone to do: we acted like nothing had happened.

We went to the New Year's Eve party but it was impossible to find any enjoyment in anything, let alone a raucous party. Copious amounts of alcohol, yes but even that wasn't doing the trick. We left and returned home after a couple of days. I was still on Administrative Leave though, waiting for the Grand Jury to meet.

Grand Juries serve for several months before they are released and a new Grand Jury is chosen. In Officer involved shootings or (OIS), prosecutors like to make their presentation to a "seasoned" Grand Jury. They want one that is almost at the end of their stint and have already heard just about everything.

By that time, the cynicism factor has risen significantly so it's very much in an Officer's favor to have their incident presented to the seasoned Grand Jury. What the Grand Jury does is decide whether the case has enough merit to be bound over for trial. In other words, it's a really big deal. And I had to be available every weekday from 0800 to 1630 hours, in the event they wanted to question me. Since there were no cellphones, I was confined to my house and next to the landline at all times.

One of the first problems was that the sitting Grand Jury was nearing the end of their term and a new group would be selected soon. That meant they could either rush my case through or wait for the next Grand Jury to come onboard. That would mean I'd probably have to wait several months until they too became hardened, so to speak.

So, what did they decide to do? They decided to push it through the current Grand Jury. I was only five days removed from the shooting when I got a call and told to report back to work. The Trial Board would do their own investigation, but if you weren't indicted by the Grand Jury then their decision was fairly routine.

In 1977, there was no such official diagnosis as Post Traumatic Stress Disorder (PTSD). There was no debriefing. There were no counselors to speak with. There was no Employee Assistance Program or Human Resources department. There was absolutely nothing in the way of services to assist an Officer who was involved in an OIS. You were expected to suck it up and carry on.

The last thing I needed to do was return to work after such a short period of time, but go back I did. The head of 3D at the time was Inspector Ronald Chase and he was holding the paperwork I needed to sign, so I could go back on the street.

I went up to his office and after some small talk, he told me that this event was similar to falling off a horse. You just got right back in the saddle as if nothing happened. Then he looked me directly in the eye and said ominously, "And you can go see the Department shrink if you think you need to. But I assure you Officer, it will put a black mark on your record."

And that was the end of that conversation. I turned around, got back in scout 98 and began patrolling again as if the event only five days ago had never happened.

64.

On the surface, I don't think I appeared any differently. But something had changed and I didn't know what it was. I seemed to have become some kind of hero to the other Officers. Many of them would approach and congratulate me on a job well done. This frequently included handshakes and pats on the back. A couple of them said, "Welcome to the club." What club! I was totally clueless until someone told me that the so called club only contained members that had shot and killed somebody. I simply didn't know what to think so I just smiled wanly and kept moving.

The more people put me on a pedestal the worse I felt. Nothing was making any sense but after what Inspector Chase said about a black mark on my record, there was no way in hell I was going to admit to anyone that there was a serious problem going on.

Even Frank didn't know. The isolation became physically painful so I addressed it the only way I knew how, by drinking more. And Frank was more than happy to match me drink for drink.

We were still pretty functional, considering the amount we consumed. Neither of us ever called in for "drunk leave," our finances didn't suffer but we were both a mess and it would continue for several more years. There was one incident though that should have been a wakeup call. We still lived on Chillum Pl NE when one day when we were both intoxicated, somebody knocked on the door. I peeked out the window and saw two Jehovah's Witnesses standing there. For whatever reason, I became very angry and decided I was going to shoot them. Frank thought that was a great idea except he announced that he was going to be the shooter. There was a gun on the top shelf of a hallway closet and we both went for it at the same time. In our drunken insanity, we started physically fighting over this loaded revolver. In the end, nobody was harmed and at the time neither one of us thought it was particularly reckless behavior.

My partner was the one with the real drinking problem. I had to cover for him more than once, when a citizen would come into 3D to make a complaint about the Black Officer in scout 98 that had alcohol on his breath. On some shifts he would tell me to drive back to 3D so he could use the restroom. He would do this several times until I finally asked him if he was okay. The look on his face told me everything I needed to know. He was going into the restroom to get away from me and

drink in peace. Once I realized what he was
doing, I'd just march into the Men's Room
after about thirty seconds and drag his sorry
ass out and back into the scout car. I don't
know why, but I never joined in and drank with
him. After work and on days off we did, but
not during work hours. Yet.

65.

I still spent most of my time on 14th
St, or in the immediate area. The location of
the shooting was less than half a block away
so I must have driven by that damn house
several times each shift. I never went back
inside though.

The time started to blur together. We
responded to countless numbers of domestics,
robberies, burglaries, assaults, rapes,
shootings, etc. You name it, we got it. One of
the few calls I didn't handle were serious
accidents. Those were investigated by Traffic
Division which was fine with me.

I got a call one night for a
disturbance in an apartment building in the
1400 block N St NW. It was on an upper floor
and fortunately the elevator was working. When
we exited the elevator, we immediately
observed an older Black female yelling and
cussing at something she was dragging down the
hall. It turned out to be her boyfriend who
she had just stabbed to death. And she was
pulling his dead body toward the elevator so
she could take him downstairs to God knows
where. And boy, was she mad! It seemed she had
caught him with another woman and the rest was
history. There was blood everywhere which we
were all slipping and sliding in.

When we arrested her she was more pissed that we had stopped her from carrying out her mission, than being charged with first degree murder. Some people just have different priorities.

Another night, I was on patrol on 14th St when I saw a car stopped in the middle of the intersection at 14th and N St. As I pulled up and stopped, I saw a White guy on top of one of the girls who was lying over the hood of his car. He was pistol whipping the shit out of her! I jumped out without even advising the dispatcher and began yelling at him to stop. He paid no attention to me and continued to beat her in the head with his gun.

I wasn't about to get into hand to hand combat with him as long as he was holding a lethal weapon. So I drew down on him with my Smith & Wesson, still ordering him to stop. He kept at it for several more seconds and then glanced my way. When he realized I was about to shoot him, he stopped. Then he announced he was a Detective who worked at Headquarters downtown as if that explained away everything. The girl was visibly injured but she just took off running. I was so angry, mainly because I had almost shot another Police Officer (not that he didn't deserve it), and that he was so nonchalant about it. Like "what's the big problem?"

I did something I'd never done before. I reported him to one of my Lieutenants, who assured me a full investigation would be conducted. But surprise, surprise. The whole thing was swept under the rug and that was the end of that.

66

The radio system was a very interesting piece of work. It reminded me of a large ballroom, where if everything was flowing effortlessly it was a sight to behold. Unfortunately, there were the Officers who insisted on cutting in when not appropriate or other Officers that were always stepping on someone's toes.

It was a matter of taking your turn and trying to judge just how important your transmission really was. Was it truly necessary to interrupt a high speed chase merely to get a tag check on a parked vehicle? It took real skill to become adept at grabbing air time. The Officers that pissed off the dispatchers with needless crap usually had hell to pay one way or the other. The dispatcher may be more prone to assign them the Unconscious Person in August than the Officer that waited their turn. You never wanted to get the reputation for being a pain in the ass on the radio.

Our Hall of Fame dispatcher was a civilian named John Gales. We always knew we were in good hands when John took charge of the mic. He was similar to the conductor of a large orchestra, and boy you better play his tune! He knew the city so well that one time we were searching for a suspect and he advised us that the third house from the corner had a hidden window well that we should check. And damn, there was S-1.

He had a deep, DJ kind of voice and even though he took no prisoners over the air, if an Officer was injured on the street he would never leave his shift without making certain that person was properly taken care

of. Sometimes he would even meet up with us
for a couple of beers in the parking lot.
I got flagged down one day, yes on 14th St. A
man told me there was someone wanted for
Homicide at 13th and Corcoran St NW. He
pointed toward the end of the block where I
could barely see a man standing on the corner.
I thanked the guy and drove down the street to
where he was. I picked up the mic to advise
the dispatcher and request backup. But, oh no!
The system was down and there I was standing
next to a Homicide suspect. No radio, no
backup, no nothing.
       I just acted like this was something
really routine so I wouldn't spook the guy. We
got engaged in small talk as if this was the
most natural thing in the world.
       "How bout those Redskins?" Come on
friggin' radio.
       It seemed like forever but finally the
radio came back up, I ran his name through and
yes, he was wanted for Homicide. He politely
turned around so I could handcuff him, got in
the transport car and I didn't see him again.
I never did find out who he allegedly killed.
I was on to the next call.

67.

       I heard every excuse under the sun from
people that committed traffic violations. One
of the most common was, "Don't you have
anything better to do, Officer?"
"Well, actually no I don't."
       Or "Why are you picking on me when
there's real crime happening out there?"
       Or "Do you realize that I pay your
salary Officer?" "Thank you very much and do

you realize I could use a raise right about now?"

"The light was malfunctioning Officer." With these people, I would make them get out of their vehicle and we would stand there and watch the traffic light go through several cycles. And it was a miracle because it was always working perfectly.

The ones that called me "Baby" or "Honey" always got the ticket.

Then there was the cab driver that insisted the light was not red. Really, what color was it? "It was blue!" As I was handing him the ticket, I implored him to go to court and tell the Judge what he had just told me. That would be entertainment at its finest. Darn, he didn't show up to contest it.

The out of town cop/tourists were some of the worse. Remember, they were only in that part of town for one reason and that wasn't to see the Lincoln Memorial under the moonlight. They would quickly flash their badge and huff and puff about what Police Department they were with. I would make them take their badge back out and hand it to me so I could look it over. Half of them were fake but they all got "the lecture" about maybe it wasn't a great idea to come down here trolling for pussy while your wife and kids were back at the hotel sound asleep.

The ones that really pissed me off were the guys that left their weapons under the seat or in the glove compartment while they were out getting a piece of ass. Then their vehicle would be broken into and the gun stolen. These guys got to return to Mayberry while we had one more stolen weapon in the hands of S-1.

I still see it all the time; those stickers that people plaster on their cars. "I support the Police." Or other stickers to that effect. They've paid a few bucks to some organization to get the stickers so they won't get tickets. Wrong! They mean nothing. Even the Thin Blue Line stickers don't mean what they used to, because so many people have them. Everyone is always looking for an edge and there just isn't one. I have Active Member Fraternal Order of Police tags and even though it's helpful, any Officer that stops me still has the discretion to write me up.

I always tell people if asked, not to make excuses or ask dumb questions. Just look pathetic and remorseful and maybe ask the Officer if he or she could possibly give you a written warning.

There were a couple of times that Frank would stop a woman and when he walked up to her window, her blouse was completely unbuttoned and her boobs hanging out. Or their skirt was hiked up so far, he could see..... Well, never mind. He would politely thank them for the free peep show and then hand over the ticket. Or so he claimed.

68.

Some of the buildings that people lived in were beyond belief bad. The stench of urine in the hallways was overbearing, the elevators were always broken and crime was rampant both inside and out. In the sweltering summer months, everyone stayed outside as long as possible to avoid returning to their oven baked apartments. Air conditioning was a luxury that few could afford.

In the winter, ovens were turned all the way up, with the doors open for added warmth. A terrible fire hazard but people did whatever they could to survive.

There were two buildings in 3D that were famous, not by their addresses but by their names.

The first was Clifton Terrace which was located on the South side of the 1300 block of Clifton St NW. It was a series of several connected, five story apartment buildings that were a large source of the crime in 3D. One thing that made them stand out, aside from the continual criminal activities was that the South side of the buildings had some of the most spectacular views of the city anywhere. A lot of people would pay a fortune to see an unobstructed view of the DC skyline from their living room. Not these people. They were too busy trying to make it.

I quickly learned that when entering Clifton Terrace or most of the other buildings in 3D, to never get too close to the walls. The reason being that the cockroaches would jump all over you. Door frames were especially dangerous. You made sure you walked right through the middle of the door and even then some of the more athletic roaches would try to get on you.

I can't forget the trash and garbage that was spread out all over the halls, along with graffiti everywhere. Some of these places weren't fit for a dog and no Officer ever lingered around for any reason.

I got a call one day to respond to Clifton Terrace for a disturbance. I was driving North on 14th St and when I got to Clifton St I saw a crowd of people on the sidewalk, all pointing upward toward the building.

When I exited the scout car and looked to where they were pointing, I saw something I'd never seen before.

On a third floor balcony, two men were dangling another man over the rail by his ankles and threatening to let go. Of course, the crowd was loudly encouraging these guys to drop him. I yelled at them to pull him back in, but being that I was significantly outnumbered I'm sure they didn't hear me. And even if they did, they weren't about to listen to a lone White female Police Officer. It wouldn't have been macho.

I called for backup and we went inside to try and get into the apartment. Luckily it was unlocked and when we got entered, they were still holding him over the railing. When they realized it probably wasn't a good idea to finish the deal, they pulled him back to safety and explained their actions.

It seemed these men had returned home from work and found this guy burglarizing their apartment. So they took it upon themselves to pick him up by his ankles and throw him over the balcony. Actually, it sounded reasonable to me but of course I couldn't say that. Unfortunately, the Po Po arrived before they could finish their plan.

Instead of arresting these two men, we locked up the burglar and proceeded to march him out the front door of Clifton Terrace. What we didn't know until we got outside was that the original crowd had now swelled to several hundred. And they were angry! Not at us, but at the burglar who we had in handcuffs. His life was again in danger because these people wanted blood.

I called for more assistance but by
this time they were throwing anything they
could get their hands on. Rocks, bottles, even
slabs of concrete were being thrown at us. I
safely got S-1 into the back of my transport
car but by the time I was able to make my
escape, every window in the vehicle had been
shattered. Shit, more paperwork and although
we were covered in broken glass, we got out
uninjured. S-1 was actually thanking me for
saving his life by the time we arrived at 3D.

69.

The other building was the Whitelaw
Hotel located at 1839 13th St, or at the SE
corner of 13th and T St NW. It was originally
built in 1919 by Black men for Blacks in a
fully segregated city at the time. Many famous
entertainers stayed there when they were
booked to perform at the various theaters on U
St, which was then referred to as Black
Broadway. The name Whitelaw came from the last
name of the builder's Mother.

When I arrived at 3D in 1973, the
Whitelaw was one of the most crime ridden
buildings in the city. It was one of those
places that an Officer would never go in
alone, and that was saying a lot. Most of the
time there was no running water or electricity
but that didn't keep anyone out. Heroin
addiction was rampant and the majority of
apartments were used as shooting galleries.
You just never knew what you were going to get
involved in at the Whitelaw, but you knew it
wasn't going to be good.

One time Frank and R.C. went there on a
call and they knew nobody would answer the
door when they knocked. So Frank came up with

an ingenious idea. As he was knocking, he would announce they were collecting for the Star. As if anyone at the Whitelaw was having the Evening Star newspaper delivered. But wouldn't you know it, the door opened.
When Frank and R.C. stepped inside, they were immediately surrounded by about thirty junkies, many of them armed with guns. And they were all very unhappy. Being that Frank and R.C. were completely outnumbered and hesitant to use the radio to call for help, Frank just waved and said they would come back next month to collect for the Star. Apparently the druggies thought that was a good idea so the two of them backed out the door and got the hell out of there.

Just across the street, in the 1300 block of T St NW, was one of the biggest 10-33s I had ever been involved in. A 10-33 call is for an Officer in Trouble and when somebody puts that call out, it usually means all hell has broken loose.

On this particular day an Officer got into something he couldn't get out of so he radioed a 10-33. And when you hear that call, you drop everything and respond as fast as possible. This happened to be a very hot day so everyone on all sides were irritable to begin with. It didn't take much for the entire block to come out and join the fray. It seemed like every Third District Officer was fighting every resident of the 1300 block of T St. It was so out of control that members of the Second District were also instructed to respond and that was totally unheard of. I'm sure they were more than happy to get in on the action. A change of scenery is always good for the soul.

Finally, I think everyone got too hot and too tired and it ended as quickly as it started. Sure, a few people had to go to jail for the obligatory Disorderly charge but for the most part we all got a good, healthy workout.

70.

Just north of the 1300 block of T St, is a one block street called Wallach Pl NW. As with most other blocks in 3D, this entire block was covered entirely in small row houses. Almost without exception, they were all rundown and in need of major renovations. One night the dispatcher put out a 10-33 inside a home on Wallach Pl. It was a little unusual that the Officer him/herself didn't actually make the call themselves, but not totally unheard of.

All the Officer on the street hears is that a fellow Officer is in trouble and needs immediate assistance. Everybody fights to get on the air to advise the dispatcher they are responding, but that's usually an act of futility since only one person at a time can transmit. So it turns into a case of "the hell with it, I'm going whether dispatch hears me or not."

Within seconds, the entire block was flooded with scout cars, cruisers and transport wagons. We all rushed through the front door and saw something completely unexpected. The whole first floor was filled with people, balloons and cake. WTF! It was a friggin' birthday party and someone had called 911 yelling that an Officer had been shot at that location. Kind of a joke on the birthday boy to see his face when the dumbass cops came barging through the door. Everybody was drunk/high and laughing their heads off, but guess who wasn't laughing? Or rather, guess who got the last laugh?

We filled up both wagons and every transport vehicle so they could continue their party in jail for the night. An added bonus were the extra tight handcuffs they got to wear for a very long time.

Speaking of handcuffs, no matter how loose you may put them on someone, they always complain about how tight they are. And they always wear them in the back, no matter what. Some people, if they think the Officer is a rookie will make all kinds of excuses as to why they have to be handcuffed in front. And sometimes it works, which is a really bad idea. Conceivably, an Officer could be choked to death with the metal chain that hooks the cuffs together.

If S-1 is particularly obnoxious, the tightness of the cuffs can make a grown man cry. It depends on their demeanor and/or the type of offense they're being charged with. Crimes against children, the elderly, and rapists are at the top of the list. You get the idea.

There was a little grocery store on the East side of the 1900 block of 14th St. I got a call for a shoplifter being held for transport to 3D. When I arrived, I was directed to the rear of the store where the shoplifter was sitting on a box. The owner had caught him stealing some meat and wanted him arrested. Not a problem, or so I thought. I directed him to stand up and turn around so I could search and handcuff him. It was then I noticed he was missing an arm. How in the hell was I supposed to handcuff somebody with one arm? This wasn't taught in the Academy either. Hmmmmm!

Then it came to me. I put one cuff on the only wrist he had left, and the other cuff to his belt. And it worked perfectly. There are so many ways an Officer has to improvise on the street. They just can't teach you everything at the Police Academy. Did this scenario ever come up again for me? No, but I was prepared if it did.

71.

I was patrolling one night in the North alley of the 1700 block of Rhode Island Ave NW. It was a cold night and if I recall, there wasn't a whole lot going on. As I was driving slowly down the alley, I noticed a rolled up carpet directly in front of me, completely blocking my path. It sort of reminded me of a speed bump, and nine times out of ten I would have just run over it. But for whatever reason, this time I didn't.

I exited that nice warm scout car into the frigid air and bent down to pull the carpet out of the roadway. Damn, this rug was heavier than I anticipated. I gave it another tug and that's when I saw there was somebody inside the thing. It was a drunken homeless guy that had rolled himself up like a cocoon to keep from freezing to death. He didn't fully think it through though, or he would have moved it out of the middle of the friggin' alley. I woke him up with a few choice words and sent him on his way. Why I didn't run over him, I'll never know and he never fully comprehended how close he came to a physical catastrophe.

The only part of 3D that was somewhat upscale was the East side of Connecticut Ave NW. Everything to the West was the Second District. Along with the world famous Mayflower Hotel were many expensive stores, just begging to be broken into. Many S-1's committed "smash and grabs" and burglaries where they broke in any which way they could.

One night I was again patrolling in an alley over by Connecticut Ave. This particular alley ended up behind the Raleigh department store. Raleigh's, now long gone, was a retail institution in DC for many, many years. As I pulled up behind Raleigh's, I noticed a pickup truck that seemed somewhat suspicious. I got out of the scout car to take a closer look but it was the view above me that caught my eye.

Apparently, Raleigh's had just been burglarized and the suspects were on the roof throwing fur coats in the direction of the pickup truck. It was actually raining mink coats and the back of the truck was their target. Unfortunately, the damn Police ruined their plans. K-9 was called in and everyone was apprehended without incident. I couldn't help but try on a couple of coats before turning them over to the store's authorities. Actually I looked pretty good with that Sam Browne belt wrapped around a $10,000 full length mink coat.

72.

I would be remiss if I didn't spend some time on the Presidential Inaugurations. These were by far, the biggest events DC Police had to handle because there simply was no room for error. The whole world was watching, and everyone in law enforcement had a part in making it happen without security issues.

When I was a teenager, I attended the parade on Pennsylvania Ave for Lyndon Johnson in 1964. And also, Nixon's second inauguration in 1973. There were so many angry protestors at that one, I almost got swept up in mass arrests taking place at 13th and Pennsylvania Ave. Little did I know that just nine months later, I would be joining the same Police department that nearly put me in jail.

The first inauguration I worked in uniform was Jimmy Carter's in 1977. I can still remember the excitement of being an active part of this historical event.

Everyone was in dress uniform, even the Detectives who NEVER wore a uniform except every four years. The rest of the city had to be covered for 911 calls, but it was by a skeleton crew because the Higher Ups wanted as many Officers as possible downtown.

This year, 3D Officers were to report at 0700 hours to Pennsylvania Ave at 19th St NW. I should have known something was up since this was three blocks past the end of the parade route. But I didn't give it a thought because suddenly I heard glass breaking and then laughter. What the hell? I looked over to where the sound was coming from and saw Officer Patrick Eastman standing in a pool of liquid and broken glass. It seemed he had brought a bottle of hooch to ward off the cold and had stashed it inside his coat. Somehow, the bottle became dislodged and went crashing onto the pavement. Everyone, including the Sergeant, thought this was very funny. Well, if they found it amusing then I guess I did too, so I joined in the laughter.

We just hung around for hours with nothing to do and why in God's name the President is inaugurated in the dead of winter is beyond me. He isn't sworn in until noon, then there's a luncheon at the Capitol and the parade begins around 1400 hours. And we're on fixed posts, three blocks past the White House.

Finally, after endless hours of doing nothing, we saw the parade coming toward us. There are always lots of horses and most of them are trained not to crap when they're prancing down the street. So they've been holding it for quite some time. And here we were at the very end of the parade and they needed to go. I think every friggin' horse in the 1977 Presidential Inaugural parade took a shit and piss right in front of me. And we're talking about a lot of horses. By the time the day was over, I kinda wish I had hidden a bottle in the front of my coat too.

The next Inauguration was in 1981 when Ronald Reagan was elected President. This time I was in a specialized group called the Civil Disturbance Unit or CDU. I was still assigned to 3D but if something out of the ordinary happened, CDU became involved. It was kind of like a SWAT team with none of the fancy equipment.

My assignment in '81 was to ride in a cruiser that was always parallel to the Presidential motorcade and one block away. The idea being that if an incident occurred, we could swoop in and assist in any way we could. Whoever was driving the cruiser monitored the radio so he would know at all times where the President's limo was. I can still hear the dispatcher saying, "Rawhide has just crossed 7th St." Or, "Rawhide is approaching 15th St."

It was very exciting to be a part of history even though the only thing we really saw was the back of thousands of people watching the parade.

In the evening were all the Inaugural Balls, which the President and First Lady attend. The term "Ball" is used with a grain of salt. Each one is a mad house, packed so tightly with Party supporters that Fire Marshals inevitably show up and either shut them down or make people leave. The food and drinks have already been consumed by the "locusts" so those in the know have eaten before arriving.

Downtown is solid gridlock because of all the limousines and half the drivers don't know where the hell they're going. In other words, it's a total free for all. But I was still in the cruiser, one block away from each event. When the President and Mrs. Reagan left one Ball to go to another we shadowed them, not knowing when they would call it a night. By this time, everyone was exhausted and hoping they would cut the party short and go back to the White House.

Around 0130, word came that the Reagan's were leaving the last Ball. Once we knew they were safe and sound within the White House grounds, there was a collective sigh of relief and we checked off and went home.

73.

Thinking of CDU back in the day reminds me of how low tech it really was. There were some openings in the late 70s and of course I had to apply just to see if they would take a woman. And they did. I don't think I had any interest in joining the unit, but what the

hell? It was another opportunity to piss off
the establishment because they were forced to
take a certain percentage of women.

The only thing I remember about the
training was we had to go back to the Lorton
firing range for additional instructions. That
meant "mastering" the shotgun which included
badly bruised shoulders from all the shooting.
As a treat, we got to shoot clay pigeons.
Whoo! Whoo! They could have fired a clay
elephant out of that thing and I would have
missed. I was such a bad shot they should have
dismissed me right there and then. But no, the
worst was yet to come.

We had to go through a course with our
revolvers. The clay pigeon fiasco wasn't used
against any of us but the scores using our
38's on fixed targets would be. And being that
we were CDU candidates, we had to do a lot
better than the routine qualifications. I was
pretty nervous because I didn't want to wash
out in front of all those men.

I went to the line and fired
innumerable rounds. Sometimes the targets were
twenty five yards away, fifteen yards and
seven yards away. Strong arm, weak arm and
kneeling.

When we were finished and the line was
clear, we walked up to our targets to see how
we did. The Range Instructor started at the
far end of the line with his clipboard and
counted holes in the targets. At this point I
just knew I hadn't made the grade, so I did
something I'd heard you could do to always
qualify.

I had a pencil in my pocket which I
discreetly removed and poked several holes in
my target. Hmmm, were there enough? I sort of

panicked and poked a few more just for good luck.

When the instructor came to score my target, he gave me a funny look. Then he told me to follow him to the office. This was not going to be good. When I got inside, he announced that there were sixteen extra holes in my target, along with traces of pencil lead. I wanted to suggest that maybe they came from the Officers on either side of me but looking at his expression kept me from saying anything.

The other Range Instructors entered the office which further humiliated me because I knew they weren't done yet. One by one, they all let me have it, but in the end I was permitted to stay after I swore I would never do such a lamebrain stunt again. And I didn't.

I was now an official member of the Civil Disturbance Unit and could rightfully carry a shotgun, wear a helmet and big, bulky body armor. Now I could really be a part of the action, as if I hadn't been already. Still, the tip of the iceberg. Still, the tip.

74.

Washington DC is not only our Nation's Capital, it is also The Place people come to protest and demonstrate their pet causes. Sometimes these demonstrations can be quite large. During the Viet Nam War, over a million protesters took to the streets to voice their dissension against the War.

I have to confess that I rode in a school bus from my college in Ohio to DC in 1970 to be a part of that mass demonstration. It seems that everyone has a cause and feel the need to come to DC to show the world just

how important it is. And who is better
prepared to handle these masses than the DC
Police, National Park Police, US Capitol
Police, Metro Transit Police, etc.
        The fact of the matter is that nobody
here gives a shit about protesters and their
all important issues. It's just something
these people do to feel good about themselves.
"We marched in Washington and now everything
is going to change!" Yeah, right. You walked
down the street carrying a sign and whatever
legislation you're for or against is
automatically going to be enacted. And God
forbid, the Police who estimate crowd figures
put the number lower than you think it should
be. Here come the lawsuits. It actually got so
bad that Police quit reporting it. Ok, so you
want to say that ten million people showed up
to protest against strawberry ice cream, then
so be it.
        Here's the truth of the matter: The
only thing people in the District of Columbia
care about is parking and how to get from
point A to point B with the least amount of
resistance. Your stupid ass protests endear
you to nobody. You can go home now.
On the other hand, it was a great way to make
overtime pay.
        As a member of CDU, I was once assigned
to escort a group of demonstrators who were
walking from Adams/Morgan to the White House.
I have no recollection of their particular
cause, but I didn't care because I was being
paid a lot of money to go for a walk. There
were about fifty of them and they seemed
peaceful enough, but as we got closer to the
White House we all noticed a distinct change
in their demeanor. Many began picking up
debris along the side of the street. Debris,

such as rocks, broken bricks, bottles, you get the picture.

Everyone's antenna went up at this point. Helmets were strapped a little tighter, riot sticks gripped firmer and name tags removed. It looked like this might get down and dirty.

As we approached the White House in Lafayette Park, every member of the group turned toward us and began throwing all the crap they had been collecting along the way. The minute the first missile was thrown, all hell broke loose. After they threw whatever they were holding, they went into hand to hand combat mode. But that didn't do much against the three foot long hardwood riot sticks.

Some of them ran into the nearest Metro station which was a mistake since the Transit Officers could now become a part of the action. It was truly a crazy scene but there was one sad component to the whole situation. US Park Mounted Police responded to Lafayette Park and some of the protesters had nail bombs which they used and ended up injuring a horse so badly, he had to be put down. At least, that's what we had been told.

A lot of S-1s went to the hospital that day, and for what? How did attacking the Po Po and killing a horse promote their cause? Dumbasses!

To really make some kind of change, you have to get in the trenches and devote a large portion of your life to whatever it is that interests you. It's hard, thankless work with no guarantee that anything will come of it. I'll be the first to admit I don't have the tenacity for it. Are the people who live in and around DC cynical? You bet, and proud of it!

75

In 1973, the same year I was sworn in, a man arrived in town to start a group called the Community for Creative Nonviolence (CCNV). His name was Mitch Snyder and he became a fixture in the local community with his endless energy in advocating for the homeless and disenfranchised. CCNV members were always coming up with imaginative ways to help people and even today the largest homeless shelter in the city is named after Mitch Snyder, who sadly killed himself in 1990.

I received a call one day to respond to the Safeway at 17th and Corcoran St NW for some shoplifters that were being held by a security guard. They turned out to be a couple of young women from CCNV who had lifted day old bread to give to the needy. I felt it was a total waste of time to lock them up but the guard insisted, and if he was willing to do all the paperwork then I was willing to transport them to 3D.

They didn't give me any trouble and I think we actually had an interesting conversation about what CCNV was all about. The whole thing was pretty uneventful and I never gave it another thought. Until about a year after my shooting on Q St in 1977.

I was in roll call one night when a Sergeant handed me an envelope with CCNV written in the left-hand corner. It seemed very odd that anyone from there would be sending me anything. But I tore open the envelope and inside was a letter from one of the women I had transported, oh so long ago from the Safeway.

She wrote that she had seen the
Washington Post article about the shooting
incident and wanted to contact me. She said I
had been very kind to her and very much
appreciated the way they had been treated. She
knew that if I had to use deadly force that
December night, then it had to have been
totally justified. The letter ended with her
writing that she was praying for me because
she believed I was probably adversely affected
by the entire ordeal. She was the first and
only person that got it! And she was a member
of the Community for Creative Nonviolence! I
never saw or heard from her again but I'm
still profoundly touched by her gesture of
support.

76.

Back to the infamous 14th St. While the
poor girls were selling their booty in all
kinds of weather, their pimps were comfortably
lounging in the local bars. If asked, each
girl would insist their man was in love with
them. It didn't matter if they were beaten to
a pulp for not meeting the night's quota. At
least he was paying attention to her, or so
she claimed.

And yes, some of the pimps looked just
like you saw in the movies. With their disco
polyester clothes, hat and high heeled shoes.
The real "fashion" at the time was to drive a
big ass Cadillac with some sort of coach light
on top. Of course, these were referred to as
Pimpmobiles with Pimp Lights. It was so
entertaining to mess with them. Failure to use
a turn signal: Ticket. Not making a complete
stop at a stop sign: Ticket. Passing through a
yellow light: Ticket. The funny thing was that

these guys became excellent drivers because they didn't want to get any more tickets. There was one pimp though named Ronald Givens (AKA- Gizmo). Gizmo had a habit of parking his Caddy in an alley off the 1400 block of Church St. This was illegal so I wrote his car a ticket. The next night he did it again so I wrote another ticket. This went on for several nights until finally I decided to take this thing up another notch. I called for a wrecker and had his precious ride towed to 3D. I knew that would get his attention and boy, was I right.

Before I knew it, I was summoned by a Sergeant to respond to the station. As I walked through the side door, I saw Gizmo at the front counter in deep conversation with Sergeant Hal Gordon. He was a friend of mine and I was confident he was setting Givens straight. I couldn't have been any more wrong. When he noticed me, he immediately began chewing me out---right in front of Ronald Givens! The longer it went on, the more Gizmo smirked. I just stood there and took it but I knew even then that the War was on.

One of the first things I did was pull up his driving record from DMV. It's still hard to believe, but he had 36 points! He had been revoked for years but I didn't know it. I knew it now though. And if it was the last thing I ever did, I was going to lock that SOB up.

I put the word out I wanted to catch this guy behind the wheel, and to call me if anyone did. Somehow he must have gotten wind of this because he was no longer driving that 1973 White Cadillac with DC tags 250-166. I can't tell you what I had for breakfast this morning, but I still remember Gizmo's license plate number all those years later. Go figure. He was still a prominent figure on the strip but he just couldn't drive. Every time I saw him in his car, one of his buddies would be driving. If I caught his eye, he would merely do his now familiar smirk and keep moving. I was patient because I knew the time would come when I'd catch him.

It took two friggin' years but finally it happened. There he was tooling down 14th St driving DC tags 250-166. As soon as I turned on the red lights he stopped, exited the car and put his hands behind his back. It was all very anti climatic and I think I was a little disappointed. I was expecting a bit more drama but at least he got to spend the night in jail.

Years later, I read in the paper he had escaped from the DC Jail by tying sheets together and going out a window. I hope he didn't mess up his 'Fro squeezing through the bars. I had long ago let bygones be bygones.

77.

Every place of employment probably has a Hank Madison in one form or another. This is the person who knows everything, been everywhere and has done everything. I think our Officer Hank Madison had been an astronaut, decorated Green Beret, fighter pilot, spy, doctor, etc, etc, etc. Why he was now a lowly street cop was always explained in the vaguest of terms. No doubt he was on an undercover mission to save the world from mass destruction.

One night he was on the corner of 16th and L St NW, trying to make an arrest. A struggle ensued and somehow S-1 got Hank's gun out of his holster. As they were both fighting for control of the weapon, some dumb ass tourists across the street stopped to gawk. Really a bad idea because the gun accidentally discharged and one of the tourists was shot in the throat. No, he wasn't killed but he certainly had a story to tell back home. The massive settlement he undoubtedly received from the District government didn't hurt either.

So, why am I telling a story about Hank Madison? There is a reason and I wasn't even involved in the event, or so I thought. Hank's gun was seized by Mobile Crime and processed for the investigation that was being conducted. Everyone at 3D talked about it--- for about five minutes and then went about their business.

A few months passed and then one day in the middle of the shift, I was told by the dispatcher to respond to 3D to see the Watch Commander. As I made my way to the station, I racked my brain trying to think of anything bad I might have done. Nope, not this time. When I entered his office, I saw a Smith and Wesson .38 service revolver on his desk. He asked me if I knew who it belonged to and I said no. Then he dropped the bombshell and told me it was mine. How could it belong to me when mine was sitting safely in my holster which was hanging at my side?

He stated it was my gun that had shot the tourist down on 16th St. Furthermore, the gun had a hair trigger and it was a miracle that whoever carried it had never inadvertently shot themselves.

I was told to withdraw my weapon and read off the serial numbers to him. And guess what? I was carrying Hank Madison's .38 and he had been carrying mine. How in the hell did that happen?!

You just don't switch weapons with someone for any reason. It didn't make sense but there it was. It remained a mystery for several days until somebody came up with a bright idea.

For security reasons, whenever you came into the station with an arrest, you turned your weapon over to the Desk Sergeant before going into the cellblock area. At some point, Hank and I must have made lockups at the same time and when it came time to return to the street, we were both handed the wrong firearm. The only way to know if this had occurred was to pore over the arrest book and see if this was indeed the case.

It turned out that it was. I had been carrying that damn hair trigger piece of shit for years until Hank and I made the inadvertent switch-a-roo and he ended up shooting a tourist in the throat. We both got new revolvers and the policy was changed at 3D in regard to securing your weapon upon entering the precinct. I wonder if it's still in effect.

78.

Burnout was a big problem, as it is with many jobs. We had a Sergeant Bowles that had been on the Department for about a hundred years and he was one of the most burned out individuals I ever met. Being that he was truly Old School, he didn't hide the fact that he absolutely hated female Officers working the street. I just stayed out of his way as much as I could.

One morning at about 0700 hours, I came into the front door of 3D and saw a young Black man engaged in an intense conversation with Sgt. Bowles. He was becoming very angry with the man and finally told him to quit wasting his time and get the hell out of the station. The young man kept saying, "But it's true. I really killed him." The more he said it, the madder Sgt. Bowles became. When the guy saw he was getting nowhere, he just threw his hands up and left.

I couldn't contain myself so I asked Sgt. Bowles what was going on. He told me this guy came in the station and confessed that he had just killed his roommate in their apartment at 15th and Euclid St. He went on to say the man was crazy and besides, his breakfast was getting cold back on his desk. I had to tread carefully on this one but after Sgt. Bowles stomped back to his office, I asked the Desk Sergeant if he caught the address the guy was talking about. Yes, he had and he gave it to me.

I grabbed another Officer who wasn't busy and we made our way up to the Hilltop apartments on Euclid St. When we knocked on the apartment door, the same young man I had seen at 3D, answered and politely invited us in.

The other Officer and I immediately saw an obviously dead body lying on the kitchen floor. Oh sorry, unconscious person. It was a pretty bloody crime scene and after advising the subject of his Miranda rights, we asked him what had occurred. He told us they had had an argument and somehow he ended up jamming his roommate's face into a hot burner on the stove while beating him to death. I could have done without the hot burner part because the

smell of burning flesh is not something you're
going to forget---for a very long time. But
the guy was very cooperative and this time he
returned to 3D in handcuffs and was turned
over to Detectives in the Homicide branch
downtown. I never said a word about it to Sgt.
Bowles but he was so burned out I don't think
it would have had any impact on him.
He officially retired after this incident. Was
it because of his appallingly poor judgment? I
had no idea. I was just glad he was gone.

79.

One day, while working the 1500 to 2300
hour shift in scout 98 with Clarence Black, we
received a call to "Investigate the children
playing with a human hand."
We weren't sure what we had just heard
so I asked the dispatcher to repeat the
assignment. And she came back with the same
thing, "Investigate the children playing with
a human hand in the 700 block of P St NW."
So off to P St we went. When we
arrived, we saw a young boy chasing another
boy with a broom handle. On the end of the
handle was something that strongly resembled a
hand. We called the boys over and they said
they had found it back in the alley. I took a
closer look and damn, it really was a human
hand. These boys didn't have much in the way
of toys so they had stuck the hand on the end
of a broom handle and were playing tag! For a
second, I actually admired their ingenuity.
The question now was, where's the rest
of the body? It wasn't long before another
call came out for a pair of legs in someone's
backyard in the 1800 block of Wiltberger Pl,

which was just a couple of blocks from where we were.

Eventually, the remainder of this person's body was recovered. All except the head which was never found, as far as I knew. Some of the things that kids were exposed to in the inner city were pretty horrific. The fact that these boys thought it was perfectly normal to play tag with a human hand spoke volumes. Violence, especially domestic violence was a way of life. Guns, drugs, robberies, assaults and the like were the norm rather than the exception.

One night, a group of us executed a search warrant over on 12th St. It was believed there were guns in the apartment so the entering Po Po's, after using "the key" (battering ram) came inside like gangbusters. It was a very noisy and tense scene until the occupants were safely secured. At one point, I entered a room that had about three or four kids watching television.

They barely looked up but I remember one kid turning toward me and saying coldly, "Will you motherfuckers shut up! We're trying to watch TV!"

They were not fazed in the least that there were eight Police Officers running through their apartment with guns drawn, and dragging half the people out in handcuffs. In this case, the insanity had become the norm.

80.

Two stories that have absolutely no connection to each other: The first was one of the most bizarre incidents in my whole career, and that's saying a lot.

I was transporting a prisoner down to
CCB (Central Cell Block) by myself during a
day work shift. As I was driving South on 13th
St below Logan Circle, my prisoner began to
kick out the back window in an attempt to
escape. This happens every once in a while and
usually they are subdued before they can
actually get out of the car. The guy was very
methodical and just kept kicking and kicking
at the glass. I knew I needed some assistance
but as I picked up the radio mic, I heard a
loud unidentifiable noise coming from behind
my scout car. I looked in the rear view mirror
and could not believe what I was seeing. There
was a marching band coming down the middle of
the street!

The closer it got, the louder it became
and there was no way the dispatcher would be
able to hear my transmission for help. I
leaped out of the car, opened the back door
and began wrestling with the man who by this
time had broken out the window and was trying
to escape. There was blood and glass
everywhere, but the marching band never missed
a beat as they passed us by without a glance.
I guess you could call it "Music to fight a
prisoner by." I finally got him under control
and radioed for another transport car because
I had a lot of paperwork to do with the
Destruction of Property report and additional
charges for S-1. I never did find out any more
information about that friggin' marching band.

The other story involved some kind of
injury in an apartment in the 1400 block of
Harvard St NW. When I arrived, I was met by an
elderly Black couple at the door. The wife
explained that her husband had been badly cut
but she was taking care of it until the
Paramedics arrived. I asked what type of first

aid she was administering and she replied that
she had covered his hand in cobwebs. Say what?
Apparently it was an old Black Southern custom
to cover anything involving blood with
cobwebs. Her husband seemed quite agreeable to
this and it wasn't long before I was helping
pull cobwebs off the ceiling and adding them
to her growing collection. Ever since then,
whenever I get a cut I always think of that
old couple and their cobwebs. Who knows, maybe
it works but I could never bring myself to try
it.

81.

One evening, I was patrolling in the
1600 block of P St, when I observed a car
directly in front of me weaving back and
forth. I turned on the red lights and tapped
the siren so the operator would know to pull
over to the side of the street. When the car
stopped, a youngish White woman exited and
quickly walked back to my scout car.
#1: This was a no no. You need to stay
inside your vehicle unless instructed to do
otherwise. A potential safety issue for the
Officer but people still do it all the time.
I told her to return to her car but she would
have none of it. Nobody was going to tell her
what to do!
I noticed she was wearing a uniform
identifying her as a United Airlines flight
attendant and asked her to show me her license
and registration. She became more indignant
and stated she did not have one, looking at me
as if that was the dumbest question in the
world.
I then inquired if she had been
drinking, which of course was even a dumber

question. I guess she didn't consider the fact that her breath reeking of alcohol may have further piqued my interest.

By this time though, I had had enough of Miss United Airlines and told her I was arresting her for DUI. She was ordered to turn around and place her hands on the hood of my car so I could search and handcuff her. As she was screaming obscenities and calling me every name in the book, I just stood there until she wore herself out. Or so I thought.

Suddenly, I heard a familiar guttural noise coming from her direction. Before I could react, she spit right in my face and quickly reloaded so she could spit again. Wrong! I immediately grabbed her and had the handcuffs on in record time. It was all I could do to keep from smacking the crap out of her but I did the next best thing. I tightened the handcuffs and called for the Police wagon to transport her to the station for processing.

You Never, and I mean never spit on a Police Officer! When we got to 3D, I called her supervisor who responded in record time. She was horrified to hear what one of "her girls" had done. And wearing the United uniform to boot. If she could have, I think she would ripped it right off of her in the Precinct. This stewardess had just been permanently grounded.

82.

Washington DC has lots and lots of embassies. Many of them are located on Massachusetts Ave NW in 2D, also known as Embassy Row. With the embassies, come lots and lots of Diplomats. Their vehicles were easily identifiable because the license plates all had DPL on them, along with a two letter code showing what country they were from. For example, the letters SG may signify France, or BL may mean Germany. We all knew the Russian Diplomat tags because their embassy was located in 3D, in the 1100 block of 16th St NW. Their tag code was FC, which struck me as very funny because I just knew it stood for Fucking Commies. I could never prove it for years, make that decades but I knew I was right. And then one day as I was reading the Washington Post, there it was. That is exactly what it meant and when the Russians finally caught on, they demanded a change of letters.

I was driving around Logan Circle one night and saw that the car ahead of me did not have any headlights on. It had DPL tags but I thought I would pull it over just to tell the driver to turn his lights on. He continued around the circle and stopped at Rhode Island Ave. I exited the scout car and walked up to the driver's side window. Inside was a middle aged Black male who appeared to be from Africa. As I began to tell him why he was being stopped, he began yelling and cursing at me. I couldn't get a word in edgewise as he continued his rant. I asked for his license and registration and, like Miss United Airlines, he was having none of it. All I wanted to do was tell him to turn his lights on and he wanted to start WWIII. Finally, he got on my last damn nerve so I called for a transport unit because this guy was getting a free trip to 3D, in handcuffs. Two Officers responded and it took all of us to drag his ass out of the vehicle and into the back of the scout car.

As I was driving to 3D to process my prisoner, the dispatcher came over the air and announced that the guy was in the so called White Book. This meant he had full Diplomatic immunity and could not be arrested. I advised her he was already under arrest and she told me to stand by for further instructions.

A few minutes later, she told me a representative from the State Department would be meeting me at the station. All kinds of phone calls had to be made, people notified, papers signed, all because this jerk didn't want anyone telling him to turn on his headlights. I don't like to pull the gender card but I really think it was because, God forbid, a woman was telling him what to do. He did indeed have Diplomatic immunity and was able to leave without any further action. But the only redeeming thing in my mind was that he was inconvenienced for several hours. That was the best anybody could hope for.

83.

All the adventures I've written about make it seem like it was all violence and insanity, all the time. That was a large part of my story but there were times when it could also be pretty quiet.

This was when we were able to slow down and patrol at a much calmer pace. We could go into businesses and get to know the owners and employees. Let people know that we were more than just an anonymous face inside a scout car. All the banks and financial institutes had green books that the Police used to sign, showing that the Po Po were making sure everything was okay.

On the day work shift during the school year, we transported lots of truants back to school. Many of them were hanging out at the corner stores and some of them were turned in by their parents who couldn't get them to go to school. It was kind of a joke because most of them probably ran out the back door as we were exiting through the front. Quite a few would run away when they saw us approaching and there was no way I was going to chase down a thirteen year old with fifty pounds of equipment around my waist.

Eating a meal during any shift could be quite challenging. For one thing, we couldn't eat during rush hour. Or at least go out of service during rush hour. They wanted as many Officers available as possible to get those commuters safely in or out of town. 13th Street even became one way, in that it was Southbound in the morning and Northbound in the afternoon. Many major streets did not permit parking during rush hour and tow trucks were out in full force. For awhile, the DC city tow truck drivers would pick up an Officer at 3D so they could write tickets and keep the driver from being assaulted by irate motorists. I enjoyed the assignment because when someone was being a jerk, I'd pop out the door and threaten them with arrest, along with a hefty ticket and tow to the impounding lot on the other side of town.

There were a few restaurants that loved the Police and would give them a substantial break on their bill. But you really had to keep these places a well-guarded secret because if word got out, every cop in 3D would show up and expect the special Police discount. Next thing you knew, the Po Po weren't welcome there anymore. Nothing like a

bunch of cheap ass cops to ruin it for
everyone.

There was a carryout on Georgia Ave NW
that was open until 0400 hours. This was
pretty unusual because most everything closed
by 0200. The place was called Thrifty's and it
was a joint that specialized in grease and
more grease. The barbeque was okay but we
couldn't be picky so Thrifty's it was.

I was working with Jimmy Malloy one
night and he wanted to get something to eat at
Thrifty's. It was almost 0400, so we hurried
up there before it closed. I pulled in front
just as they were locking the door. When they
saw us, the owner signaled for us to come in.
I wasn't hungry so I told Jimmy to go ahead
and I would wait outside. He was let in and
the owner locked the door behind him so nobody
else could enter. I decided to get out of the
scout car and stretch my legs. There weren't
many people on the street at the time, so I
did something really stupid. I actually let my
guard down for a minute. Big mistake because
out of nowhere, some guy who was walking down
the sidewalk decided to sucker punch me. I
went down but I took him with me. Jimmy must
have seen the commotion because he ran to the
front door so he could assist me.

Problem: When the owner of Thrifty's
locked the door after Jimmy, he took the key
with him. And now Malloy was locked in and the
owner was way back in the kitchen. As S-1 and
I were doing battle, I could hear Malloy
trying to break the door down with no luck.
Finally, the door was unlocked and the guy was
arrested for Assault on a Police Officer,
which of course was knocked down to Disorderly
Conduct when it went to court. That was the
dirty little secret: hit a cop and it'll only

cost you ten bucks. That's how little we were
thought of then, and I know it hasn't gotten
any better over time.

84.

One crime we had that was fairly common
was the Robbery-PBS. That stood for Pocketbook
Snatch and I took more reports for that
particular offense than I care to remember.
Too many women, even today carry their purses
so casually that they're just begging to be
ripped off. Added now are smartphones and
tablets in phenomenal numbers. Pay attention
people! That call can wait, or at least go
somewhere safe.

But back to the Robbery-PBS. If we were
lucky, we'd find the pocketbook in a nearby
dumpster, minus the money and plastic of
course. If S-1 was really determined or if the
victim fought back, she would invariably be
knocked to the ground and possibly injured.

All those stupid self-defense classes
for women are ludicrous and can cause way more
harm than good. They're taught a few simple
moves and S-1 is totally incapacitated and
begging for mercy. Not quite. It's a good way
to really piss off the perpetrator so he
causes grave bodily injury or worse. Just give
up the friggin' bag, call the credit card
companies, go to DMV and thank the Good Lord
you weren't killed. Those self-defense classes
are nothing more than money makers that result
in women having a false sense of security.

There was a Baptist church at 1225 R St
NW that started having a PBS problem after
services, when the old ladies were exiting the
building. It happened several Sundays in a row
and we couldn't seem to catch the bastards.

Finally, the male members had had enough and put their own undercover mission into operation. Several of the younger members wearing casual clothes, staked out the entrance and waited for the services to end. And wouldn't you know it, along came S-1 who immediately grabbed a handbag and began running East toward Vermont Ave. There was an apartment building on the corner of Vermont and R St which he ran inside of.

Obviously, the undercover team was right on his tail. And right behind them was the entire congregation, which included the Pastors, children and nurses.

Sidebar: Almost every Black church I've been in has nurses. I don't think they're actually nurses but they dress in White uniforms and are at the ready, in case somebody falls out after being overcome by the Holy Spirit.

While everyone was running down the street, someone called 911 and that's where I came in. When I arrived at the building where the suspect was, the place was surrounded by the congregation. As I got out of the scout car, the choir began singing hymns and a large group held hands and started loudly praying.

Boy, I needed backup for this one. Reinforcements quickly came and when we went in the building, we found S-1 hiding in the basement and the purse behind the furnace. As we took him out in handcuffs, the choir and praying got louder. I think this little jerk probably thought twice before messing with the R St Baptist church. Or maybe not.

Three more unrelated stories:

Several times while working the street, we'd be looking for S-1, who had made his escape after committing a crime. Being that this was in the middle of the city, there were a million places to hide. Hopefully you were able to get a slew of Officers to assist you in the hunt, but that wasn't always possible. Especially when it was really busy out there and everyone was tied up with their own assignments.

I remember searching for a robbery suspect who was last seen running into an alley in the 1400 block of Rhode Island Ave NW. I looked everywhere for that SOB and was about to give up until the dispatcher came over the air with, "An older woman who wishes to remain anonymous believes that the person you are searching for is hiding under the blue vehicle next to the stockade fence." This alley was completely surrounded by apartment buildings and somewhere, in one of those apartments was an old lady who had seen the whole thing go down. She must have realized I couldn't find this guy and did her civic duty by calling 911 and turning him in. And yes, he was hiding under the blue vehicle next to the stockade fence. After I got him securely handcuffed, I waved toward all the buildings as a show of thanks to my anonymous friend.

Another time, I got a call for a robbery report in a home at 11th and Vermont Ave. It's essential to arrive there as soon as possible and get a lookout over the radio, so units could begin searching for S-1. I wasn't far so I arrived in no time. As I entered C-1's (Complainant) door with notebook in hand, a terrible feeling came over me. I was about to be hit with a major case of diarrhea! Now! What in the hell was I supposed to do? The complainant was standing there expectantly waiting to give me information.

The dispatcher and scout car Officers were waiting for the lookout.

I told C-1 to give me a description as fast as he could and then asked where the bathroom was. He looked at me oddly but pointed down the hall. I was becoming too sick to be humiliated so I ran into the loo and slammed the door. Luckily by then, we had portable radios because as I was sitting on the toilet, I was able to transmit S-1's information. Other than the dumbfounded complainant, nobody had a clue about the circumstances that were going on in that house on 11th Street. I think I kept that story to myself.

When I was still fairly new and that time of the month came around, I'd be all modest and make up excuses as to why I had to go to the station every hour. If the weather was cool, I'd have Tampax hidden inside my jacket so it would be readily available.

One day I was taking a report somewhere on Connecticut Ave and you know where this is going. I'm standing next to my partner, interviewing C-1 when it happened. A Tampax become dislodged from my jacket and fell on the floor right in front of my partner and the complainant. Oops! I hate when that happens. All three of us totally ignored what had just occurred and I kept my head down and continued writing. It was then I made the decision that I simply didn't care anymore. There is zero dignity in this job anyway so I decided it was time to go with the flow. Sorry, I couldn't help it.

After that, when it was that "special time," I just told my partner, "Look, I'm on the rag and I need to go to the station." They

never said a word which was probably a very
smart decision.

85.

I hate to admit it but there were a few
times when I was a total jerk on the street.
I went through a period when I was hell-bent
on enforcing all the taxi regulations. There
was a manual with information about what
hackers could or could not do. And I was
determined to learn and enforce every
infraction.

If you were ever in downtown DC, you
wouldn't see advertising or bumper stickers on
cabs. None of those gaudy roof signs you see
in other cities. DC was tough on outside
signage although it looks like today they've
lightened up a bit.

Standing more than five feet away from
your cab while waiting for a fare. Violation.

Improper manifest. Violation.

Wearing shorts. Violation.

Dirty cab. Violation.

Bumper sticker(s). Violation.

One time Clarence and I were driving up
14th Street and I saw a cab with a Blood of
Jesus sticker on the back. Violation. I told
Clarence I was going to pull him over and
write a ticket. Clarence always went along
with the program but this time he sat straight
up and looked at me like I was crazy.
"You can't do that! It says Blood of Jesus."
I didn't care what it said. He was in clear
violation and I was going to write him up.

By this time I had pulled the guy over
but before I could get out, Clarence and I got
into a shouting match over the stupid Blood of
Jesus bumper sticker. He was absolutely

horrified that I would consider writing this good Christian soul a ticket. I thought we were going to come to blows but I wrote the ticket anyway. I think it was several days before he spoke to me again.

There is one incident though I will always regret. I saw a cab in the 1300 block of Corcoran St with four stickers in the back window. Each one identified a different college and in my eyes, this guy was toast. He pulled over and when I told him he was in violation of the hack regs he apologized. He then explained that these were the colleges his children attended and being that they were the first ever to go past high school, he wanted to proudly display them for all to see. No. No. No. A clear infraction and I told him he had two choices. Either take the ticket or remove the stickers right then and there. He chose the latter and I stood there until all four were taken off. Was what I did legal? Yes. Was it one of the most classless things I ever did? Absolutely yes. At that point, everything was totally black and white with no room for gray. To this day I wish I could find that gentleman and apologize for being such a total asshole. Certainly not one of my finer moments.

86.

As I wrote earlier, Washington DC has so many demonstrations that they all kind of blur together. But there was one in particular I will never forget.

In January 1979, a large number of farmers came to town to protest against something they thought was highly unfair. What made their group stand out a bit more than the others was that they all arrived on their tractors. And I mean a lot of tractors. All different colors and sizes. They had decided they were going to shut down the city until they got their way. But first, there was going to be a big rally in front of the U.S. Capitol. All the tractors were parked on the National Mall, while the farmers gathered together in protest.

I have no idea who came up with this idea, but it was truly brilliant. Unbeknownst to the farmers, while they were at the Capitol every available DC government vehicle was parked bumper to bumper all the way around the Mall. The tractors were totally blocked in, with only one place to exit which was controlled by Police. Boy, were they in for a surprise after the rally.

When the last speech was completed, the farmers returned to their tractors so they could go out and shut down the District. Well, that wasn't going to happen and that's when a five week standoff began.

It was quite a sight to see endless numbers of city busses, and garbage trucks ringing our Nation's National Mall. At 3rd and Constitution Ave NW, was an opening so emergency vehicles could enter and exit.

To put it mildly, the farmers were very unhappy. Some said, "Screw this. I want to go home." And they were allowed to leave under Police escort, to either the Maryland or Virginia state line.

Most though dug in and set up camp. They weren't going anywhere until they got what they wanted. Or so they hoped.
As a member of CDU (Civil Disturbance Unit), I was ordered to report there, in case things got out of hand. My group was assigned to sit

in an old DC Transit bus in front of the
National Gallery of Art. We started out with
sixteen hour days, doing nothing more than
waiting. And waiting some more. No days off
and yes, the money was good but it got really
old, really fast. A lot of gambling was going
on in the back of the bus, but that just
wasn't my thing.

I had a very primitive, handheld
electronic football game that I wore the hell
out of. At the time, it was considered very
high tech, which I guess it was.

A couple of weeks in, we went down to
twelve hour shifts, still with no days off.
The farmers were getting pretty bored too, so
they started a makeshift tractor competition
on the Mall. This included races, wheelies and
burnouts. All of which totally tore up the
grass, but nobody went in to stop them.

Then, sometime in February twenty four
inches of snow fell on the city. The joke
around here is if the "S" word is even
mentioned in the winter, the entire
metropolitan area goes into panic mode.
Everything shuts down, including all the
schools and Federal and local governments.

So, for Twenty-Four inches of snow to
come down was nothing less than catastrophic.
Anyone that lives around here knows I'm not
exaggerating.

The city's plows couldn't possibly keep
up, so another ingenious idea was hatched.
Since the farmers, by this time were
practically comatose from boredom, they
volunteered to plow the DC streets with their
tractors. It was agreed that each tractor
would have an Officer onboard with them to
make sure things went smoothly. Plus, they

would have been lost in about thirty seconds
without an Officer to help navigate.
I was assigned to ride this huge piece of
equipment with an older farmer from the
Midwest.

It turned out to be a win-win for
everyone. The city streets were plowed in no
time and when the Farmer's Detail (as it came
to be known) finally ended, the Po Po and the
farmers had become pretty friendly with each
other. During the entire five weeks they never
gave us any real trouble.

Even today, when I drive past the East
wing of the National Gallery of Art, I think
about the Winter of '79 when I froze my butt
off with a couple of hundred American farmers.

87.

I was never into high speed chases for
a couple of reasons. First, the vehicles being
pursued were usually stolen and I was not
going to kill myself over something as trivial
as that. Just call your insurance company and
let them handle it. Plus, I really didn't want
to run over innocent bystanders. Unlike today,
the rules back then were pretty loose. If you
could justify that a felony had been
committed, then the chase was on whether it
was into Virginia or Maryland.

I started a few chases but as soon as I
told the dispatcher what I had, I just pulled
over and let the "cowboys" take over. And they
were more than happy to oblige. My favorite
pursuits were the ones where the Officer
radioed, "He's heading for the Wilson Bridge."
The dispatcher didn't need any more
information because they immediately called
the bridge operator, who also knew what to do.

Until recently, the Woodrow Wilson was a drawbridge on the Capital Beltway (I-495), and one of the few routes to quickly reach Virginia. As S-1 made his approach to the bridge, the operator raised it just enough that he wasn't going anywhere except to jail.

Now, one time I got into a chase. A slow speed chase. I observed a guy on a moped swerving in traffic. When I attempted to pull him over, he just kept on going. I turned on the red lights and tapped the siren but nothing. I blasted the siren to no avail. Now what? I knew if I advised the dispatcher of my slow speed pursuit I would never hear the end of it. So I kept following him, hoping he would finally stop. This went on for what seemed like a really long time.

Finally, in the 1400 block of Florida Ave NW, he pulled into a parking space, got off and walked up to the front door of a row house. I ran up behind him as he was trying to enter the premises. When I asked him what the deal was, he said the moped was his and that he lived there. Wrong! The moped was stolen and he did not live there. J-A-I-L for you Buddy.

There was a popular restaurant at 17th and Q St NW called Trios. Trios was right on the corner, the Fox and Hounds bar was connected on one side and Trios Carry Out was on the other. What they all shared in common was the kitchen which sat in the middle. I was having a sit down meal with Mike Hubbard one evening at Trios. Our scout car was parked directly in front of the carry out and it was a treat to actually be able to sit and eat like a regular person. Did I really think that was possible?

Of course something had to happen just as our food was served. One of the cooks came running out of the kitchen, hysterically yelling and pointing toward the street. I guess that meant dinner was over. We were able to ascertain from him that Trios Carry Out next door had just been robbed at gun point. Now that was ballsy, being that our marked car was parked right in front of the entrance. S-1 knew the Police were next door at that very moment and could have waited until we left. But he didn't. Maybe that was part of the thrill. I handled countless robbery reports in my time, but that was one I never forgot. It was probably a long time before I tried to sit down in a restaurant again. It was just easier eating in the car. And maybe safer.

88.

In early 1979 there was a rumor that the Motor Squad and K-9 were being forced to admit women to their ranks. Since I had become quite adept at being one of the first female patrol Officers, I thought this might be another good opportunity to be harassed by an all new group of angry White men.

My question was, which unit was I going to go for? I had been riding a motorcycle since I was eighteen so the thought of being paid to ride a big Harley Davidson was very tempting. But not tempting enough.

The K-9 Division was at the Police Academy, where Officers from DC and other jurisdictions came to train their dogs. The Fairfax County Sheriff's Department had requested that one of their female Deputies, Cindy Kreticose join the next class.

The DC Higher Ups then decided that the first female shouldn't be from an outside agency. Since it was inevitable they were going to have to admit women anyway, this would be the right time to put two of their own in the same class.

At the time, the K-9 office was in a tiny cinderblock building, across the parking lot from the Academy.

I made the decision to apply for entrance to K-9 by this time and one day while at the Academy, I decided to wander over to the K-9 office to ask some questions. As I walked toward the building, I saw an older Officer approaching me. As he came closer, I asked him if the building straight ahead was where the K-9 Sergeant had his office. He looked right at me and kept walking without saying a word. I found out later his name was Ken Chatham and he was one of the K-9 trainers. Oh boy, here we go again.

At the time, every decision within the Department was made not only on qualifications but by race. In this case, one Black and one White was going to be chosen as the first female DC Police K-9 handlers.

I put in my application and within a short period of time, I received a time and date to report for an interview at the K-9 office.

I made sure I looked good and when the day came, I was really nervous. I entered the office on time and inside was Sergeant Sid Michelin, Ken Chatham and a very old Officer named Walt Forrester.

Sgt. Michelin seemed fairly friendly but the other two were shooting daggers my way. I answered the usual questions and after a few minutes, Officer Chatham pointed to a

large, fifty pound bag of dog food sitting in
the corner. He told me that if I was accepted,
I would have to be able to pick my dog up for
any number of reasons. He said that bag of
food was representative of a dog's weight and
ordered me to lift it in the air to prove I
was strong enough for the job.

As I stood up and walked over to the
corner, I noticed that they had chosen the
dirtiest bag in the bunch. And I was wearing
new clothes just for the occasion.

That wasn't going to slow me down one
bit though. I was so psyched I not only picked
that Bad Boy up, I lifted it over my head a
couple of times as if it weighed nothing. I
was doing so much with that friggin' bag they
had to tell me to stop and return to my seat.
Afterwards, I think I was sore for a week.

89.

We still had the same neighbors and
knew it could cause a lot of problems if I
showed up with a German Shepherd just like the
infamous Sparkle. But the worry I felt wasn't
enough to make me withdraw my application.
It was not long before I received word that I
was in, and the class was going to start in
mid-April of 1979, only a couple of weeks
away.

There were two female Officers that
were infuriated by the decision. One, who had
"accidentally" shot her husband years ago
complained that I should be disqualified
because of Frank's dog shooting incident. Even
though he was cleared, she reasoned that a
German Shepherd would not be safe in this
hostile environment. What?!?! Hello!

The other female, Barbara Alexander apparently had the ear of the Chief and convinced him she should be included in the class. A grievance was made through the Police Union and she was booted out of the class in a matter of hours.

On the first day of class I met Cindy and the other DC Officer, June Maddox. We clicked immediately, knowing we were in for a long fifteen weeks. Our trainer was a big, reddish haired Officer by the name of Dave Haskins. I think he was the only one that would agree to teach a class with women in it. Ken Chatham said that if all three of us completed the class, he would publicly admit at our graduation he was mistaken and women could actually be effective K-9 handlers. At the time, I think he was fully confident it would never happen. Little did he know this would just make us more determined.

The other members of the class were Charles, Brad and Kirk from DC and Barry from Arlington County, Virginia. That put the class at seven, which was about average.

I don't know how they assigned the dogs, but I got a German Shepherd named Klink (after Colonel Klink from the old TV show, "Hogan's Heroes"). June got Sam and Cindy got Shep. Bobby brought his own dog from the county and the DC boys all got Shepherds too. The first thing we did was walk with our dogs to get them used to us. And walk we did---for miles and more miles. Through neighborhoods in DC, into Prince Georges County, and back to the Academy.

Every dog was donated to the Department for a variety of reasons. The most common was that the owners were moving and couldn't bring the dog, or the dog wasn't good with their kids. All sorts of reasons, most of which were probably lies. Nobody was going to confess they had been beating their dog with a shovel or doing some other horrendous abuse. So we, for the most part inherited dogs with an array of problems that we had to figure out how to deal with. And the dogs weren't talking. Over time most of these problems could be dealt with, but not always. And sometimes Officers got hurt.

When I went through class with my second dog, an Officer ended up at the ER because he simply gave a slight tug on the leash. The dog did a full blown attack and put the guy on the ground. You can only imagine what his previous owner had done to him to react like that. The good news was that they eventually "kissed and made up" and the dog went on to become an excellent member of the K-9 corps.

90

When the dogs were first brought to K-9, two things were immediately done. They were x-rayed to see if there was hip dysplasia, a very common issue with German Shepherds. If they passed this, they were then tested to see how they reacted to the sound of gunfire. The dog was put on lead and the trainer, holding a revolver behind him shot blanks into the ground to test the dog's reaction. If the dog appeared curious and unafraid, then he was accepted into the class. Obviously, if he showed fear and/or tried to get away he was given to a good home. There was a list of people who wanted to adopt these guys. My feeling was they probably told their friends the dog had come from the DC Police K-9 Corps, which technically was true. Most probably failed to add that the dogs washed out before the class even began.

There were two Seventh District K-9 Officers that were known to pick up strays, walk them through the back of their cruiser and give them to people as retired Police dogs.

For every dog that actually made it to the end of class, there were untold numbers that didn't make the grade. Nowadays, most of the dogs are purchased from reliable breeders for a lot of money but back then, we had a motley crew of some unusual looking dogs.

In the beginning, we did a whole lot of obedience. Half of the handlers had been through this before, but then there were "the girls," and Bobby from Arlington county. Bobby was a big guy that had played a little football for the Pittsburgh Steelers. What was funny was that he ultimately turned out to be the biggest wimp in the class. Go figure.

Dave's job was to train us as much as train the dogs since we had no clue as to what we were doing. Every morning would start with tracking, since the grass was still wet which made it easier for the dogs to pick up a scent. We would take turns scuffing our feet down long imaginary lines and then another handler and their dog would track the scent. The dog wore a special tracking harness that was used only for this particular exercise.

After tracking, we did obedience which was a major part of the training. Then agility, where the dogs were jumping over fences, climbing ladders, walls and crawling through tunnels.

Article search next. The dogs learned to search for things by scent. This could be

anything from a gun used in a crime to a
screwdriver a burglar may have left behind.
Watching a dog work using his nose is
fascinating to see because they are so adept
at it. And the "only" reward they received for
a job well done was lots of praise and "atta
boys." On the street, if they did something
above and beyond, a juicy steak was probably
in the cards.

91.

       In the back of our minds, we knew this
was all leading up to the ultimate test:
Attack work. Today, that type of training is
referred to as "Criminal Apprehension." God
forbid we might offend anyone with the harsh
reality that a dog may bite a fleeing felon.
Give me a friggin' break. Well, that's the
last time you'll see those two ridiculous
words in my narrative.
       When word came down that we were going
to do attack training one afternoon, it was
interesting that almost every K-9 handler in
the city "magically" appeared to observe how
the girls were going to do. At least half of
them believed we would chicken out and quit
when faced with a snarling ninety pound German
Shepherd just waiting to bite the shit out of
us.
       Cindy, June and I had a quick meeting
and we each vowed that no matter what, we
would do this.
       Back then, there were no fancy bite
sleeves, pants or suits like they now have.
When I go to competition today, the people
running from the dogs look like the Michelin
Man. They have so much padding I don't know

how the dog can even get his mouth around anything.

I know it sounds like ancient history but this was the kind of padding used back then: Someone would go to the loading dock of a downtown office building and "borrow" any canvas mail bags lying around. The mail bags would find their way back to K-9 where they would be cut up into long strips, about eight inches wide.

These strips were wrapped around the runner's arm, from the hand to just below the elbow. Then, twine was wrapped and tied around the canvas. Hopefully, it was done just right so the dog couldn't get his teeth between the canvas strips, thereby injuring the runner. Finally the time came and all I remember is being terrified and determined. The worse that could happen was I'd end up in the Emergency Room. I had come too far to wimp out now.

Dave put the canvas around my right arm and tied it tight, but not too tight. He told me that on his signal, to start running down the field. About five seconds in, turn around and feed your arm to the dog that is about to nail you. Make sure that the right arm is the only appendage he can get to, otherwise you'll be bitten in an area with no padding and that will hurt really bad. "MOMMY!"

I walked about twelve feet away from the line and turned around to face a very hostile German Shepherd and his handler. In my left hand I held a long tree branch which I started waving toward the dog while hissing menacingly. If the dog wasn't angry enough before, he was really pissed off now.

Dave gave the signal and I dropped the stick and began running for dear life. I could hear the Officer yell, "Git em. Good boy!" and

I knew we were at the point of no return. By sheer luck, I turned around just as the dog was leaping through the air. He caught my arm halfway between the wrist and elbow and then I was supposed to shake him in a back and forth motion. This movement would hopefully keep him on the sleeve and not come off and try to bite me on another part of my body.

It seemed like he was on me forever but then I heard the handler yell "Out" as loud as he could. Of course the dog didn't listen because this was a new exercise so he had to be pulled off of me.

When I looked down at the sleeve I saw it was all dented in, but I Did It! And so did Cindy and so did June!

The infamous "protective" sleeve made of burlap and canvas

92.

One very important aspect in training a Police Dog is to keep it from becoming boring for him. That was one reason we did the mundane exercises in the morning because they were smart enough to know that after lunch came the attack work. And they never got tired of that. You could actually see their disposition change as you were taking that last bite of your sandwich.

We took turns running from one another's dogs and you got to know each dog so well you could actually gauge where the dog was going to aim for and hope for the best. We had to run every two or three days and after a while it got a little easier, but not much. Our arms would be so black and blue from the 750 pounds of pressure being exerted, we were continually in pain. And just as we might be feeling a sliver of relief from having a couple of days off, it was time to run again. There was no going to the Police and Fire clinic unless blood was drawn and even then, it had to be pretty bad.

One day, I was running from June's dog Sam, and he caught his tooth inside the sleeve and into my hand. I didn't realize I had been bitten until I looked down and saw the canvas becoming blood soaked. Sam was being uncooperative and refused to disengage from the sleeve. Every time June would go in to pull him off me, he would swing around so she couldn't get to him. By this time, I was in a lot of pain but there was nothing I could do to remove Sam from my hand. He was just having so much fun at my expense. Finally, she got ahold of him by the collar and yanked him away as hard as she could. I guess I was bleeding sufficiently enough because I was allowed to go to the clinic for first aid. But be sure and return to class as soon as possible. I think as a reward for my battle wound, I got one extra day off from running.

Another part of the attack work is that after the dog hits the sleeve and comes off either by physical extraction or verbal command, the runner (bad guy) has to be searched. The dog then goes into a Sit next to his handler, about fifteen feet away from the decoy. If the bad guy makes any evasive moves, the dog is supposed to reattack without command to protect his handler. Sometimes, in an effort to mix things up, the runner would push the Officer just to see how the dog would respond. The dogs were constantly trying to out think us, so we could never keep doing the same things in the same order.

93.

Not all the original dogs made it through to the end for various reasons. One of the most common was that they simply were not tenacious enough. You wanted a dog that was aggressive but not psycho, and that could be a fine line sometimes.

My dog Klink was doing very well and it looked like he might turn out to be an excellent patrol dog. But then the unthinkable happened.

One day we broke for lunch and tied our dogs to the chain link fence outside the K-9 office. They all had water and sufficient shade and it was something we had been doing since class started.

After we returned, we did the attack work and then went home for the day. Klink seemed fine for a while but then I noticed he was becoming sick. He could not stop vomiting and appeared to be getting weaker and weaker. I didn't know what to do so I called Sgt. Michelin who told me to take him to the vet as soon as possible. Fortunately, the vet's office was close to our house, so I drove Klink there immediately. The vet told me to leave him and he would call me when he knew something.

I went home and paced the floor for a couple of hours until the phone rang. It was the Doctor who told me to return ASAP. As soon as I got there, he called me into his office and told me that Klink was dead. WTF! What do you mean Klink was dead?! He didn't have any answers as to the cause, but suggested an autopsy be done to clear up the mystery.

Klink's body was transported to the University of Maryland where an autopsy was conducted. It turned out he had ingested a massive dose of poison. But how? My first thoughts turned to my next door neighbors, but the timeframe would not have made that possible. And let me say, they were damn lucky to be eliminated because Frank and I were both on the Warpath. Who the hell poisoned my friggin' dog?

The potential answer came after a while, although we could never prove it. While we were on our lunch break that day, prisoners from Lorton Prison were spraying the Academy grounds with pesticide. Somehow that poison got into Klink's system. I always believed one

of the inmates sprayed the hell out of Klink.
Since he was tied up, there wasn't a lot he
could do to escape. It was heartbreaking and I
cried my heart out, in private of course.

The class was about a third over and
now I had no dog. There were "spares" in the
kennel and I was assigned a couple of them but
none out. At this point, I was beginning to
panic because I thought they would make me
leave the class and join the next one which
hadn't even been planned yet. I had to
graduate with this class no matter what!
And then, there he was! Duke! Our lives would
never be the same again.

94.

All the dogs have a number behind their
names. When K-9 was initially established in
the early 1960's, the first dog's names had
the number one with it. For example, the first
dog with the name King, became King1. Then the
next dog that was donated with that particular
name, became King2. There was a big green
book in the Sergeant's office that kept track
of all the names and numbers.

One day, Sgt. Michelin received a call
from Donald Bartell who was a K-9 trainer for
the Smithsonian. It seemed he had a fully
trained dog that he could no longer keep
because the dog had bit several tourists. And
could Sgt. Michelin use him in the current
class? Well yes, as a matter of fact he could.
I was called into the K-9 office and asked if
I would like to take a trip out to Silver
Hill, Maryland to pick up this dog. They
didn't have to ask me twice. So out to Prince
Georges County we went.

When we got there, Don was waiting outside with a dog on lead. My expectation was that he would be a blindingly handsome German Shepherd. Boy, was I in for a surprise. First, this dog was definitely not a pure bred. He sort of resembled a Shepherd although his legs were so short he could have had some Bassett Hound in him. But he was mine, all mine except technically he belonged to the DC government. His name was Duke and when we returned to the Academy, we had to go to the green book to find out what number he would be.

As Sgt. Michelin thumbed through the pages he suddenly stopped and said, "NO." What? It turned out that the last Duke they had was number sixty eight. Sid was such a complete prude that he refused to have a Duke69 in his Department. Duke70, yes. Duke69, no. Word quickly spread throughout K-9 about what Sid was going to do and several handlers came into the office to tease him mercilessly. I stayed out of the fray since I was a nobody but it was fun to watch.

I guess Sid couldn't take it any longer because he finally slammed the green book shut and with raised voice announced, "Okay dammit, he can be Duke69. Now everyone get the hell out of my office!" And Duke69 he became. Frank was taking a class at the Academy that day and we had ridden in together. We had a little 1976 Chevy Chevette that cost all of $3,000 brand new.

Duke seemed to take to me right away and I spent the rest of the afternoon walking him around, as I had done with Klink on the first day of class. So far, so good.

At 1500 hours, it was time to go home so I waited in the parking lot for Frank to come out. He had been a K-9 handler in the Air

Force and had been stationed in Okinawa and
Viet Nam in the 1960's. With his experience,
he was really the one who should have been
accepted into the class. But he was the wrong
color and gender so it never came to be.

   He was aware I had a new dog that was
going to come home with us, so he came out as
soon as he could to meet the newest member of
the family. As he approached Duke with his
hand out to pet him, Duke's demeanor suddenly
changed. His hackles went up and he lunged
toward Frank in an effort to rip his face off.
Oh great! Now what?

   The Chevette had a hatchback and I was
able to tie him in the back. As Frank drove
home, Duke spent the entire trip snarling
within inches of his head, just hoping the
rope would break. Not a great start to say the
least, but Frank was a good sport and knew
that with time their relationship would
improve. At least we hoped so. It ended up
taking three months before Frank could get
near him. Everyday, it was Frank's job to feed
Duke in his kennel, so that eventually Duke
would associate food (good) with Frank (also
good). Frank would open the kennel door and as
Duke was tearing toward the opening, Frank
would throw the dish inside and slam the door
just as Duke was making a flying leap. The
running joke was that Duke had Long Fence
embedded in his forehead from hitting the
kennel door so often.

95.

   Class continued and the dogs were
really coming along. Frequently, we would
leave the Academy grounds and go to vacant
buildings all over the city. This was where

the dogs learned to do building searches, which was a large part of what K-9 handlers do on the street. Someone would hide in a building and it was the dog's job to find him. When he was successful, the "bad guy" would jump out and the dog was allowed to attack the sleeve as a reward. We went to vacant schools, stores, bus stations, anywhere we had permission to train. If it was decided we were using one particular building too often, we'd go on to the next. One time we even drove out to a large abandoned mental hospital in Prince Georges County. It was really creepy and easy to get lost in. You could almost sense crazy ass ghosts in there. I was very happy when we didn't go back.

Finally, the fifteen weeks were coming to an end and graduation was on the horizon. All the donors were invited to attend an informal ceremony that included a demonstration of what the dogs had been trained to do. One man, after seeing how well-trained his donated dog was, decided he wanted him back. Sorry Dude, but that ain't going to happen. Here's the piece of paper you signed, relinquishing ownership to the DC Police department.

After the K-9 demo, we went inside where a few people were set to speak. June, Cindy and I remembered what Ken Chatham had said he would do if we all completed the class.

The Chief was there and briefly spoke, Sgt. Michelin thanked the donors and Dave Haskins said a few words. Then Ken stood up and announced he had something to add. He looked at the three of us and said, "I never thought women could complete these fifteen weeks and go on to be successful K-9 handlers.

But I was wrong. You girls did well and I'm
proud of you." He could have left off the
"girls" part but who was I to complain?
We were now the first female K-9 handlers in
the whole area. I have to admit, I was feeling
pretty good about what the three of us had
accomplished.

Frank, Duke and I returned home and
celebrated with beer and Milkbones. A new
phase in my career and life was about to begin
when I returned to 3D as the rookie K-9
handler. Were Duke and I up for the task? I
certainly hoped so but time would tell.

96.

Almost all the K-9 handlers drove
pickup trucks so Frank and I decided the
Chevette had to go. We went out shopping and
ended up buying a new 1980, bright red Datsun
pickup. We had a cap put on the back and I was
now ready to go.

On my first day at 3D, I was assigned
an experienced K-9 Officer to show me the
ropes. His name was Harry Armbruster and he
turned out to be one of the finest Police
Officers I ever worked with. He wasn't real
tall and had a buzz cut that made him look
like he'd been in the military. I'm sure he
wasn't real thrilled to be stuck with me but
he never showed it. He had a Black dog named
Sabbath and he was one ugly dog. Even worse
than Duke but he was one hell of a Police K-9.
He was probably so mean because he had some
kind of complex, and he certainly didn't take
to Duke. Fortunately, there was a barrier
separating them in the cruiser.

What I didn't learn in the Academy, I
learned from Harry. We did lots of building

searches and it was always in the back of my mind that when the shit hit the fan, how would Duke react? Would his training kick in or would he turn tail and run away?

Every once in awhile a dog would go all the way through the fifteen weeks of training, do great in class and be a total washout on the street. Then the handler had to start all over again with a new dog which was Not Fun. One day we got a call for a burglary at a Church over on Ontario Rd NW. When we arrived, we discovered that there had indeed been a break in and the subject(s) could possibly still be inside. Harry told me to take Duke out of the car because we were going to do a building search.

The protocol at the time was to enter the building and announce in a loud voice, "Metropolitan Police K-9. Come out or we're going to release a dog!" Then we waited for a reasonable period of time in the event the subject wanted to surrender. The word "reasonable" was certainly open to interpretation for every handler. In this case, since a Church had been burglarized, "reasonable" may have been no more than half a second. In any event, there was no response so Harry signaled for me to take Duke off lead and give the command, "Find him. Good boy."

When you search any kind of building, it must be very methodical. You have to make sure that anything behind you has already been searched so the bad guy can't escape and/or attack you from the rear. And this is what we did. Inside, it appeared that things had been stolen from the altar and office which made me more hopeful we would catch S-1 on the premises.

After searching for a while with no results, something about Duke caught my eye. His ears stood straight up and he inhaled deeply through his nose. Was this his indication that someone was in the next room? Harry nodded and signaled with his hand that this was it! He opened the door and Duke went bounding in. I ran inside just as S-1 punched Duke in the face.

Bad idea! Duke was all over him and the guy gave up. But not before receiving several souvenir dog bites which resulted in a trip to DC General for stitches.

Afterwards, Harry said that Duke did exactly what he was supposed to do. I think he might have said something nice about me too but I don't remember. I was too happy that all this training hadn't been for naught. Good Boy Duke!

Frank and I at a Third District picnic in 1976

Harry and The Mighty Sabbath

97.

Frank was still doing his best to try and make friends with Duke and after about three months, Duke finally relented and grudgingly decided that maybe Frank wasn't so bad after all.

That was a relief for both of us because the ordeal had been one big pain in the butt. One weekend, Frank and I decided to go on a picnic at Great Falls Park in Virginia. We took Duke with us since he had been behaving himself lately.

It turned out to be a nice day and we returned home late that afternoon. As soon as Frank parked the truck in the backyard, I went upstairs to use the bathroom. As I was taking care of business, Frank began unloading the truck and bringing things inside. As he was

walking toward the house, he accidentally
dropped a brown paper bag on the ground. What
he didn't know was that there was leftover
fried chicken in the bag. But Duke knew and
when Frank reached down to pick it up, Duke
immediately attacked him.

I was still indisposed in the bathroom
but I could hear all this commotion and
yelling in the backyard. I instinctively knew
what was happening but there was nothing I
could do at that very moment. When I could, I
ran downstairs and out the backdoor as fast as
I could.

By this time, Frank had been able to
pull Duke up by his collar and was holding him
off the ground so he could do no further
damage. As soon as Duke saw me, he jumped out
of Frank's grasp and ran over to me. He sat
right in front of me, tail wagging wildly with
a look on his face that said, "I'm a good boy,
aren't I?"

I looked at Frank and his arm was
covered in blood. We both knew he had to get
medical attention, so we drove over to
Providence Hospital in the Brookland section
of Northeast.

It turned out Duke bit him about
thirty-seven times. The Doctors did what they
could to stitch him up and he was off work for
a couple of weeks. But it was classified as a
line of duty injury so Frank didn't have to
burn any of his sick leave.

He actually was a real trooper about
the whole thing and never held the incident
against Duke. But there was no taking food
away from him again either.

98

A couple of things we were taught early on in K-9 was to be able to "read your dog" and "believe your dog." Each dog had a special way of indicating they were on to something, and you better not miss it. Some dog's indications were very obvious. If he started madly barking and pawing at a closed door, the odds were that the bad guy was hiding on the other side. Those dogs were great to have because there was no way you'd miss his message. Of course, Duke was not one of them. When he discovered something that might be of interest, his ears would go up and he would take a deep breath. No barking or scratching. Nothing more. Most of our searches were at night in dark buildings and yes, we had flashlights but he made it really difficult because there was no room for error.

One night I got called to respond to Meyers Elementary School at 11th and Clifton St NW for a burglary. The school had been broken into and the Officers on the scene wanted a Police dog to make a sweep to be sure the premises were clear. So Duke and I went through all the hallways, making certain that he pressed his nose under each classroom door. Luckily, the building wasn't real big so fatigue was not a problem. Some of the buildings we searched were so large it would take more than one dog to adequately do the job.

When we completed the search, I had to make a phone call to the station, so I went into the school office to use the landline. As I was dialing the number, Duke began tugging at his leash which was uncharacteristic of him. I looked over at him and he had his nose to the carpet and was taking a deep breath. When his ears went up, I remembered the "Believe your dog" mantra. But the carpet was perfectly flat so nobody could be hiding underneath it. Could they?

Duke looked up at me with an "Okay, I did my part now you do your part" look.

I bent down and examined the carpet and lo and behold, there was a faint outline about three feet by six feet. I put my hand down and it was then I discovered (or rather, Duke discovered) a hidden trapdoor. With gun in hand, I pulled open the door and there huddled in the bottom of the crawlspace were two juveniles. Duke would have been more than happy to bring them up by his teeth but they were compliant and surrendered without any problems. If Duke had not been there, I'm not so sure how agreeable they would have been. Without him, I would have never found these guys. Good Boy, Duke!

99.

Sometimes we were called to other Police Districts to assist if they were shorthanded.

I got a call one night to respond to a burglary over in 5D at a Safeway grocery store. When I arrived, the Officers wanted Duke and me to search the premises in the event S-1 was still inside.

I stood in the doorway of the store and made the usual announcement about surrendering or a dog would be released. And yes, I waited a reasonable amount of time. When there was no response, I unleashed Duke and he immediately took off like a bat out of hell.

My intention was to begin searching the store from front to back but Duke was nowhere to be found. Then I heard some commotion in the back which made me think he had already located S-1. Well that was fast!

I ran down an aisle toward the noise so I could assist Duke with his apprehension. When I got there, I could not believe my eyes! There was Duke in the middle of the refrigerated meat section having the time of his life. He was practically doing swan dives from the steaks to the ground beef to the pot roasts. I yelled at him to get his ass out of the meat case and all he did was turn toward me, growl and get back to business. Which did not include searching for any burglars. I took a deep breath, hoping he wouldn't bite me and physically dragged him out of his little piece of heaven. I tried to get him back into search mode but he had lost all interest, so I had to search the damn store by myself with negative results.

As I exited the building, all the Officers wanted to know how it went inside. Since I didn't know any of them, I just mumbled that Duke did a great job and didn't miss a thing. I then put him in the back of the cruiser and made a hasty exit back to 3D.

100.

My drinking at this point was getting where I couldn't ignore it any longer. I broached the subject with Frank and we both agreed to cut back. Whatever that was supposed to mean. I tried my best but I was absolutely miserable. All I could think about was alcohol and how was I going to live my life without it? I would go a day or two, but then I was right back into the bottle. I felt like a mouse on one of those spinning things in a cage. Running a hundred miles an hour but going nowhere.

It seemed like everyone around me drank heavily too and appeared perfectly fine. Hell, I had scraped so many drunks out of the gutter and taken them to Detox on N St it wasn't funny. I certainly wasn't That Bad!

Finally, in May of 1980 I made a decision. I had a female Lieutenant who I felt I could approach with my situation. Maybe she had some ideas.

It took all the courage I could muster to ask her if we could meet in private. She agreed and once I sat down in her office, I told her everything. She said she would make a phone call and get back to me.

It wasn't long before she told me to go down to an office on G St NW and speak to someone who worked there that could help me. I was working with Harry that day so he drove me there and waited out front in the cruiser. I located the office and went inside where I was greeted by an older Black man who identified himself as Reverend Walker. When I told him that I thought I had a problem with alcohol, he looked at me intently and said, "You don't look like you have a problem." I didn't realize it at the time but that was absolutely the Wrong thing to say to someone asking for help! I was ready to leave since he had just told me he didn't think I had a problem. But he told me to wait because he wanted to phone somebody named Jim and have him speak to me.

He made the call and when Jim answered, the good Reverend handed the receiver to me.

After a couple of pleasantries, Jim said to me, "You need to go to meetings."

There was a pause as I waited for him to continue but all he did was repeat, "You need to go to meetings."

I thanked him, turned toward the Rev and said, "Jim told me to go to meetings." This seemed to please him so I said my goodbyes and walked downstairs to where Harry was still patiently waiting.

He of course, wanted to know what had just transpired in that mysterious office. I told him that some guy named Jim told me to go to meetings. Harry asked me what kind of meetings? And I said, "He never told me." Looking back today, if I really wanted to know I would have asked.

After work, Frank and I rode home together and he inquired about the same thing. I think I asked him if he knew what meetings were but he didn't have a clue either.

It was off to the races again for what turned out to be another six years.

101.

Then I figured it out. If we moved out to the suburbs, everything would be okay. Since I was originally from Montgomery County and Frank from Prince Georges County, it seemed pretty obvious we would head to Maryland.

One day I was talking to Lt. Gildon about different places to move and she suggested coming to Virginia, where she and her family lived. Now there's a general rule of thumb that people from Maryland stay in Maryland, and those from Virginia stay in Virginia. For some reason, neither side wants to cross the Potomac River. So it was a big deal that we would even consider making such a drastic decision.

She recommended her neighborhood in Fairfax and it wasn't long before we found a nice house just a couple of blocks away from her. The price was a little on the steep side but we figured we could swing it and in September of 1980, Frank and I moved into our new house on Gainsborough Drive.

All the neighbors were very friendly and welcoming and I just knew that this was the solution to all our problems. What I did not know was that this was merely a "geographic cure." Same problems, different location. The good times lasted all of three months.

I was back at work with Harry and we were inside the Fox and Hounds enjoying a soda when we got a call for a burglary in the 600 block of Rhode Island Ave NW. The Officers wanted a dog to search a row house to make sure S-1 wasn't still inside. I said I would take the run and proceeded to drive over to the location.

When I arrived, I parked directly in front of the premises and took Duke out of the cruiser. The front door of the house was open but there were no Officers around, so we waited on the sidewalk until someone advised me of the situation.

It couldn't have been more than a few seconds when suddenly a large dog came tearing out the front door, right toward us. He immediately attacked Duke, who was quite a bit smaller than him. Shit, this wasn't good. Almost before I could react, a second even larger dog came running out the same door and assaulted Duke. Behind him, was a Black man in hot pursuit. I remember thinking that this guy would help me stop this two on one dog fight. But when he got about ten feet away from us, he suddenly stopped and just stood there. I yelled at him to get his Goddamn dogs off of mine but he didn't move. I looked down and saw that they were getting the better of Duke, who by this time was looking at me like "are you going to help me or not?"

These two dogs, (which I later learned were Akitas) were about to do serious, if not fatal damage to my dog if I didn't do something. I pulled out my service revolver and looked over at Numb Nuts one more time but he still had not moved.

I then made one of the hardest decisions I've ever made in my life. I shot both dogs. They fell in a heap on top of Duke, both dead. Duke, who was seriously injured was trapped underneath so I had to physically pull him out to safety. There was blood everywhere from all three dogs but foremost in my mind was getting Duke to the vet as quickly as possible. I carried him to the rear of the cruiser and carefully placed him inside. I advised the dispatcher of where I was going and without waiting for permission, drove Code One to the other side of town where the vet was located.

When I arrived, they rushed him into surgery where they were able to patch him up.

102.

A Sergeant, not known for being particularly bright came to the Vet's office and demanded I turn over my service revolver to be processed as evidence. I knew that in this type of case my weapon did not need to be seized, but he was insistent so I just handed it over. Before he left, he told me I was in trouble because I had left the confines of 3D without receiving permission from an Official. Whatever. This guy had been promoted in the early 70's when they pretty much promoted anyone with three years, whether they were qualified or not. And it showed with several 3D Sergeants.

I left Duke at the Vet's office for observation and returned to 3D, not knowing what to expect. After I parked behind the station and was walking toward the back door, I ran into Lt. Fred Wilmott. He asked me if I had been injured during the incident and I told him no. I knew he heard me but oddly enough, he repeated his question and I repeated my answer. He then looked me right in the eye and said slowly, "Are you sure you weren't injured?"

At that point, the lightbulb went on and I finally understood what he was implying. The only way this shooting would be justified is if I had been hurt too. It did not matter about Duke, because he was seen as just another Department issued piece of property.

As Lt. Wilmott turned to leave he said, "Chief Richards wants to see you in his office ASAP." Now I had another difficult decision to make. And I had to make it fast. I went back to my truck and retrieved a knife which I kept under the front seat.

Making certain that nobody was looking, I took the knife and stabbed my uniform pants hard enough that I also cut my leg. I'm not really into self-inflicted injuries, but I had to make this look believable. And I did just enough damage that blood was running down my leg as I entered Chief Richard's office.

I sat down in front of his desk and related everything that had happened on Rhode Island Ave. He seemed somewhat sympathetic but he ended the conversation by saying that the shooting would only be justified if I had been injured during the melee.

And as much as he liked dogs, the Police K-9's were really only property owned by the District government. Before I left, I dutifully showed him my bloody wound and torn pant leg.

Several days later when I went down to the K-9 office at the Police Academy, I was met by several handlers who made it perfectly clear that if I had not protected Duke the way I had, I would have been permanently ostracized by the entire unit. Then, I think they took me out for a few congratulatory drinks.

This is the end of the story and then I'm done with it:

The man who came running out the front door was the boyfriend of the dog's owner. He was too frightened to get involved and that's why he just stood there. A true Chickenshit because he could have taken a few punctures to save the Akita's lives. If I could have broken up the fight by myself, I would have. But there was simply no way.

The owner, who was working in Georgetown at the time immediately filed a lawsuit against the District government. And speaking of Chickenshits, rather than posing any kind of defense, the Powers-That-Be caved in and settled for $10,000.

And then there was the Review Board that met to investigate my Use of Service

Revolver. That took a while but eventually they voted in my favor.

Of course, there still was no assistance available to anybody who might be feeling the effects of taking a life (or two), especially because these were "just dogs." Another "Suck it up" incident that was not supposed to have any impact whatsoever. Since I had a lot of practice at this, it was becoming easier and easier. At least on the surface. Hey, everybody thought I could handle anything thrown my way. And in a way I could. But the price was getting higher. And the drinking was getting worse.

One thing that was helpful was getting involved in K-9 competition. I threw myself into it and even though I didn't do too well at the beginning, I enjoyed the camaraderie and friendships I was making.

Sometimes we traveled as a team to other jurisdictions such as Atlantic City, Norristown, Pa, and Philadelphia to compete. There were even National Dog Trials but I was too intimidated to try that. At least then.

Harry was a great dog handler but couldn't seem to win the top prize. As with many things in life, there were a lot of politics involved and apparently Harry didn't kiss enough ass to be on the A list of competitors. What he did to somewhat get his comeuppance was brilliant. He decided to teach me everything he had learned, knowing that if I (a woman no less) won, it would truly piss off a lot of people. And that's what he did. He taught me every nuance, every trick, every single thing to make Duke come out on top. Or so we hoped.

That particular year, 1982, the competition was held in Vienna, Virginia. Duke and I were as ready as we could be. There were about 30 competitors and of course I was the only female.

We were doing pretty well until we came to the event that Duke was weakest in. It was a wooden, six foot wall that the dogs were expected to scale. Remember, Duke had the legs of a Bassett Hound and there was no way in hell he would ever conquer the wall. And he didn't either. I gave him three shots at it to no avail. My score was still toward the top but this certainly did not help.

The last event was the attack work which everybody badly wanted to win. Who wouldn't want the baddest dog of the bunch? Duke was very good at this but I knew it would be close. My decoy, Bob Rau was an excellent runner and would do everything he could to make Duke look his best.

The field was pretty wet from a recent rain storm and there were puddles everywhere. This was going to make the event a bit dicier but we were all at the same disadvantage.

When my turn came, Duke did great. He even knocked Bob down causing him to fall in the middle of a large mud puddle. I think he may have fallen on purpose but I didn't care. That was called Taking One for the Team.

Finally it was time to learn who had won. It Was Me!!! Thanks to Harry, Duke and I won the top prize which included Best Attack work! I beat all the men! I had only been in K-9 three years! I heard later that some of the Judges were so horrified that they tried to juggle the scores so someone else would win. But it didn't happen. I never won again but my name is somewhere on a plaque and trophy from 1982. A great memory in the midst of some pretty bad ones.

Duke and I receiving our award for winning the
Police K-9 competition by 3D Commander Catoe
in 1982.
I was praying Duke wouldn't bite anyone.
(Photo courtesy of Linda Wheeler)

103.

Sabbath continued to barely tolerate
Duke, and at times that became a problem.
One day we were over in the Georgetown area
walking the dogs on a path called Lovers Lane.
I have no idea why we were in the Second
District, but it may have been that we wanted
a change of scenery.

At any rate, it was a pretty day and it
was nice to be out of the inner city for a
while. But then, out of nowhere Sabbath
decided to attack Duke right in the middle of

the path. This was a bad one and Harry and I couldn't separate them. We were both rolling around on the ground with these four-legged warriors and not getting anywhere. Out of the corner of my eye, I could see the la dee da rich folks in their designer digs just jogging past us without barely a glance. If this had happened today, it would have been all over You Tube. Finally, we were able to get the upper hand and pry them apart. When Harry and I stood up, our uniforms looked like we had just been in a war. Which in a sense, we had been. We were totally covered in dirt from top to bottom, and the dogs hadn't fared much better. I think we quietly returned to 3D and kept a low profile for the rest of the shift.

Another time, we were doing an off lead building search at HD Cook Elementary School in Adams/Morgan. It was at night and for some reason there was no electricity in the school so we had to use our flashlights. Both dogs entered the premises and headed down a long hallway. The next thing we heard was the familiar sound of a dog fight. We both ran in the direction of the K-9 altercation and it was at this time my flashlight went completely dead. Here I was floundering in the dark and Harry was trying to hold onto his flashlight with one hand and pulling Sabbath with the other. Then were back on the floor, rolling around with two pissed off dogs. I believe that was the last time we ever had these two bad boys off lead again.

It's important that you get along with your partner's dog in the event something happens and you have to take charge of him. I got along with Sabbath fairly well. At least he had never attacked me. Until I did something really stupid at the Police Academy.

Harry and I happened to be there at the same time for retraining (kind of a two day tune-up for the dogs and handlers every six weeks).

It was lunchtime and Sabbath was sleeping in the back of Harry's pickup truck. I was walking through the parking lot with some friends when I spied the Mighty Sabbath. He had the well-earned reputation of not being lovable toward anyone but Harry. But hey, this was my partner's dog so I naturally had to brag that I could handle Sabbath too. You know where this is going.

I reached into the back of the pickup to give Sabbath a little pat on the head. Well, he not only bit my hand, when I tried to pull away his tooth became snagged and I couldn't disengage it. We were having a tug of war with my hand and I think after a while Sabbath became tired and/or bored because he finally let go. It looked like a bloodbath in the back of Harry's truck. All of it of course, being mine.

The Police and Fire clinic was just up the road so somebody hauled me there where I was stitched up and put on light duty for a couple of weeks.

Poor Harry, not knowing any of this returned from lunch only to find out that Sabbath had just "shown some love" to his partner. That one hurt but it was 100% my fault. Sabbath was merely protecting "Daddy's" vehicle. It wasn't the first time I had been bit by a Police dog and it certainly wouldn't be the last.

One of the many "perks" of being in K-9.

It was almost impossible to do any kind
of tracking work in 3D because it was such a
high density area. But sometimes we would give
it a try, mainly to appease a Complainant who
insisted on it. Most of our successes were in
buildings where the dogs could more easily
pick up and follow a scent.

One night on the midnight shift I got
called to respond way up in 2D, on Oregon Ave
NW. There had been an armed carjacking and it
was believed that S-1 ran into the woods of
Rock Creek Park. For whatever reason, 2D K-9
was not available so I got the request.
Oregon Ave is almost into Maryland so it took
me a minute to think about how to get there.
When I arrived, the vehicle in question was
sitting on the grass with the driver's side
door wide open. The Officer's thought Duke
might be able to sniff the seat and track down
S-1, who they suspected was hiding somewhere
in the woods.

Oh sure, we can do that. Not a problem.
I put Duke's tracking harness on (after I
dusted it off) and we were off. It was really,
really dark and my flashlight seemed barely up
to the task but we kept going. I turned my
radio down far enough that it wouldn't give my
position away. And Duke kept pulling me
further and further into the woods. Did I
mention it was really dark?

After awhile I took a close look at
Duke and realized that if there had originally
been a good scent, it was now lost. I didn't
want to give up just yet so we continued on.
By this time, I was all scratched from tree
branches and wet when I nearly fell into a
creek.

Alright, I was done. We gave it our best shot. I keyed the radio mic to advise the dispatcher that I was terminating the track and we would be returning to the scene. No answer. I tried again and then realized I couldn't get a signal out there in the wilderness. Alright, I would just walk back and advise the dispatcher and Officers when I got there.

I looked around to see what direction I had come from so I could head that way. It was then I discovered I had absolutely no idea where I was. I was totally lost in of Rock Creek Park. In the middle of the night with a radio that was completely useless. Help!!!

Duke and I wandered around for awhile but if you've seen one tree, you've seen them all. I had no idea what to do. I thought maybe if too much time passed, somebody might come looking for me and I would never live that down.

I kept keying the radio and after what seemed like forever, the dispatcher finally answered. Now, no matter what you're involved in they always want the exact address so they can type it into the computer.

I didn't think telling her I was standing by the 644th Oak tree, Southeast of Oregon Ave would be acceptable. So I swallowed my pride and announced I was totally lost for all the world to hear. Now what?

One of the 2D Officers came up with the bright idea that he would turn on his red lights and tap the siren so I would know which way to walk. That siren was better than a beautiful symphony and Duke and I stumbled as fast as we could toward it.

When we finally emerged from the Haunted Forest, I threw Duke into the back of the cruiser and headed "home" to 3D where we belonged.

105.

A big part of the job was responding to burglar alarms, of which the vast majority were false. But once again, you could never become complacent because you could end up dead. It did get really tiresome though.

I got an alarm one day in a Catholic services building in the 1300 block of Massachusetts Ave NW. I drove around back to check for any signs of a break in and when I didn't find anything, I started to return to the cruiser.

As I was walking in the alley, I heard glass breaking. Maybe there was a burglary going on after all. I looked closer at the building in question but couldn't see anything out of the ordinary. Hmmm. Very odd, but then I heard more glass breaking. And it sounded like it was coming from the apartment building next door. I radioed for another unit to respond to my location and as I waited for my backup, I walked toward the sound. As I turned a corner, I saw that all the windows of the basement apartment were broken out.

By this time, additional Officers had arrived and we carefully approached the gaping holes to peer inside.

In the apartment and you can't make this stuff up, was a Black man tightly holding another Black man in a choke hold with one arm. In his other hand, he was holding a sawed off shotgun against the man's head. It was kind of dark in there but there was no question about what we were seeing. The guy in

charge was yelling at the other man to pay up
or he would kill him.

    We all started yelling at him to drop
the gun but everybody was shouting at the same
time, so it all just sounded like a lot of
white noise. To get a better look, I shined my
flashlight on the two of them all the while
imploring S-1 not to shoot.

    Suddenly, the hostage made a break for
it and as I was about to pull the trigger to
shoot at the suspect, my flashlight went dark
(I knew I should have bought those Alkaline
batteries). Now we couldn't see much of
anything but fortunately S-1 surrendered
shortly afterwards and was arrested.

    I seized the shotgun as evidence and
instead of promptly putting it on the property
book like I was supposed to, I took it home
until the next day.

    It was a very "cool" sawed off shotgun
and Frank and I took pictures of each other in
our Bonnie and Clyde poses. Then the next day
I entered it on the property book and never
saw it again. I have no idea where those
pictures are today.

                    106.

    Duke was not exactly Officer Friendly
when it came to patrolling the streets. So it
came as a surprise when Sgt. Raycraft called
me into his office one day with a request.
Well, actually an order. There was a preschool
just up the street that wanted a K-9 Officer
to come with their dog and do a show and tell
for the kids. Apparently I was the only one
available, so he told me to go over there and
do a short presentation. Maybe the children
could even pet Duke. I looked at him like he

was nuts and reminded him that Duke was the last dog to be around anyone, especially a group of crazed toddlers. But he wouldn't listen and told me to get over there. Now!

So I made the short drive over to the 2100 block of New Hampshire Ave and parked out front. I gingerly walked Duke through the front door into an empty room. One of the teachers came out to greet me and told me how excited the kids were. Before I could give her a heads up on how the children should behave, a rear door opened and about thirty screaming three year olds came running into the room.

Duke took one look at this imminent threat and instantly went into attack mode. He almost pulled my arm out of its socket trying to get at these little monsters. Within half a second all thirty children made an immediate u turn, still screaming and crying hysterically, trying to get away from this four legged maniac.

A complaint was made by the head of the preschool and I got yelled at by Sgt. Raycraft but I never, ever was ordered to do one of those things again.

We did have a team that went around the city to do demonstrations. It was a great opportunity to show off what the dogs were trained to do and I was chosen to be the token female on the team. At this point, I didn't care anything about that because I really deserved to be a part of the group.

One Sunday during the NFL season, we got to do the halftime show for a Redskins/Patriots game at RFK stadium. As part of the show, it was decided that our runner (Bad Guy) would be wearing the Patriot's #14 Quarterback jersey. The dog chosen to do the

attack work would be wearing a Redskins
jersey.

The entire first half of the game, the
weather was terrible. Pouring rain and very
windy. But the show had to go on. Just as
halftime started, the rain stopped and the sun
attempted to come out. The field however, was
a disaster because of how soaked it was. We
did the best we could and the crowd seemed to
enjoy the show.

What we didn't realize was how
intoxicated so many people were but we found
out real quick. When Jimmy Corcoran came out
on the field dressed in Steve Grogan's jersey,
the crowd took notice. Then the K-9 in the
Skins jersey came out and stood about fifty
feet from "Grogan." At a designated signal,
Jimmy began firing a gun (blanks of course)
while running down the field. The Skins dog
was released and did a full blown attack in
the middle of the field.

When Jimmy went down, the crowd went
completely berserk. I think a lot of them, in
their drunken stupor thought Jimmy was an
actual Patriots player. The next thing we
knew, bottles and anything else available at
the time was flung out onto the field in an
attempt to get that damn New England player. I
remember the PA announcer trying to get
everybody to calm down and quit throwing
stuff. I think the only reason they stopped
was because there was nothing left to throw.
We were freezing and wet, the dogs were
freezing and wet so we loaded the cruisers and
left.

Another successful show for the DC K-9.

107

One Easter night while working the midnight shift, I got called to respond to a burglary at the Catholic Shrine of the Immaculate Conception on Michigan Ave NE. It seemed that S-1 had broken in, hoping to steal the proceeds from the Easter services. Once again, Officers wanted a dog to sweep the building to make sure nobody was still inside.

Now this is a Big friggin' Church with a million hiding places. But inside we went. The main area was huge and there were all sorts of alcoves with burning candles that made everything really eerie and creepy.

Duke and I approached each alcove very carefully, peering in to see if it was secure. At one point, I thought I heard a noise coming from one of them, so I withdrew my service revolver from its holster and quietly approached. Those damn flickering candles were just adding to the tension but I took a deep breath, rounded the corner and yelled, "Freeze!" Directly in front of me was a White figure that wasn't moving. My finger was on the trigger but before I could fire, I realized what it was. It was a statue of Mother Mary! And I almost shot her! Now that would have been an interesting investigation.

Was that the end of it? Oh no, there was more. Duke and I returned to the main sanctuary and continued our search. As we were walking between the pews, Duke suddenly stopped. He inhaled deeply and his ears went up. The classic response that he had detected something. I looked down the aisle and saw a man standing about twenty pews away from us. I made sure it was a living human being and not another statue, before I told him to stop right there. He began walking away and it was then I took Duke off lead and sent him toward S-1. Duke made a mad dash in S-1's direction and then made an abrupt stop.

I ran over to him and noticed he looked pretty confused. I tried to get him to pick up this guy's scent but he was unable to. Whatever we saw had disappeared into thin air. Even after all these years I have no idea what it was, but we definitely saw something. I never believed in ghosts or spirits before, but now......?

At this point, Duke and I were both exhausted so we made our way to the exit to speak to the Officers outside. When I told them that S-1 had probably already escaped, one Officer piped up, "Did you search the catacombs?"

I told them if they wanted the catacombs searched, they could do it themselves. We were outta there.

108.

A couple of K-9 chase stories:
One night, the infamous Raleigh House on 13th St was robbed and Duke and I happened to be right around the corner. We were so close that as we approached the building, S-1 was running out the front door with gun in hand, toward Logan Circle. Directly behind him, in hot foot pursuit was plain clothes Sgt. Sammy Anderson.

I immediately threw the cruiser into Park and got Duke from the back. He could see what was going on and was more than willing to become an active participant. The only problem was that there was an MPD Sgt. between him and S-1.

Suddenly, I had an idea that I hoped would work. If it didn't, I was really going to be up Shit's Creek. I yelled at Sgt. Anderson to get down while at the same time releasing Duke with my standard, "Get him! Good boy!"

By the Grace of God and some good luck, Sgt. Anderson understood my intention and immediately threw himself on the ground. Duke was in full stride and as he entered the middle of Logan Circle, he actually leaped over the Sgt. He then caught S-1 at the South end of the Circle and apprehended him with a couple of souvenir bite marks. Good job Duke! I think Sgt. Anderson may have had to go back to 3D to change his underwear.

I haven't mentioned the girls in a while so I need to include them in one of my stories. They were more than willing to perform sex acts for money but boy, you better not display a gun. These girls could almost give the Po Po a better lookout than the dispatchers. I always thought they might carry little notebooks and pens in their hot pants, they were that accurate.

So here I was, cruising North on 14th St, approaching Q St which was a particularly active corner. When the girls saw me, they came tearing over to the passenger's side window. One of the girls told me that a guy had just pointed a gun at them and was now walking East on Q St.

I turned the car onto Q St and damn, there he was just as they described him. When he saw me, he took off running and this time there was nobody between him and the Dukester. I stopped, threw open the back door and Duke jumped out with fire in his eyes. This was a

K-9 handler's dream; a fully justified attack
down the middle of Q St on a confirmed felon.
S-1 was quick but Duke was quicker. When the
guy got to 13th St, he turned around and
realized what was about to occur. So he
stopped in mid stride. But by this time it was
too late and Duke was unable to stop (not that
he wanted to). He ran into S-1 full force and
knocked him down, along with the gun he was
holding. It went clattering down the street
but if the guy had any intention of retrieving
it, Duke made sure that wasn't going to happen
since he had the suspect's hand firmly in his
jaws. Another good job by DC K-9 Duke 69!

       The Fox and Hounds bar on 17th at Q St
NW, was kind of an on-duty oasis for 3D cops.
They loved the Po Po to come in for free sodas
and discounted meals. Especially when there
had been an armed robbery with shots fired in
the early 70s. On the frame of a large
painting on the wall was a hole from an errant
bullet. I bet it's still hanging there.
When I worked the midnight shift, they
particularly liked the Police around at
closing time. After the place closed at 0200
hours, the manager would exit carrying a bag
containing the night's receipts. He would be
easy pickings for anyone with a criminal mind
and an ulterior motive.
       If it wasn't real busy on the street, I
would park the K-9 cruiser out front and go
inside for a Coke and some conversation.
The entire East side of 17th St was composed
of commercial businesses and across the street
were private residences. And people trying to
sleep.
       Whenever I was out of Duke's sight, he
would bark nonstop until I returned. So the

minute I entered the Fox and Hounds, Duke had a complete fit. The people across the street were trying to sleep and were very unhappy. Apparently, somebody had had enough and telephoned the 3D Watch Commander complaining about that damn Police dog in front of the Fox and Hounds. It wasn't long before I was dispatched to the station for a little lecture. In a nutshell, it went something like this, "Shut your Goddamn dog up. He's keeping the whole damn neighborhood awake."

"Yes Sir."

Instead of staying away from the Fox and Hounds, I had a better idea. I took him inside with me and put him on a bar stool, with his paws leaning on the rail. Getting into the spirit of the moment, the bartender asked me, "What'll he have?"

Without missing a beat, I replied, "He'd like a Miller Lite and some cold cuts, please."

In no time, a small pan of Miller Lite and a plate of lunch meat was placed in front of Duke, who thoroughly enjoyed every morsel. Today, I thank The Lord that there were no cell phone cameras at the time or Duke and I would have been on a viral YouTube video.

From then on, whenever I'd drive by the Fox and Hounds without stopping, Duke would throw himself against the back door, in an effort to get out and enjoy some more treats. The good news was that there were no more complaints from the neighbors. Zzzzzzzzzzz!

109.

One of the more memorable assignments I received while a member of CDU occurred on Christmas Eve in 1979.

It seemed a boyfriend and girlfriend were having a holiday altercation in an apartment in the 1400 block of Clifton St NW. Suddenly, it went to an all new level when he put a gun to her head and decided to hold her hostage. All the screaming and yelling led somebody to call 911 and complain about the commotion. When Police arrived, S-1 refused to open the door and that's when CDU got involved.

All the 3D members, along with SOD personnel met up at 14th and Clifton St, where a large truck was parked. Inside, was the "high tech" equipment we'd be issued to help carry out the mission.

I had parked my K-9 cruiser in the middle of Clifton St and walked down to the Command Center, leaving a very unhappy Duke behind. At the rear of the truck I was handed a helmet, a big, bulky bullet proof vest and shotgun. Frank was standing next to me and after he received his gear, the SOD Sgt. gave us our assignments. I don't think he knew we were married to each other because he paired us together. Our job was to go to the apartment building next door, climb up on the roof and if S-1 happened to stand by his window, we were to shoot him.

So off we trudged, past Duke who was hysterical by now and into the assigned building. We walked up the stairs to the highest floor and looked for a door leading to the roof. Apparently there wasn't one so Frank figured we would have to go through somebody's apartment, out their window and up the fire escape. This was becoming a bit complicated but Frank chose a door and knocked on it.

We both heard a muffled, "Come in." Frank tried the doorknob and it was unlocked so we entered. Inside, were a man and woman engaged in sex. We both immediately apologized for the intrusion but after they gave us a quick glance, they went back to business. Frank and I were pushing each other in an effort to see who could get through the window and up the fire escape first.

Once we got up on the roof, we located the window in question, directly across the alley. Then it was time to hurry up and wait. And it was friggin' cold! And then it started to snow!

After about an hour of praying this stupid thing would come to an end, I started to feel funny. It was a very familiar feeling that hit me once a month. Oh my God, my period had started and all my supplies were in my locker back at 3D. And like the Morton's salt slogan "When it rains, it pours," I had no choice but to take immediate action. I ripped off the helmet and vest and handed the shotgun to Frank, saying I'd be right back. Before he could respond, I was down the fire escape and back in the "love nest." I rushed down the stairs and hauled ass toward my cruiser, kinda doing a duck walk in case S-1 decided to take a shot at me.

Amid all of Duke's barking, I could hear somebody yelling in my direction, "Officer Weinsheimer, where in the hell do you think you're going?" Any woman alive knows that you never get between them and a Tampax and I was no exception. I fired up that car and was back at 3D in no time.

After I took care of business, I returned to Clifton St as though nothing happened. I climbed up the stairs, walked back into the apartment without knocking (I think by this time they were smoking cigarettes),

and went up the fire escape to the roof. Frank
knew better than to give me a hard time so he
just handed me my helmet, vest and shotgun
without a word.

We stayed up there for a couple more
hours until we heard an all clear over the
radio. Back down the fire escape and through
the apartment where we all wished each other a
Merry Christmas. As Frank and I entered the
hallway, we heard a distinctive click behind
us. It was the sound of the door being locked
and bolted.

110.

We were really only allowed to use our
dogs for felony-related assignments. In other
words, if someone was being disorderly, you
weren't permitted to put your dog on them (as
much as you may want to). And a lot of S-1's
knew that. Hell, a lot of them knew the
General Orders better than some of us.

An example of that came when I was
cruising down U St one afternoon and
discovered a dice game in an alley. It must
have been a very slow day because normally we
didn't have time to waste on such a nothing
violation. But for whatever reason, I decided
to flex my muscles and break up their little
activity. Maybe even make a couple of arrests
which would be called by many as "hummers." A
hummer is an arrest that is a complete waste
of everybody's time. Locking someone up for
spitting on the sidewalk might be considered a
hummer. And you certainly didn't want to get a
reputation for making a lot of those type
arrests.

But here I was pulling up to a dice
game in my K-9 cruiser, as if I was the

baddest Mo Fo in town. The men barely glanced my way which was an affront to my authority, so I thought, "I'll show them."

I exited my vehicle, opened the back door and took Duke out to help reinforce how big and bad I was. The men gathered up their money and slowly stood, as if they didn't have a care in the world.

Well, I'd had enough by this time. I told them to stop or I would release the dog. I think one of them yawned as he said, "You're not allowed to do that. This is only a misdemeanor." And they walked away, slapping each other on the back and laughing. Talk about being put in your place because he was absolutely right. I couldn't ask for backup to assist me with these "mass" arrests. The whole thing was complete BS and all I could do was slink away and pretend that none of it happened. And Duke wasn't talking. I think he was embarrassed too.

111.

Jimmy Carter was President when I was in K-9, and he and his family worshipped at a Church located at 16th and P St NW. One night we got a call for a burglary there and of course the building needed to be searched by a dog.

I went in with Duke and, as I recall, another Officer. The Church was large, but nothing compared to the Catholic Shrine. We searched all the nooks and crannies and even though it appeared that S-1 had already escaped, in the back of my mind I felt that somebody was still there.

After we had been inside for about twenty minutes, we entered some kind of

recreation room that contained two pool
tables. On the other side of the room were a
couple of doors that I believed may have been
a closet. Before I could take another step, I
heard Duke take a deep breath and start
hauling ass across the room. When he got to
the closet doors, he leaned down and put his
nose inside the crack at the bottom. Another
long breath and ears straight up.

As my partner and I stood on either
side of the door deciding how to go about
this, the door was suddenly flung open. A
youngish, Black male jumped out, tightly
gripping a pool cue. Duke immediately went
into attack mode but before he could get to
the guy, S-1 cracked him over the head with
his stick. So hard, in fact, that it broke
over Duke's head. Duke, who was obviously in a
great deal of pain fell backwards, shaking his
head. I had no idea what he would do next so
the other Officer and I started to move toward
S-1 to make the arrest.

Well, it turned out Duke wasn't going
to let that happen. The look on his face was
one of complete fury and nobody was going to
end this thing except him. He was on S-1 so
fast it was like a blur of fur.

Let's just say that when it was over, a
lot of blood was spilled in the recreation
room of Jimmy Carter's Church. Probably 25% of
it Duke's and 75% S-1's.

When we got the guy outside, the
minister was standing there waiting to talk to
us. We kept it short and sweet. Better get the
janitor in the rec room with plenty of
cleaning supplies. And sorry about the blood
on the newly laid carpet. Kept moving without
giving the Pastor any opportunity to ask
questions.

I kept a close eye on Duke for any signs of something serious but other than a few knots on his head, he seemed fine. The boy was tough and I was proud of him.

112.

I was patrolling in Adams/Morgan one afternoon when I heard the dispatcher call for any available unit to respond to All Souls Unitarian Church at 16th and Harvard St NW. It seemed that Marion Barry was there with one of his cronies, and wanted this person driven to National Airport in one of the Police cars. Since he was the Mayor, there was nobody to tell him the Po Po were not there to serve as his personal chauffeur. So a scout car was dispatched to drive this "all important" somebody to the airport.

Apparently I was bored, because I decided to drive over to the Church to see who this person was. As I was pulling up front, I saw that the scout car had not arrived yet. I would just sit there and wait.

But as soon as I stopped, Marion Barry and a man carrying a suitcase hurriedly approached my cruiser. Oh shit, they thought I was the one providing the transportation! Before I could pull away, Marion Barry's friend reached the back door and yanked it open. And came face to face with Duke the Dog, who was more than willing to make his acquaintance.

Who was this mysterious man, you ask? It was none other than Jessie Jackson. Dogs are colorblind so there was no pulling the race card on this one. Jessie Jackson just about crapped when he saw that there was a very unfriendly Police dog about to rip his face off. He gave a wild shriek as he slammed the door shut. I knew there was going to be hell to pay but I never heard anything about it.

Whenever I see the Rev. Jackson on TV, I can only think, "What could have been?" Even though I'd probably be serving a life sentence, wouldn't that have been a sweet sight? Insert smile.

113.

Speaking of Adams/Morgan, there was a tailor's shop just North of Columbia Rd, on Calvert St NW. It was owned by an older Jewish man named Murray.

Murray loved the Police, especially K-9 handlers and their dogs. He had a small refrigerator in the back that was stocked with cold sodas for any Officers that happened to stop by. There were also a couple of comfortable lounge chairs that made the place even more inviting. The only catch was that Murray expected all the latest gossip, either what was happening in the neighborhood or better yet, the latest shenanigans going on in the Third District. He was a good guy and everyone seemed to like and trust him.
One day, Duke and I were walking a foot beat along 18th St, and after awhile I decided it was time to take a break and head over to Murray's to put my feet up and have a Coke. I also needed a restroom break and when you were with a dog, it became a little more complicated.

As I entered Murray's, he immediately offered me a soft drink. I told him thanks but I needed to use his bathroom first. I knew Duke and I both wouldn't fit into the tiny space, so I looked for a safe place to tie him while I took care of business. Nothing could possibly go wrong, could it?

Unbeknownst to me, while I was indisposed, a Lieutenant entered the tailor's shop to take a break too. His last name was Campbell but his friends called him Bull. Between him and the cold sodas was Duke the Dog. Murray told him that I would be out of the loo shortly so I could get Duke out of his way.

As I later learned, Bull Campbell glared at Duke and said, "Fuck that dog" and roughly pushed him away with his leg. Not a good decision, Bull! Duke took his pant leg in his mouth and totally ripped it off Bull's body. By the time I got there, Lt. Campbell was standing there wearing something that resembled a Navy colored hula skirt. It was that bad!

Bull immediately cursed Duke and me out and told us to get the hell out of there. I looked over at Murray before making my escape and saw that he could barely contain himself. Good thing he was a tailor although I think those pants were well beyond repair.

114.

We're not leaving Adams/Morgan just yet. Our K-9 cruiser must have been in the shop because one day Harry and I found ourselves walking a foot beat with our dogs. I remember it was a hot day and we had to be particularly careful with Duke and Sabbath not overheating. Those burning sidewalks could be brutal on their paws. We also had to be sure they had enough water to drink. All in all, not a great situation for any of us but there's an old saying that a good cop never gets hungry, tired or wet.

Another concern for the two of us was that some dumb ass would approach and try to pet either one of the dogs. And people tried more than you would think. In some areas, the sidewalks could get quite crowded so even an inadvertent push could set them off. These boys did not have a sense of humor but then again, that wasn't part of their job description. When they hit the street, they were all work and no play.

After we wandered around Adams/Morgan for a couple of hours, Harry and I decided we had had enough. It was time for an air conditioned break. At the corner of 17th and Columbia Rd was a movie theatre that was nice and cool inside. The manager was more than happy to see the Po Po. Free security for him and a dark, air conditioned place to hide out for us.

Being that it was the middle of the afternoon, there weren't many patrons inside. The four of us settled into the back of the theatre where nobody could bother us. The movie was about that cult maniac Jim Jones, who forced almost 1,000 of his followers to drink poisoned Kool Aid and die. It wasn't something I particularly wanted to watch but it was free and cool.

The dogs settled in on each side of us and we sat there, half watching the movie. There was a part of the story where a California Congressman flies into the area (somewhere in Africa), to investigate complaints his office had received about the mistreatment of Jim Jones's followers. Unfortunately, Congressman Ryan and others were shot and killed on the runway before they could escape.

Everything was fine until that scene in the film. As soon as the gunshots started, Sabbath and Duke immediately went berserk. Remember, these dogs were trained to attack at the first signs of gunfire and they were unable to distinguish between real and not real. It was all Harry and I could do to keep them from leaping over the seats and attacking the movie screen. Between all the gunshots and the K-9 hysteria, the poor patrons didn't know what the hell to think or do. I believe some of them may have thought it was part of the show.

Harry and I each gave our dogs a hard tug and ran upstairs to the nursery which fortunately was vacant. Since it was soundproof, we could all enjoy the rest of the movie in peace. I think the manager missed the whole thing because when we finally left, he thanked us for coming by.

Attending court could sometimes be a problem if you were in K-9. When the weather got hot, you had to be oh, so careful with the dog being inside your Police cruiser. The Third District was particularly bad because it was covered in roughly 99% asphalt and concrete. If it got too hot, we would notify the dispatcher and head over to Rock Creek Park so the dogs could get some relief. It was an unofficial rule that we would respond to calls only when absolutely necessary.

One afternoon, I received word to respond to court for a meeting with an Assistant US Attorney about a case I'd made. I was about to go home and was not happy about the added distraction. It was pretty hot outside but I'd been told that the meeting would be short and I'd be out of there in no time.

I put Duke in the back of the Chevette and when I arrived downtown, I was able to find a parking place without much hassle. The problem was that I couldn't possibly leave Duke in my hot car. Luckily, the Chevette had a hatchback so I was able to raise it and tie Duke so that he was able to get some shade.

I wasn't happy with this arrangement and when I entered the attorney's office, I told him so. He then informed me I would probably have to stay for several hours since he had found a glitch in the case.

Well, that was not going to happen and I told him so. We went back and forth for a couple of minutes, and finally I lost my cool. I told him I could not safely leave my Police dog in the car any longer and he would just have to continue the case. Before he could reply, I was out the door.

I rushed back to my car and saw that Duke was panting profusely. It scared the crap out of me and I knew I had to do something fast. But what?!?!

I noticed a deli across the street and made a split second decision that may have saved Duke's life. I picked him up and ran into the deli yelling," Get me all your ice! Now!" They looked at me like I was crazy but I didn't care. The customers that were in there made a beeline for the door but I didn't care about that either.

They brought out some ice but it wasn't nearly enough. I laid Duke on the floor and ordered them to bring every friggin' ice cube they had and put it on the floor. I took all the ice and completely covered Duke with it until I could see that he was feeling better.

Then I had him stand up and I thanked the owners for their help as we left. I remember looking back as we went out the door and observing that the place was totally covered in melting ice and water. A complete mess but thankfully there were no complaints or camera videos to record the incident. Sometimes drastic events call for drastic measures.

Looking back, I can see how life had become a never ending Twilight Zone marathon. But nobody knew it at the time. It wasn't necessarily a bad thing but it certainly contributed to an unbalanced life out in the real world. It also didn't help that two cops from the same District were married to each other and frequently worked side by side. We simply couldn't get away from the job. We'd even speak in Police codes to one another.

"Did you see that 10-50 on your way home from the store?"

"10-4. I was going to assist but when scout 134 showed up, I decided to 10-22."

And it all seemed perfectly normal. That's probably why so many Officers stay with their "own kind." Even today, I find I have to filter myself if I'm talking about something that someone might find disturbing. I'd have to guess it's the same with combat veterans.

One particularly crazy incident occurred after the midnight roll call and Officers were released to go out front of the station to relieve the evening shift. This was usually a bit chaotic with a lot of noise thrown in. The evening group wanted to get the hell out of there and sometimes the midnighters had to virtually jump in their

Police vehicles and peel off for pending calls. Hot weather and weekends were the worse.

This shift change started out just like the last thousand, except for one thing. A man and woman who lived across the street decided to have an altercation. This was nothing unusual except the man took it to another level. He pulled out a gun and began chasing her down the sidewalk toward about twenty five cops standing in front of the Precinct. If that wasn't bad enough, he started shooting at her as she weaved among the Officers. They both hauled ass to 17th St and then turned the corner toward U St. By that time, the gun was empty and all twenty five Po Po were hot on his tail. Well, maybe not all twenty five. There were probably a few that said "Screw this, I'm going home."

It looked like something out of the Keystone Kops and of course, the guy was eventually taken down and locked up. Surprisingly, nobody was injured except for one Officer who claimed he sprained his ankle and ended up being granted a couple weeks of free sick leave.

If this dumbass had just waited a couple more minutes, we would have all been gone. But what's that saying? "Time waits for no one."

115.

Almost everyone was injured on the street at one time or another. Frank was hurt several times, through no fault of his own.

Once while he was attempting to make an arrest, he got one handcuff on S-1's wrist and before he could complete the job, the guy was able to swing the loose cuff with such force it knocked Frank's front teeth out.

Another time he was fighting S-1, trying to get his ass into the back of the Police wagon. In the ensuing melee, Frank fell and broke his leg.

Then there was the man he was trying to arrest in front of the Washington Hilton. The guy bit Frank so hard in the hand that his teeth went all the way to the bone. And then it got badly infected. Attention: Human bites can be far worse than animal bites.
Unless it was something debilitating, most injuries were viewed as just part of the J-O-B.

But once in awhile, the worse happened. Arthur Snyder was a 3D Officer that was sworn in about three years after I was. He was a really goofy looking White guy that took the word "serious" to a new level. He had a reputation for not cutting anyone a break-- ever. Everything was Black and White to him and at times it caused him problems.

One time, a woman overdosed on pills and Arthur rode in the ambulance with her to the hospital. That was highly unusual because if we were going to the hospital to write a report, we drove our Police vehicles. It seemed that Arthur was in the ambulance so he could arrest her for possession of illegal narcotics. And he was getting in the way of the EMTs who were attempting to save her life. By the time they arrived at GW Hospital, Police and Fire Officials were on the scene to break up the altercation that had now become physical. The rest of us would have just waited until the woman was tended to and then made a decision on how to proceed. But not Arthur.

On February 12, 1980, Arthur and Officer Constant Pickett were assigned a foot beat in the 14th and U St NW corridor. As they were walking along 14th St, they observed a drug transaction take place. Constant decided to approach S-1 from one end of the block and Arthur from the other end so that he could not escape.

Arthur reached the man first and as he got closer, S-1 pulled out a gun and shot Arthur. The first round hit his body armor and the second, his belt buckle. The impact knocked Arthur to the sidewalk and as he fell, the POS shot him in the head and killed him. The guy was able to make his escape on foot but a couple of days later, he got into a shootout with Police and ended up on the losing end.

It was a terrible blow for everyone at 3D, especially Constant Pickett who apparently blamed himself for years.

I never personally worked with Arthur but we knew each other well enough to joke around and tell stupid jokes. Today, the community meeting room in the Third District is named after him.

Arthur P. Snyder was twenty-nine years old, married and had two Beagles. RIP Buddy!

116.

I was working the midnight shift one
night at the end of March in 1981 and when
0700 hours finally rolled around, I was more
than happy to turn the cruiser over to my
relief. That morning, the K-9 Officer
relieving me was Tom Delahanty. He was a
veteran Officer with dark, greasy hair, all
slicked back from his forehead. Kind of a big

guy who didn't have a whole lot to say to me.
Not rude, but rather indifferent.

Apparently, during his tour of duty,
his dog Kirk got sick so he found our K-9
Sergeant and asked him what he should do until
checkoff. Sgt. Schaefer told him to go over to
the Washington Hilton where President Reagan
was going to give a speech. Tom and a group of
other Third District Officers would be
assisting the Secret Service with securing the
area.

And the rest is history. As President
Reagan was exiting the hotel, John Hinkley
reached out from the crowd and shot the
President, James Brady, Timothy McCarthy and
Tom Delahanty. In a split second, Hinkley was
overpowered by the Secret Service and 3D
Officers.

Tom was taken to the Washington
Hospital Center where he underwent surgery for
a bullet wound to the back of his neck.
Afterwards, while he was in his room
recuperating, all the Third District K-9
handlers took turns sitting outside in the
hallway keeping away people that might want to
bother him.

When my turn came to "stand guard," I
would go through the endless number of
mailbags that were being delivered. Inside
were thousands of get well cards, and it
turned out that some of them were from very
famous people. I opened one card with a
handwritten message from Frank Sinatra.
Another one from Barbra Streisand. It kinda
became a game to see who could find the most
famous celebrity. A lot of people sent crosses
too. And I mean a lot! There were so many
crosses we didn't know what to do with them
all. But nobody was going to throw a single

one away. Just in case. I have no idea what happened to them.

I also don't why, but many of the incoming envelopes contained cash. That was all handled according to the General Orders because everyone was paranoid it was a setup by Internal Affairs. Every dime was accounted for, not that it wasn't tempting.

Tom eventually recovered and the rumor was he was promoted to Captain on paper, so when he retired on disability he would receive a larger annuity.

Tom was treated by the press as a hero, wounded while attempting to protect the President of the United States. The sad truth was that at the time of the incident, Tom Delahanty had his hands in his pockets and was facing away from the crowd. All you have to do is look at the video and the video doesn't lie. I'm sorry he got shot but Tom Delahanty was certainly no hero. And there were plenty of real heroes that day. When I revisit that video today, I still feel a great sense of pride when I see the many members of law enforcement running toward the active shooter with no regard for their own safety. That's what suiting up every day is all about.

117.

In May of 1982, I discovered I was pregnant. Frank and I were excited and nervous at the same time. I knew the minute I told anyone at work, I would immediately be put on light duty. So I kept my mouth shut for as long as I could get away with it. And Duke wasn't talking either. I considered it an advantage that my weight was always fluctuating, so it wouldn't raise any suspicions if I showed a few extra pounds.

One night, I was called to do a track near Sherman Circle in the Second District. There had been an armed carjacking and the suspect took off running toward Massachusetts Ave NW. When I got there, I took Duke out of the cruiser, put his tracking harness on and had him try to pick up S-1's scent. He seemed to be having some difficulty since the area was so densely populated, but as he was walking alongside a row of bushes in front of an embassy he suddenly dove into the shrubbery. Before I could react, I heard a scream and saw a figure come running out onto the sidewalk. He continued to run toward an alley in an effort to escape but by this time Duke was hauling ass after him. He caught up with him in no time and S-1, with his infinite wisdom kicked Duke in the head. Not a good idea. At all! I think that just added a few more stitches to the ones he was already going to receive at the hospital.

Which reminds me of the burglary call I got in Adams/Morgan. The house had been turned inside out and the Officers on the scene wanted a dog to make a sweep of the premises before leaving. For whatever reason, I decided that we could go through the house quicker without the dog because it was so small. So we did a cursory search without finding anything.

As I was walking out the front door and back to my cruiser, the homeowner came running after me. He told me he had heard a noise coming from the basement and would I please come back in with my K-9 and take a look around? I agreed and reentered the premises, this time with Duke in tow.

We went down the stairs into a half finished basement, filled with furniture that was scattered everywhere. As soon as I loudly announced my presence and with no response, I released Duke to search the area.

He immediately honed in on the far corner of the room and quickly made his way over there. As he approached an old sofa, a man jumped out from behind it brandishing a lamp over his head.

He started swinging it at Duke as he began moving toward the back door in an attempt to escape. Duke stepped back and was able to turn his head so he wasn't clobbered. S-1 swung the lamp again at Duke and missed.

It kind of became this crazy dancelike situation, all through the basement.

Swing. Sidestep. Forward.

Swing. Sidestep. Forward.

By this time, Duke had lost all patience and grabbed the guy by his "lamp hand" before he could continue.

Did this Bozo really think he was going to incapacitate Duke the Dog and make good his escape? I'll give him a little (and I mean little) credit for trying. FYI: Never fight a Police dog because the odds are overwhelming you're gonna lose. And get stitches.

118.

It was during this period that Harry had completed his twenty years on the Department and had the audacity to retire. I was not happy because he had taught me so much and I considered him to be a good friend. But I couldn't really blame him. He had done his whole career on the street and that will take a toll on anyone. He found he couldn't stay out of law enforcement completely though. It wasn't long before he became Chief of Police in the small town of Shenandoah, Virginia.

My new partner was almost the exact opposite of Harry. His name was Bill Gregory but everyone called him Bigfoot. The best word to describe him was "Goofball." He had no common sense whatsoever but he was an excellent Police Officer and K-9 handler. He had a young German Shepherd named Dylan that had a much sunnier disposition than Sabbath, although that wouldn't have been hard. "Foot" and I got along well although there were many times when I wanted to kill him. He could be so stubborn but I guess I could be too. He did have an uncanny knack for thinking ahead of S-1. If there was a lookout for a subject or vehicle, Foot could almost predict which way this guy would be going.

One time we were searching for a vehicle and as we were passing N St, Foot yelled "Stop!" He pointed toward a car that was so far down the block I could barely see it.

"That's it! Turn! Turn! Turn!"

I started to argue with him but I knew it would be useless so I turned onto N St just to prove him wrong.

Of course, it turned out to be the right vehicle with the right suspects. We still argued but I was less inclined to disbelieve him after that.

The time was fast approaching when I would have to tell on myself and go on light duty, because I was now five months pregnant.

In October of 1982, Bigfoot and I received a call to respond to the Foggy Bottom Metro station to do an underground search for a suspect wanted for armed robbery. There's a third rail down there that can electrocute the shit out of you but we were assured it had been deactivated. Yeah, right. There was no way we were going to take a chance so we proceeded down the tunnel with our dogs on lead.

There were all kind of ladders leading up to emergency exits and ledges that would make great hiding places. As I was climbing up my fifth ladder it finally dawned on me, "What in the hell was I doing?"

I was five months pregnant and actively searching for armed robbery suspects. This was it! I had to spill the beans. Now! Bigfoot and I didn't find anyone so we returned to our cruiser to drive back to the Third District. On the way, I turned to him and confessed that I was pregnant and expecting in February.

I had no idea how he would respond but it was almost immediate. He went absolutely ballistic because I hadn't told him before. That I was endangering the life of my newborn baby. On and on and on. Of course he was correct on all counts.

That cruiser was up at 3D in no time and Foot hightailed it into the Sergeant's office to tell on me. Thinking back, it really was a selfish, stupid thing for me to have done. And light duty started immediately.

Sidebar: I find it interesting that my last call on the street while pregnant with Michael was down in a Metro Transit tunnel. And then, years later, Mike became a Metro Transit Police Officer. Coincidence? I like to think it wasn't.

119

Light duty was as bad as I expected it to be. I was assigned to the Detective's office where it was my job to file index cards and answer the phone for eight hours. Also, prisoners were frequently brought in to be processed for arrests. Since they were handcuffed to a desk, security was not a big issue.

The problem was that when each arrestee made an outside telephone call, they used the phone on my desk. Remember, this was when AIDS was at epidemic proportions and this particular population was not exactly the healthiest group you'd ever want to be around. They'd all be hacking and coughing into the receiver of the phone I was expected to use. It was totally disgusting and there was no way I was going tolerate it. After all, I had my baby to protect (yes, I had finally come to my senses).

I went to the Lieutenant to ask if there was somewhere else I could be assigned and he gave me an emphatic "No." Fortunately, I had a friend who was a Lieutenant in the second floor Detective's office. His name was Bruce McDonald and he had been my Sergeant many years ago. He could be a real Hard Ass but he always went the extra mile for Frank and me. When I asked if I could come and work for him, he immediately said "Yes."

So upstairs I went and basically did the same job of filing index cards and answering phones. But this time, none of those stinky S-1's got anywhere near me.

Under the circumstances, I had a lot of fun in that office. The Detectives, all men took me under their wing and made sure I ate lunch and had several breaks during the day. When it was time for business, they were all business. But when it was time to lighten up, these guys were the funniest and dirtiest I'd ever been around. Political correctness was not in the vocabulary then and although sometimes it appeared that a line was about to be crossed, everybody seemed to 'Get It.' People weren't tiptoeing around each other then like they do today. And that was okay.

Another good part about this whole pregnancy thing was that I quit drinking as soon as I found out. Cold turkey and it wasn't hard at all! Maybe I had just been exaggerating all these years. I could take it or leave it. Well, that was certainly a relief. Life was good!

120.

Frank and I faithfully attended birthing classes at Fairfax Hospital and did everything the Doctor told us.

Duke was not real understanding about any of this. He was forced to stay at home when I went to 3D to do my light duty stint. He just wasn't the kind of dog you could take in and put under your desk. He would have everyone backed into a corner, just daring anyone to move.

Desk duty was pretty uneventful so I enjoyed listening to the Detectives talk among themselves about cases they were working on. Even monitoring the Police radio helped relieve the boredom, although it made me want to get back into the middle of it. But of course, that wasn't going to happen anytime soon.

During the third week of February in 1983, Frank and I were invited to a married couple's home for dinner. They were both Lieutenants, Vance and Caroline Boggs, and Caroline and I had become pretty good friends. As we were entering the block where they lived, Frank pulled over and informed me that it was really a surprise baby shower. Thank goodness he told me, because I hate surprise parties.

There were a lot of people from 3D in attendance and it turned out to be a lot of fun. I have a picture somewhere of me sitting in a chair and I am Huge with that baby weight. The time was getting close but I had no idea that day just how close.

We got home about 2230 hours and as I was standing next to the bed changing into my pajamas, I noticed I was standing in a pool of water.

Hmmm, that seemed odd. I asked Frank if he knew anything about why there would be liquid on the floor and he said no.

Then it dawned on me. My water had broken and very soon, I was going to have a baby. I excitedly told Frank who had just fallen asleep. He mumbled, "You're just imagining things. Go back to bed."

But I made him get up, call the Doctor and drive me to Fairfax Hospital. At least that was his intention. He got so flustered, he entered the Capital Beltway in the wrong direction. But that was Frank. He had always been directionally challenged, so it was only appropriate he get lost on the way to the hospital.

Ten hours later, 7 pounds, 3 ounce baby boy Michael Frank Weinsheimer was born on

February 21, 1983. He was absolutely perfect and we were both thrilled.

Two days later, I was released and sent home with this bundle of joy. Neither one of us had a clue as to what to do with a newborn but fortunately my sister Marcia flew in from Ohio to help out.

I stayed at home for Michael's first five months but then it was time to return to work. Luckily, I had found a wonderful woman, Ann Hall who provided care in her home while we were gone.

Since we both worked such odd hours, Ann Hall, or Mama Ann as she was fondly called, was a particular Godsend. Her husband John, drove a truck for Pepperidge Farms and had to get up unusually early so it was alright to bring Michael over unusually early too.

On the one hand, returning to work was great but on the other hand, I felt guilty for dragging this baby out at all hours so I could go to work. Duke was happy though. One thing about working dogs is that they want to work until they take their last dying breath. It seems to be their sole purpose in life, unlike many people who usually can't wait until the day they retire.

My best example of that was the day I took Duke to work for what turned out to be an uneventful tour of duty. When we came home, Duke jumped up on my bed as I was changing out of my uniform. When I was getting ready to exit the bedroom, Duke got off the bed to follow me. From the corner of my eye, I saw something red on the bedspread. I looked closer and noticed that it was blood. And there was a lot of it! What the hell?

I went over to Duke and ordered him to lay down. I didn't see anything out of the ordinary until I rolled him over on his back. That's when I saw a deep gash on his stomach, about twelve inches long. Once again, what the hell? How in the world did this happen?

I knew he needed immediate medical attention so I rushed him to the local vet where he received fifty five stitches. He was going to be okay but I was still racking my brain as to how this injury occurred. And of course, an official report had to be made for the Police Department.

I'll never know for sure but this is what I think happened: Before I left for work every day, Duke would run out in the back woods to take care of business. In the middle of the woods was a creek that had a rather large beaver population. It's my thought that Duke and a beaver(s) had a physical altercation and Duke sustained the stomach injury in the process. Somehow, he knew it was time to leave for work and there was no way he was going to miss that. I guess to him it was just a minor flesh wound.

So he went and did a full eight hours, without giving me any indication he was seriously hurt. Now if that had been me with the same type of injury, I would have been off work for months.

Unfortunately for the Dukester, Fairfax County Animal Control made me quarantine him for ten days to make sure he didn't come down with rabies.

During that time, I would try to sneak out of the house when I was going to work so he wouldn't see me. But every single day, he would conveniently position himself in front of the door to the carport to make sure I felt extra guilty for leaving him behind. That was a painful ten days for us both.

Mike riding "The Killer Duke"

121

Life was good at this point. Michael was a complete joy for Frank and me. And Duke was a great "Big Brother." When Mike was in his playpen Duke would patrol the perimeter, making sure that all was safe in the Weinsheimer household. For him, it was all work all the time. Strangers could get near him only if there was a slow introduction. And then he was fine. Usually.

One time, Linda Wheeler came to the house with a date who was somewhat intoxicated. I remember sitting on the couch at the opposite end of the living room, holding Duke by the collar. Linda told her friend that he couldn't just come right up to Duke and expect a positive outcome.

This guy was evidently feeling a bit of liquid bravery and told us there wasn't a dog anywhere that he couldn't get next to. I tried to tell him that Duke wasn't exactly like any other dog and to just chill out for a few minutes. Of course, that made this man more adamant and he kept pushing until I'd had enough.

"Okay Asshole, pet the nice dog." And I let go of Duke's collar.

He was on the guy's expensive suit in a split second. Before Mr. Know It All could react, Duke ripped the entire sleeve off and then looked at me for permission to finish him off. Permission however was denied and Duke grudgingly returned to me.

Well, so much for the nice evening Linda and her date had planned. I think this little event sobered up and embarrassed him enough that he couldn't exit the front door fast enough. I don't think Linda ever went out with him again either.

Duke was beginning to show his age at this point. Unfortunately for large breed dogs, especially German Shepherds, it's usually the hips that go first. I always said that when the time came where he could no longer walk, I would have to make the decision nobody wants to make. He was still walking alright, but his hips were starting to sway a bit. This was an early indication of what was going to happen down the road.

At the DC K-9 office at the Police Academy, when one of the dogs had to be put down there was a rather macabre ritual the handler went through beforehand.

Another handler would put on the attack sleeve and the dog would get his last bite before receiving the needle. Some of these dogs were in pretty bad shape but when they saw that sleeve, there was always a brief rejuvenation and then the final walk into the vet's office. Afterwards, everyone would go sit up in the old K-9 cemetery and get good and drunk.

122.

Periodically, Frank, Michael, Duke and I would travel to Yardley, Pennsylvania to visit my parents. At first, Duke was not exactly Mr. Congeniality but that was nothing new.

One time, I took my Mother out shopping while my Father had to run some errands in the opposite direction. Duke remained in their house which should not have been any problem. But of course, it was.

My Father happened to arrive home first and when he attempted to enter his own house, Duke went on High Alert and put an immediate stop to that. There was no way this "stranger" was going to come into these premises. Apparently, Father went to every door and was met with the same set of teeth, just daring him to come any closer.

This was way before cellphones so there was no way to get in contact with us. A few hours later we returned only to find my Father sitting on a picnic table, staring with resignation at the back door.

With time and patience, Duke and my Father became fast friends mainly because he walked him about ten times a day. On these walks he would fervently hope that someone would walk by and ask about Duke.

Then my Father would pull the lead close to him and announce, "This is a fully trained DC Police K-9. Don't come any closer or you will be bit." This would totally make his day and Duke couldn't have been happier to get all the attention.

When Duke finally died, my Father cried like a baby. This was coming from the ultimate narcissist who treated most of the family with complete indifference. Even years later, he would tear up at the mention of Duke. Of course, in his eyes Duke built him up and massaged his ego and reputation like we could never do. Whatever.

Duke's last day on the street at Blagden
Alley, NW. 1984
(Photo courtesy of Linda Wheeler)

123.

Finally it became obvious that Duke was
going to have to retire and I would have to
train a new dog.

I was asked if I wanted to keep him,
which of course I did. Some handlers choose to
surrender their dogs and they are then placed
in a good home. Linda Wheeler actually took in
a couple of retired dogs where they lived the
rest of their lives in the lap of luxury. But
there was no way in Hell I was going to give
up the Mighty Duke.

To make the transfer from DC property to private citizen I had to sign documents agreeing to assume legal liability in the event Duke was a Bad Boy. And with him, that could be taking on quite a responsibility. Now I had to get a new dog and wait for the next K-9 class to begin. During that time, I went back on the street and performed the duties of a scout car Officer. That meant responding to 911 calls but I didn't mind because I knew I wouldn't be doing it for too long.

After a couple of weeks I got a message that there was a dog at the Academy that might be suitable for the upcoming class and would I like to come and take a look? I certainly would so I made the trip across town to see what was waiting for me in the kennel.

When I arrived, I walked through the Sergeant's office and back to the kennels where the dogs were kept. I immediately saw a beautiful all Black German Shepherd quietly standing on the other side of the kennel door. I took an instant liking to him but there were a few hurdles to go over before he could get into the class.

First, his hips had to be x-rayed to see if there was already a predisposition for future problems. Then, if he passed that they would see how he reacted to the sound of gunfire.

This dog passed both tests and I asked Sergeant Ritter if he would assign him to me. He said that would be okay but there was something he needed to tell me. That sounded ominous but I said, "Go ahead."

"Well, it's about the dog's name?"

"What are you talking about, his name?"

"Yes, his name is Wimpy." And he began laughing uncontrollably.

"What?!?!?!

"The donor's kid named him after that fat guy in the Popeye cartoons that ate all the hamburgers. His name was Wimpy and you're not allowed to change it. Do you still want him?"

Wimpy??? Like I'm really going to take a Police dog on the street named Wimpy! "Get him Wimpy!" That was not going to happen! I asked if there was anything I could do to correct this horrific situation. I was told that if I got the donor's permission, I could change his name to anything I wanted.

I couldn't get to the telephone fast enough. "Uh lady, do you think I could change that dumbass name you let your dumbass kid give this dog you donated?"

I didn't exactly word it that way but in the end she was agreeable and Wimpy then became Chief. I had to go to the so called Name Book to see what number he would be. Ladies and gentlemen, I would like to introduce you to Chief 5.

Chief 5 and Duke 69

124

I put Chief in the back of my 1972 Chevy Chevelle and proceeded to drive home via the Capital beltway to Fairfax. As I was crossing the Wilson Bridge, I heard a heaving sound coming from the back seat.

Oh Shit, he's puking all over the car and I'm doing 65 in the left lane. He threw up all the way home, until I finally pulled up in the driveway. This dog vomited every day, both going to the Academy and coming home from the Academy. Even after we graduated from class, Chief would periodically heave ho in the back of the Third District K-9 cruiser.

As when I went through class with Duke, the fifteen weeks of training were very intense and physically draining. The modern attack sleeves were still not the norm so we continued to cut up pilfered mail bags to use as protection around our arms.

Chief was much more "handler conscious," which meant he was extremely sensitive to me. If I raised my voice a decibel too loud he would get upset. He was definitely not the Hard Head that Duke was, so I had to turn my entire thought process in another direction. I couldn't hurt the poor baby's feelings or he would simply shut down.

One exercise we did was the Recall and Chief was not cooperating in any way, shape or form.

The Recall goes like this: The bad guy takes off running and the dog is sent to make the apprehension. While the dog is in full pursuit, a "little old lady" walks in between the two. The goal is to call your dog back before he nails the "little old lady." This is probably the hardest thing to train a dog to do because he does not want to come back.

If the dog repeatedly refuses to return to his handler, a special collar is placed on him. If he still continues with the pursuit, a low voltage shock is sent via remote control to the collar and hopefully he will get the message and return to the starting line. This usually works but not always.

When it was time for Chief to partake in the Recall, I just knew that he would come back to me. After all, this was the dog that would basically freak out if "mommy" raised her voice too loud.

When the exercise began, the bad guy started running and I sent Chief to apprehend him. At a certain point, I yelled, "CHIEF, COME" and then waited for him to make a u turn and return to my side.

Wait a minute! He never even slowed down. Just continued on as if he never even heard me. I tried a couple more times with the same results. Okay, so now it was time to try the special collar. This would certainly do the trick.

The collar was adjusted around his neck and Jimmy Corcoran stood behind us with the handheld remote. The bad guy took off running and once again, I sent Chief in his direction with the command, "GET HIM! GOOD BOY!"

When Chief got about twenty yards from the starting line, I yelled, "CHIEF, COME!" Nothing. Jimmy hit the button as I yelled again. Not only did Chief not respond to the sudden jolt, he began running faster toward the bad guy. Just as he was about to attack the sleeve, he kept on running toward the Fire Academy which was next door. Jimmy kept pushing the button on the remote until it

either lost all its juice or Chief merely got
tired. By this time, I had lost my voice so
it was only by the Grace of God that Chief
decided to come back and not run into the
middle of I-295. What the hell was that all
about?!?!

125.

The remainder of the fifteen weeks were
uneventful. More obedience, more scent work
and more attacks. It was all about repetition
and it was cool to see these dogs go from
nothing to fully trained Police K-9s.
After graduation, one of the handler's had a
party at his house so we could finally let off
steam in a big way. This involved getting
stupid drunk and I was more than happy to join
the fray. And so was Frank. We didn't know it
at the time but we were about to snowball back
to our old ways.

I returned to 3D, this time with Chief.
I didn't have the full confidence in him that
I had with Duke, but somehow we would make it
work. There was no way I was going to turn him
back in, wait for a new class and go through
those fifteen weeks all over again. Not going
to happen. It almost did though.

When Michael was about eighteen months
old, he was in our TV room by himself eating a
hotdog. Chief decided to investigate the
enticing smell of food and went in to check it
out. Mike thought it would be funny to stick
the hotdog in front of Chief's face and pull
his hand back just as Chief went to eat it.

Apparently this happened a couple of
times, until Chief had had enough. As Michael
pulled his hand back for the last time, Chief
bit him in the face.

When Frank and I ran into the room we
saw Mike covered in blood and Chief finishing
the last remnant of hotdog, without any trace
of guilt.

We rushed him to the ER in Fairfax City
and were relieved to be told that it looked
worse than it really was. A couple of stitches
and he'd be good as new.

An internal investigation had to be
conducted and I was found at fault for not
properly supervising my dog. Nothing else was
done except I was ordered to report to the K-9
Sergeant's office at the Academy.

He told me that if I felt I could no
longer work with Chief, I could turn him in
and train another dog.

Hell, no! I loved my kid but I wasn't
going to start over in a new class if I could
help it. I told the Sergeant we would all be
fine and got out of there before he changed
his mind. After all, it was this toddler's
fault for teasing the dog. Nah, just kidding.

126.

The Third District had two K-9 cruisers
so sometimes it was just Chief and me in one,
and Bigfoot and his dog Dylan in the other. If
one of the cars was out of service, we worked
together in one cruiser.

Dylan was a very cool dog that had a
great personality. But when it was time to
work, he was all in. He and Chief got along
fine which was an added bonus.

My favorite story about Bill Gregory
and Dylan actually happened not long after I
retired. Bill was flagged down on U St one
night by someone who said they'd just been
robbed at gunpoint. The man pointed North on

10th St toward a guy running on the sidewalk and told Foot that was the one who robbed him. Being that it was the middle of the night, there were no other people anywhere in sight. Bill exited the cruiser, opened the back door and took Dylan out. He pointed Dylan in S-1's direction and released him with the prerequisite, "Get him! Good boy!"

At the corner of 10th and V St NW, a car was parked with the back door open and the motor running. This was apparently the getaway car and just as S-1 got there, Dylan nailed him. Instead of surrendering, S-1 pulled out a gun and shot Dylan five times.

Bill had just run up on the scene and when he saw what the POS (Piece of Shit) had done to Dylan, he opened fire and shot S-1 in the shoulder. The other guys gave up and were arrested by Officers who had quickly responded to the scene.

An ambulance arrived to take S-1 to the hospital but when they saw how badly injured Dylan was, the EMT's said, "Screw this guy. We're taking the dog. This POS can wait for the next ambulance."

And that's what they did. Dylan was loaded onto a stretcher and transported to the nearest emergency animal clinic where he was successfully treated for his gunshots.

Just for the record, another ambulance arrived in short order and took S-1 away to have his wounds attended to also.

Somehow, the media picked up on the story of how medics took a DC Police K-9 in their ambulance after he was shot five times. It got a lot of attention by the public, especially all the dog lovers who thought what the medics did was great.

Unfortunately, some people in the upper echelon of the DC government saw it differently and promptly fired the people who decided to take an injured dog over an injured person.

That decision lasted all of about twelve hours, when a couple of well-placed phone calls were made and the firings were quickly rescinded.

Dylan recovered from his injuries but was forced to retire when arthritis set in, keeping him from fully able to do his job. Somebody, somewhere, decided that Dylan should receive a Purple Bone of Courage and Mayor Marion Barry should award it to him at a ceremony at 3D.

Lights. Cameras. All of the local media showed up for this feel good story and when Barry was instructed to stand next to Dylan and place the Purple Bone of Courage around his neck, he could be heard hissing, "That fucking dog better not bite me." But Dylan was a good boy and Barry can be seen in a picture with a clenched smile and hand tentatively placing the medal around Dylan's neck. I wish I had been there.

Bill (Bigfoot) Gregory and Dylan

127.

It was hard to believe, but the 14th
Street corridor was actually getting worse in
the early 80's. When I got on the street at
2300 hours, all hell had usually broken loose.
14th Street and the surrounding side streets
were solid gridlock with all the horny men and
people that wanted to check out the scene. If

the girls thought they could get away it, they'd run into the street to stop cars and make arrangements for their "date." If they got caught and there wasn't a backup of radio runs, it was off to 3D in handcuffs with the tried and true charge of Disorderly Conduct. They were usually back on their corners within an hour and "on the stroll" as if nothing happened. Sometimes even before we got back there ourselves.

We had a Lieutenant, Fred Billings, who decided to take matters into his own hands. Word was that Fred enjoyed liquor a little bit too much but what he lacked in sobriety, he made up for in his enthusiasm on the street. One night, he came up with the brilliant idea that we were going to totally shut down 14th Street, lock, stock and barrel. Now how was he going to do this? He got all the 3D midnight troops together and told us to block the streets by any means possible. The only people that could enter this restricted area would be Metro busses, residents (with valid photo ID) and anyone else that had a legitimate reason to be there.

What could we use to block the streets? Someone suggested a stealth trip down to U.S. Park Police Headquarters where they had lots of wooden barricades we could "borrow." So, our two Police wagons made several trips to Southwest and loaded up the back with as many barriers as they could. The fact that each one was marked "Property of U.S. Park Police" was of no significance. We were on a mission. Back at 3D, the barricades were set up and the streets were effectively closed down. Most of the busiest corners were manned by Officers who made the decision of who got in and who didn't. At first, the girls were merely curious but when they found out what we were really up to, they became enraged. There were a few physical altercations with the Officers but in the long run, there was nothing they could do but wait and stew.

The residents in the Logan Circle area were delighted by this new turn of events. At last, they could have some peace and quiet. If all they had to do was show their driver's license to the friendly Officer blocking the 14th St strip, then so be it.

Park Police quickly discovered their barricades had been pilfered, but it took awhile for them to find out just who the culprits were. And Lt. Billings was able to talk bureaucrat speak to the point where they believed the barriers may have actually been on loan to us after all.

This little event went on for an entire summer, and looking back it's amazing to think we were able to pull it off as long as we did. After all, even though it was completely effective, it was also 100% illegal. But we made our point and the girls may or may not have learned a lesson. At any rate, I'm sure things went back to the old ways in no time. It was a hell of a lot of fun while it lasted though.

128.

Further up 14th St, between V and W St were a couple of ghetto carryouts that the drug addicts liked to hang out at. There was such a large open air drug market that over a hundred junkies would congregate in that one block alone. And that was no exaggeration. In its own way, it was as bad as its hooker counterpart eight blocks to the South.

When the radio was quiet Officers would park their scout cars and try to move them off the corner, usually to no effect. The city had no loitering laws other than an obscure charge of "incommoding the sidewalk." This meant that if three or more people were hindering someone's passage on public space, a ticket could be issued for "incommoding...." It was also referred to as a hummer or Bullshit charge that nobody really bothered with.

The Hummer King in my time was Officer Bob Thompson. He walked a beat one night and shined his flashlight into every parked vehicle as he walked along. If the emergency brake had not been activated, he wrote them a ticket. Now that was a Hummer with a Capital H. In the morning, there was a stampede of infuriated motorists who stormed the station demanding to know who the idiot was that had written these. Thompson was advised to cool it but if a violation was on the books, he was going to enforce it.

Once again, Wild Fred Billings got a case of the ass in reference to the junkie convention on 14th St. He had us all gather a couple of blocks away and then on his signal, we swooped in with lights and sirens. Some of the junkies were able to escape but the ones that could not were lined up against the wall. This was quite a sight because they went all the way from V to W St. Must have been seventy five to a hundred of them and everyone was searched and generally inconvenienced. Names were run through the computer and there were always a couple that came back with Bench Warrants.

Some nights, Bigfoot and I would head over there for some fun with the dogs. He and Dylan would get out of the cruiser at one end

of the block and Chief and I would get out at
the other end. Then we would slowly walk
toward each other, watching the junkies
scatter like cockroaches. What two dogs could
do to disperse the masses was a wonder to
behold. You could have put every 3D Officer
out there and they wouldn't have been able to
do what these K-9's did in a fraction of the
time. S-1 tended to be overly mouthy with the
Po Po but not with the dogs or handlers. And
no, nobody got bit. It was merely a show of
presence. Plus, we were bored and needed some
entertainment.

129.

You just never knew what you were going
to get with a 911 call. The dispatcher would
try to make it as accurate as possible, but
they could only go with the information they
received themselves.

One night, some scout car Officers
received a call for the Unknown Complaint in a
building at 10th and N St NW. Well, that could
certainly be open for interpretation. My
curiosity was piqued so I decided to ride over
and check it out for myself.

When we all entered a small apartment
at the location, it became instantly apparent
that there were two dead bodies lying on the
living room floor. Nobody else was on the
premises to give us any information so we
looked around to gather any clues. There
wasn't any blood or signs of a violent
confrontation. No obvious bullet holes, stab
wounds or the like. We would have thought it
might have been natural causes except there
were two bodies. Only an autopsy would reveal
the true cause of death so Officers called for

Detectives and the Medical Examiner's wagon. And I left and went on my way, not giving it another thought.

The next day, a call came out for the very same address. This time it was dispatched as "Investigate the Unconscious Person." What the hell?!?!

Once again, I hightailed it over there to see what was going on. This time when I entered the same apartment, I saw three deceased bodies. They too, appeared to have died of natural causes but there definitely had to be more to the story.

They were transported to the Medical Examiner's Office where the autopsies were expedited since the situation was so unusual. It turned out that the first two people had died of carbon monoxide poisoning. But since nobody knew that at the time, family members arriving the next day to make funeral arrangements were also overwhelmed by carbon monoxide and died.

The area I worked in was generally so poor, that people were more concerned with putting food on the table than installing a carbon monoxide detector. Five family members lost. Very sad and I never forgot them.

130.

Anyone who was connected to the city from the late 60's to 2014 had a Marion Barry story, and I certainly had mine.

During the summer in the 1980's, 3D had an overtime foot beat detail in one of its drug-infested neighborhoods. I signed up and Chief and I were assigned to the 1400 block of W St NW. The entire Southside of the block contained several five story apartment buildings that were inundated with crime, mostly drug related. The thought was that maybe an Officer walking the area with a Police dog would give the "innocents" a brief reprieve.

It was a really hot day and there was very little shade because the addicts had destroyed the few trees that were left. The whole area was extremely depressing but it was also extremely dangerous, so Officers always had to be on their toes.

Chief and I walked around for awhile, with me trying to look like a Tough Girl. But I knew darn well that if I didn't have Chief by my side, I would have little credibility. It was so hot that Chief and I stood at the corner of 14th and W St catching some shade from a corner liquor store. As we were standing there, I noticed a large Black vehicle approaching us on W St. As it got closer, I noticed the license plate read "DC 1." It was Mayor Marion Barry's friggin' limousine!

The car pulled alongside us and stopped. The automatic rear window went down and there he was. Mayor for Life, Marion Barry himself. He said, "Afternoon Officer. Beautiful Black dog you have there."

Me: "Thank you Sir."

Mayor: "Tell me Officer, what kind of things is he trained to do?"

Me: "Well, he finds lost children, tracks down criminals, that type of thing. And Sir, we recently completed a special class at the Police Academy."

Mayor: "Excellent Officer. And what kind of class would that be?"

in my life. Old, young, even the infirm were on this guy. Some of them were stepping on me to get in on the action. I think I was able to roll my body to the other side of the room to save myself from further injury. When the melee finally ended, S-1 went to the hospital and I had a black eye. Rule of thumb: You don't attack a Police Officer in their own home. I never did find out why he hit me.

132.

Thoroughly searching prisoners was of course, a number one priority. Before they were placed into a transport vehicle, a pat down was supposed to be done by the arresting Officer and again by the transporting Officer(s). Once S-1 entered 3D in handcuffs, the transport Officer should check the back seat of the scout car or wagon. Occasionally, weapons and/or drugs have been known to be found under the seat even then. You can never be too careful.

Unfortunately, I got bit in the ass because of my carelessness. I had to transport a prisoner from 3D to Central Cell Block one night and thought I had properly searched him. I drove to the cellblock downtown, discharged him to the awaiting Officers and went my merry way.

It wasn't long before I got a call from the dispatcher to landline CCB immediately. I knew something bad had happened but I didn't know what. I went to the nearest pay phone and reluctantly dialed their number.

And it wasn't good either. It seemed that my prisoner had been able to secret a razor somewhere on his body and I had missed it. Absolutely no excuses whatsoever. I was actually shaking as they ripped into me over the phone. After that, I didn't care how intrusive I was when I searched someone. This was never going to happen again. Thank God, nobody was injured because of my mistake.

It wasn't that long afterwards I was sent to 16th and S St NW to do a transport for Uniform Secret Service Officers. When I arrived, they had a guy in handcuffs standing on the sidewalk. As I stopped the car, one of the Officers quickly opened the back door and directed his prisoner to get in.

"No, no, no. I need to search him first."

"Oh, he's been searched. We're good."

"No, we're not good until I search him."

That's when I got The Look, which I was quite familiar with. It was the You Stupid Bitch Go Back Behind A Desk Where You Belong look. What they didn't know was that I had enough street time and confidence by then to call them on their shit.

"Ok, if you don't want me to search him, then go find someone else to do your transport cause I ain't doing it."

I then got into the car and before I could pull away, I heard, "Wait, wait. Don't leave."

I got back out of the car and walked over to the Already Searched prisoner. It couldn't have been more than ten seconds before I pulled a buck knife with a six inch blade out of his boot. The look on both of those Officer's faces was one of complete horror and embarrassment, as it should have been. Did either of them apologize? Of course not. I was just the Dumb Bitch who belonged behind a desk.

133

Duke was extremely unhappy in his forced retirement. Every night as I was getting ready for work, he would lay in front of the side door to the carport. And every night I would have to step over him with a heartfelt apology. Chief turned his head away, because it was just too painful to look at Mr. Miserable.

After awhile though, I got an idea that I thought could work. I decided to take Duke with me too. Only he had to remain in the cruiser when there was work to do. Kind of a K-9 ride-along. He wasn't overjoyed with the idea of not being able to participate in the action but that was the best I could do.

I was able to do this for about a year but Duke's hips were starting to go bad, and it was becoming harder for him to get in and out of the cruiser. I always said that when the time came that he couldn't walk, I would have to make the horrendous decision nobody wants to make.

And finally that day came. His hips were continually swaying and he was having more and more trouble walking. Basically, Duke's quality of life had diminished to the point I knew I had to call the office at K-9 and make arrangements to put him down. They told me to bring him in the next morning which I did.

Everyone was very quiet and respectful when I arrived. They had all been through it themselves and knew just what I was feeling. Without asking, someone put on the attack sleeve and gave Duke his last bite.

I then took him into the vet's office and held him in my arms while the Doctor gently put him to sleep.

This was the one and only instance in my career that I openly showed any emotion, because I cried like a baby. I simply didn't care who saw me or what people would think. My heart was broken but I knew I had made the right decision.

He was later cremated at the Medical Examiner's Office and the remains returned to me so I could bury him in my yard. God, I loved that dog!

134.

So now it was just Chief and me.

We got a call one night to respond to an armed robbery at 10th and M St NW. A 3D Officer, Perry Caldwell arrived on the scene just as S-1 was making his getaway on foot. As Perry chased him North on 10th St, the subject turned around and fired a shot in his direction. Luckily he missed and Perry shot back, also missing. Contrary to public perception, it's pretty damn hard to hit a moving target, especially when you're moving too. Your adrenaline is pumping, your breathing is labored and the dark of night all contribute to the difficulty of this type of scenario.

When S-1 reached N St, he turned right into the 900 block of N St. At this point, he jumped off the sidewalk and into someone's front yard. These were all row houses and separating each front walk from the other was a wrought iron decorative fence. The fences were about waist high and approximately every foot or so there was a sharp point, about eight inches high.

For whatever reason, S-1 began vaulting over these fences in his attempt to escape. It would have been a lot easier to have just run down the sidewalk, but I learned early on not to try and figure out the mind of a dumbass criminal.

He got over about half of the antique fences when it happened. As he was about halfway in the air, he tripped and came down hard on the wrought iron point. And that pointy thing completely scalped all the skin off his penis. Kinda like peeling a banana except it was this guy's dick.

Chief and I got there immediately after it occurred and observed all the male Officers cringing and gripping their "packages" to make sure they were still there. The guy was lying there in a pool of blood, apparently in shock.

Then the ambulance arrived and when the EMTs saw S-1's condition, they too started cringing in horror. It was actually kind of funny to see all these Manly Men so severely traumatized. Being the only female on the scene, I had to take charge of the entire situation.

S-1 was transported to Howard Hospital where I guess doctors were able to sew the skin back on. Since he was under arrest, there was a guard detail outside his room but this was one prisoner we had no problems with. Actually, I don't think anyone saw him move the entire time he was there.

It wasn't that long ago that I had the occasion to drive down the 900 block of N St NW. This was at least thirty years after this incident and of course I had to look and see if that fence was still there. And yes, it was, in all its glory.

I never did find out what happened in his court case. After all, he did try to kill a Police Officer. But even if he only got a slap on the wrist, justice was served on that night so long ago.

135.

In 1978, there was a crime that polarized the area so strongly that even today people remember it well.

A fifteen year old Black juvenile named Terrence Johnson, killed two Prince Georges County Maryland Police Officers after being arrested for breaking into vending machines. While being processed at the station, Johnson was able to get the arresting Officer's gun and fatally shoot him. When another Officer, Brian Swart heard the shots, he ran into the room only to be gunned down himself by Terrence Johnson.

The case became a media sensation and opinions were strongly based along racial lines. Many in the Black community thought that Johnson had been brutally beaten by White Officers and was just protecting himself. The White community for the most part, felt he was nothing more than a cold-blooded cop killer.

Emotions ran high on this one but if anything good came out of a really bad situation, it was that law enforcement had to take a look at the practice of Police taking their weapons into the cellblock area.

I don't know if the rules changed everywhere, but DC immediately put a ban on it and that was a good thing.

But of course, there's always an exception to every rule. And of course my sorry behind had to be right in the middle of it.

I had made an arrest and was processing my prisoner in the 3D cellblock. During that time, my weapon was safely secured in another part of the precinct. As I was standing with my back to the entrance of the booking area, another Officer walked in with his prisoner. He placed him in a small room to the right, and apparently realized at that time he was still carrying his revolver at his side.

Now, I completely missed all of this since my back was turned. But then, out of nowhere came a gunshot! The whole Terrence Johnson scenario went through my mind and I just knew that a prisoner somewhere behind me had just shot a Police Officer. I also knew that I was unarmed and quite possibly, when I turned around I would be shot too. What a choice! Did I want to be shot in the front or the back? What I really wanted to do was wake up from this bad dream, but that wasn't going to happen so I slowly turned around.

And what I saw, pleasantly surprised me. I hadn't been in danger at all (tell that to my blood pressure).

This wasn't a Terrence Johnson cellblock recreation. The rookie Officer standing in the small room to the right had just shot himself in the foot.

Now how the hell did that happen? Officer Dumbbell decided to take his gun out of the holster for whatever reason, and somehow lost his grip. He made a wild grab so as to not drop his revolver, and in the process shot said foot with said gun.

I got on the radio immediately and advised the dispatcher to send an ambulance to 3D. I knew that anyone monitoring the frequency would instantly wonder what in the hell had happened at the Third District station. But I wasn't going to put any details over the air and told the dispatcher I would be calling landline.

Naturally there was no first aid kit to be found anywhere, so we made do with toilet paper to try and stop the bleeding until the ambulance arrived.

The Officer's prisoner was huddled in the corner crying, "I didn't do it. I didn't do it." There was no doubt this was a big Oh Shit moment for him and he would be blamed for shooting his arresting Officer. But there was never any question about what really happened and once the Officer healed from his injury, I'm sure he had a date with the Trial Board.

As a sidebar, Terrence Johnson served nearly seventeen years for his crime and was finishing his second year of law school when he was released back into society.

In 1995, he and his brother robbed a bank in Maryland at gunpoint and when Johnson was cornered by Police, he turned the gun on himself and committed suicide. He had fooled a lot of people into thinking he had changed but in the end he was nothing but a punk, thug and cop killer after all.

Rest in peace Officer Albert (Rusty) Claggett IV, age twenty-six and Officer James Brian Swart, age twenty-five.

End of Watch: June 26, 1978

136

I was in roll call one night minding my own business, when a cellblock Officer entered the room and signaled for me to come with him. Oh great! Now what?

It seemed that there was an irate female prisoner back in a cell who was supposed to be transported to CCB. The Officers were ready to go but when they went to retrieve her, she had taken off all her clothes and was refusing to get dressed. Was I the only female working in the entire Third District at the time? Apparently so, since they came and pulled me out of roll call.

My job, should I decide to take it was to make this prisoner get dressed and ready to go. Yeah right, like I had a choice. As a rule, CCB does not accept naked prisoners. Especially, naked female prisoners.

I knew this was not going to end well for one of us, but there was nothing I could do but try and handle the situation the best way I could.

In general, my theory was that the person I was dealing with set the tone with whatever situation we were in. If they were cooperative and civil, then I was going to be cooperative and civil (usually, anyway). But if they were a jerk, then I was going to be a bigger jerk. My Social Worker mentality had gone out the window years ago.

The cellblock Officer pointed toward S-1's cell and wished me good luck. That, in itself was an ominous sign of what was to come.

I walked in front of the cell door and observed a Black female about my age, defiantly standing in front of me with her hands on her hips. And yes, she was 100%, naked.

I tried to start a general, non-confrontational dialogue to get more of a feel of her intentions. I got about halfway through my first sentence when she angrily interrupted with a heartfelt, "Fuck you, Motherfuckin' Honky!"

Well, so much for the non-confrontational dialogue. I then told her if she didn't get fucking dressed, I was going to kick her fucking ass. When did they teach us that in the Academy?!?!

She dared me to come into her cell so she could immediately kick MY fucking ass. The line had been drawn in the sand so to speak, and I knew then it was time to "get down."

I opened the door and as I entered her cell she instantly spit in my face. Remember, this was during the time when AIDS was an epidemic and her flinging bodily fluids in my face did not sit well with me at all.

I went into crazed cage fighter mode, and it didn't take long before she was fully dressed and addressing me as Ma'am and Officer. I really don't recall a lot of the details other than I wasn't going to get AIDS from this stinking Bitch.

After she left 3D to be transported to Central Cell Block, I must have washed my face for ten full minutes. The paranoia among all of us was real and there was more than one Police Officer in the United States who contracted the AIDS virus on the street. Were we ever provided protective gloves or masks at any time? No, never.

137

Every evening as I was getting ready to go to work, I would try to prepare myself mentally as I was putting on my uniform and equipment. Without trying to sound overly dramatic, you really had to put yourself into a warrior frame of mind. Complacency has been the undoing of many a fine Officer. And even then, doing everything right can still lead to serious consequences.

Just ask Shirley Gibson. Her son, DC Police Officer Brian T. Gibson was doing nothing more than sitting at a red light, in full uniform in a marked cruiser at about 0300 hours. An irate man who had just been ejected from a nearby club at Georgia and Missouri Ave NW, decided to take his anger out on Brian and assassinated him on the spot. This occurred on February 5, 1997. Ever since then, Mrs. Gibson and her family have put out a huge holiday spread in December in their Southeast home. Any and all law enforcement Officers are invited as a way to honor Brian's memory. It has gotten so big that the Police Academy sends it's recruit's there to assist.

So as I got myself ready to leave for the Third District and into God knows what, I frequently heard a voice coming from Mike's front bedroom window. He would be looking out at the driveway and when he would see me approaching my truck with Chief in tow, he would either call out, "Mommy, don't get killed tonight" or "Mommy, I hope you don't get shot." Well, so much for warrior mode. Sometimes it took the entire thirty minute drive to 3D to recompose myself.

Then when I returned in the morning,
Mike would greet me with, "Mommy, you're
alive!" No wonder I drank so friggin' much.

138.

A light moment that occurred amidst all
the insanity actually happened to Frank.
He got a call to respond to a club over on
Connecticut Ave for a Disorderly. That was
always such an open ended call, you never knew
what you were going to get into. He knew that
whatever it was, it would somehow be alcohol
related.
    When he arrived and went inside, he was
greeted by the manager who told him he was
having a problem with the patrons.
It seemed there had been some kind of stripper
beauty contest and all the customers got to
vote for their favorite by applauding for each
one.
    The Judge held his hand over each
contestant, listening to the level of applause
coming from the bar patrons. He then made his
decision and when he announced the winner to
the crowd, they went into a drunken frenzy.
Some of them were infuriated with the results
and some of them were happy. So, of course
that's when the fist fights started.
    When Frank got there, the place was
about to explode because now word was
spreading that the Judge was having sex with
the winner, and the whole thing was rigged.
    I have to hand it to Frank because he
immediately came up with the perfect solution.
He pushed his way up to the stage and grabbed
the mic. The bleary eyed crowd looked at him
with confusion until he began to talk.

He told them that he thought he had a
great way to solve this serious dilemma and if
they were agreeable, he would give it a try.
Serious confusion, this time.

How about if he, a duly sworn Officer
of the Law conducted a do over on the voting
and they would have to accept his judgement
without further incident?

And that's exactly what he did. He
stood behind each stripper with his hand over
her head, calculating the volume of applause
so he could make an informed decision.

When he announced the winner, everyone
agreed it was fair and square and a raucous
cheer went up for the stripper and the duly
sworn Officer of the Law, Frank R.
Weinsheimer. As Frank was leaving, the manager
happily pumped his hand and promised him free
drinks and food for the rest of his life.
But he merely returned to his scout car and
keyed the radio mic with his disposition,
"10-8. No report."

139.

Bigfoot/Dylan and I/Chief were still
doing a lot of building searches all over the
Third District. Each one had to be dealt with
as if the perpetrator(s) were still inside
waiting to do us bodily harm. You just never
knew.

We got a call one night for a burglary
at a liquor store at 12th and U St NW. S-1 had
broken in through the roof to gain access.
Unfortunately for him, he had miscalculated
and actually broke through the roof of the
vacant building next door. Well, that
certainly must have been a bummer! In an
effort to correct his error, he then broke a

large hole in the adjoining wall to get inside the liquor store.

When we arrived on the scene, we took both Dylan and Chief out of the cruiser and entered the vacant structure to assess the situation. There was the big hole in the brick wall and on the other side was the interior of the liquor store.

We decided we were going to put the dogs inside to sweep the premises. But directly across the middle of the hole was some kind of empty shelf. We could have gone underneath it, but Bigfoot thought it would be easier if he just gave it a big old kick with his notorious Big Foot. And that is exactly what he did.

What we didn't know was that this particular shelf was the key to holding up all the rest of the shelves. And when Bigfoot let loose with his size 13, every single bottle-laden shelf in the whole store came tumbling down.

Before we could react, a tidal wave of broken glass and alcohol came pouring out the hole and onto all four of us. The dogs were completely saturated with a mixture of every kind of booze possible. And Foot and I didn't get off much better. Our uniforms were soaked, our equipment was soaked and we absolutely reeked of alcohol. The only good thing was that nobody was injured by the flying glass.

Then, the K-9 cruiser was covered in booze when we got inside to return to the station to try and repair the damage. But it was no use. The station had no working showers and neither one of us had a clean, dry uniform. Plus, both dogs were eying us with that WTF look.

It was time to surrender and go home.
3D Officers would just have to call a handler
from another District if they needed a dog.

140.

Another part of the job was assisting
with raids. The most common offenses involved
drugs, alcohol, prostitution and gambling. But
it could also be something far more serious.
When we'd get the call to assist, we would
never know the circumstances until we arrived.
If it involved the illegal sale of alcohol,
the suspects were usually a bunch of old Black
men trying to make a few bucks selling bottles
of untaxed Richard's Wild Irish Rose. For the
most part, not a lot of potential for danger
but you could still never let your guard down.
Any time there was going to be a raid, the
largest Officer or Detective would bring along
what was fondly referred to as "the key." This
was a heavy Black metal round cylinder, about
four feet long with a handle for a better
grip. In other words, it was a battering ram
used to forcefully enter doors in a timely
manner.
    It usually went like this, "Po-leese!
We have a warrant! Open up!"
    Then, the briefest of pauses before the
thunder of "the key" took the door down so
that Officers could quickly enter and confine
the occupants before they could destroy the
evidence or escape.
    When I was still new and untested, they
would stick me in the rear of the premises in
case anyone tried to leave out back. It was
not an unimportant assignment, but in the
excitement of the raid itself nobody would
remember to tell me when the situation inside

was under control. I sometimes would stand outside for what seemed like forever, trying to ascertain what was going on. And by standing outside, I might have been in some rat-infested alley or backyard. Or in a rain storm, snow storm, whatever. During that time period and in that area, everything was pretty dirty and neglected. It was kind of like people had just given up and I couldn't really blame them.

One of the most ingenious, illegal ideas came about in the mid-80s when someone decided they were going to open a full service gambling casino in their home. And how were they going to get the word out about their new business venture, come one come all?

They did what any enterprising entrepreneur would do. They printed advertising flyers and placed them under every windshield wiper blade within a five block radius. Blackjack, roulette wheels, slot machines and poker. Fully stocked cash bar and restaurant. Scantily clad girls at your beck and call. There would be a special Grand Opening with fabulous prizes awarded to the first twenty five customers.

It took less than a day for one of these flyers to reach the 3D Vice office. They did all the appropriate paperwork for the warrant and when it came time to raid the premises, I happened to be in the hallway of the station as they were leaving to conduct the raid.

"Hey, do you need a female Officer to go along with you, just in case?" I was curious to see this make-shift casino, so I was glad when they told me I could tag along in the event any women needed to be searched.

The place we were going to was in a row
house in the middle of the 1400 block of Q St,
NW. The front door was not locked, so "the
key" was left in the cruiser.

Inside, were all the accouterments
necessary for a full-on gambling
establishment. In the kitchen was all this
really tempting food, just ready to be sold to
hungry customers. Okay, I'll confess to
filling a small plate.

Everything was seized as evidence, the
occupants were placed under arrest and after I
finished eating I searched the scantily clad
women. I doubt if anyone did any jail time and
these guys lost a lot of money. But I always
admired them for their ingenuity. They
actually thought they were going to get away
with this. Extra credit for the commercially
printed flyers.

141.

As with Duke, I competed regionally
with Chief in the United States Police Canine
Association Dog Trials. Although we never took
top honors, Chief did pretty well and won
several trophies.

I had also become interested in
competing in the National Dog Trials, so I
made sure we qualified locally so we could go
on to the Big Show. It was 1985 and the
competition was being held in Detroit,
Michigan. There were five other DC Officers
interested in competing so we wrote up a
request asking for leave to attend, marked
cruisers to drive out there and a credit card
for gas. We never figured the Higher-Ups would
allocate us anything but lo and behold, we
were granted every wish on the list.

When September of '85 came along, we loaded up the cruisers and a couple of POV's and headed West to Detroit. Frank and two other spouses joined us as a show of support. Or maybe it was for the partying that would take place when we weren't on the field.

This was during the time when it seemed like everyone had a CB radio in their vehicles. We did too. Not only to communicate between our cars, but to listen to all the chatter going on about those DC Police cruisers that were a bit out of their jurisdiction.

The truckers, in particular had great discussions about why we were on the Pennsylvania Turnpike.

"What the hell are they doing here?"

"I dunno. They can't write tickets, can they?"

"Fuck em. They can't do shit."

"Are you sure?"

"Well, I don't think they can do shit."

It all made for an entertaining trip out there.

We stayed in a hotel outside of Detroit that was reserved for participants, their families and of course, the dogs. The word was out that the dogs better be kept under control, but they should have been more concerned about the crazy ass handlers.

I knew there was no way Chief and I would win anything but if we placed somewhere in the middle of the pack, I'd be okay. The first day, we drove to a field on the outskirts of Detroit. This was where we'd be doing obedience, agility, box and article searches. I was pretty nervous since I hadn't competed at this level before, but there was no backing out now.

When it came time for Chief to do
obedience, we walked to the starting line
where I placed him in a sitting position next
to my left leg. The grass had been freshly cut
but there was lots of clover among the grass.
I didn't think anything of it and gave Chief
the command to Heel. He stayed directly beside
me as he had been taught and my confidence
built with each step.

Then I ordered him to Sit/Stay, while I
walked about ten yards away from him. I turned
around facing him and gave the command to lay
down by giving him a hand signal. He did this
perfectly and I couldn't have more pleased.
I then gave a hand signal to go from a Down to
a Sit. Chief immediately raised his front legs
and lowered his butt into a Sit. As soon as
his posterior touched the grass, he jumped up
and started screaming in pain. He then began
running all over the field while I just stood
there, totally dumbstruck.

I was brought back to my senses when
one of the Judges loudly said, "Get your dog,
#9. He just sat on a fucking bumble bee!"
All the hours and time I had spent trying to
get to this place and my dog was stung by a
bee in the middle of the National Police Dog
Trials.

When I finally caught him and made sure
he was alright, the Judges let me redo the
obedience phase without any penalty. And as I
recall, Chief took a long, hard look at the
grass before he sat his ass down again.
Needless to say, no trophies that year.

142.

There was a large gay population in the
Dupont Circle area of the Second and Third

District. Several gay bars on P St and Connecticut Ave NW that tended to become quite rowdy, especially around closing time. But probably not any worse than the straight bars. I got a call one night for a naked, White man huddled against a tree in front of the 7-11 at 17th and R St NW.

When I arrived on the scene, he ran over to my cruiser while trying to cover his vital parts. I put him in the front seat and radioed for anyone with a blanket to please respond to my location. Surprisingly, someone answered in the affirmative and came over to assist.

It seemed he had been picked up at one of the gay bars and went over to the other guy's apartment. During the course of this romantic encounter they had a tremendous fight and the man sitting next to me had been physically thrown out, without a stitch of clothing.

He led us back to the apartment where I banged on the door, to no avail. Through the locked door I implored him to merely give us the man's belongings. Nobody was going to jail. Just open the damn door. Well, that was a Big NO. It would have been nice to have requested the services of "the key" but I couldn't justify it in this type of situation

I advised the man to take a cab, go home and sleep it off. One more hurdle though was that no hacker in his right mind was going to pick up a naked drunk, even if he did have a blanket around him. So I had to flag down the cab myself and assure the driver it was alright to transport this man, who had my so-called Seal of Approval.

Back in those days, if you were a gay male Police Officer, you kept it to yourself.

Until DC Officer Bob Almstead came along. Bob was a young, openly gay White Officer who didn't care who knew it. And let me tell you, he was the talk of the whole Department.

He was assigned to the Fourth District so I didn't have much contact with him until one day when I walked into the 3D roll call room for an overtime detail. And there he was, sitting in the front row. The whole room was abuzz, especially among the men.

Bob couldn't help but be aware of all the tittering behind him and all at once he stood up and spun around so he could face his adversaries head on. He purposefully looked everyone in the eye and then said in a forceful voice, "Yes, I'm the gay Officer that you're all talking about. And if anyone has a problem with that, lets take it outside right now!"

There was a stunned silence and all the guys looked away as Bobby stared them down. Not a peep. With a satisfied look, Bob turned back around and sat down.

He went on to have a successful career and after several years with the DC Department, he transferred to become a San Francisco Police Officer. Unfortunately, he was a casualty of the AIDS epidemic and died in the 80's. I made a point of finding his panel on the AIDS quilt when it was exhibited on the National Mall in DC. You were a hell of a man, Officer Almstead.

143.

It seemed like there were some places that were magnets for burglaries. Nothing was off limits for S-1 and some of the ways they gained entry were fairly ingenious (and I use those words loosely). I think I saw just about everything, but a couple of them always stayed with me.

One was in a row house where an older Black couple lived. I don't recall the exact address but it was somewhere on S St, near 9th. They returned home after being gone for a few days and discovered their house had been broken into.

I got the call and when I entered through the front door, I remember having never seen as much destruction as I did that day. Every single thing in that house had been destroyed. Whoever did it must have been inside for hours, just trying to think of something else to vandalize. Every window was broken, every piece of furniture and appliance was totally obliterated. It was one of the most heartbreaking crime scenes I had ever seen and of course, these poor people didn't have insurance to cover the loss. And you know it had to have been somebody familiar with the area that knew the place would be unoccupied for several days.

Third District Detectives responded to investigate further and I left to go on to my next run. I never did find out the final disposition.

Another really destructive burglary took place at Seaton Elementary School, located at 1503 10th St NW. S-1(s) entered the school and also broke everything they could get their hands on. There was so much broken glass throughout the building that school had to be cancelled so the janitorial staff could clean it up. They did thousands of dollars' worth of damage which the District could ill afford to pay.

It's unfortunate that a Police dog didn't find anyone in either one of these premises. The end result would have probably resulted in some souvenir bite marks.

There were a few very obscure, block long streets in 3D. Unless you were very familiar with the area, you wouldn't know they were there. These included Columbia St NW, French St NW, Westminster St NW, Johnson Ave NW, and Kingman Pl NW. One street, the 2000 block of Portner Pl NW, isn't even there anymore because all the homes were torn down and the Reeves Municipal Center was built and put in its place.

A small, block long street behind the Howard Theater was the 1800 block of Wiltberger St NW. It contained mostly old warehouses that had seen better days. But the rents were pretty reasonable and the buildings were mostly used for storage.

In the middle of the block on the East side, was one of the larger warehouses. This was where the street venders from downtown stored their carts every night. In the morning, most of them would restock their carts with food they purchased from the lady that owned the building. Hotdogs, half smokes, chips, drinks, cigarettes and the like.

Unfortunately, her premises started getting broken into on a regular basis. And if it wasn't every night, it was every other night. I called that poor lady in the middle of the night so many times, she was on my speed dial (if they'd had it at the time). She would get out of bed and drive over from Arlington, Virginia to see what the bastards had stolen this time.

It got to be so bad and so frequent that finally plain clothes Officers were planted inside to end the situation once and for all. Everyone knew it was probably juveniles, and ta da, it was. They were caught the very first night the place was staked out. The lady was so grateful, she made a $600 donation to the Boys and Girls Club.

144.

One of the running law enforcement jokes contain the words, "Gee, it sure is quiet tonight." Most Officers I came in contact with would never utter that incendiary phrase.

I think one night when I was riding with Big Foot, I was dumb enough to make that observation. We were driving Eastbound in the 1600 block of L St NW, when I caught something out of the corner of my eye. To my right was a rental car office with a four story parking garage attached to the building. The garage was secured with a large, heavy padlocked gate that was pulled across the entrance toward L St.

As I turned my head in the direction of the garage, I saw a large late model car come crashing through the gate. When the driver saw the Police cruiser right in front of him, he immediately threw the vehicle in reverse and peeled away in an effort to escape.

By the time we entered the garage, we had lost sight of S-1 but we knew he had nowhere to hide. A quick look in the rear view mirror revealed Dylan and Chief brushing and flossing because they both knew it would shortly be their turn to shine. Okay, that wasn't true but they did know something was up that might involve teeth.

We could hear the screeching tires as we made our way from the second landing to the third, and then we were on the top floor. At the far end of the lot was the vehicle in question. Still running, with the driver's side door wide open. Shit, this would be like shooting fish in a barrel.

We got our dogs out of the cruiser and began to search any place we thought somebody could hide. It didn't take long before we realized nobody was up there. Where the hell could he be? Wait a minute! You don't think he jumped over the side, do you? We were on the fourth floor of the garage and if this guy jumped, he'd be dead or seriously injured, wouldn't he?

We both peered over the wall and down into an alley, holding our collective breath. No, there wasn't a body splattered on the concrete. Maybe he was able to crawl away a couple of feet where we couldn't readily see him.

I put the call out over the air and it wasn't long before the area was swarming with Po Po. Every nook and cranny in the area was searched by dogs and Officers and amazingly, we never found a thing. If I fell off the first rung of a step ladder, I'd probably break my neck and this guy jumped off a four story building and walked away. Kind of reminds me of the drunk driver who never seems to get hurt in an accident.

I think that was the last time I ever mentioned how quiet it was on the street.

145.

On the surface, it appeared as though everything was going well in my life.

Mike was doing great over at Mama Ann's house while Frank and I were at work. She was so accommodating with our schedule; we were just so fortunate to have found her. And when he became old enough, we enrolled him at a preschool run by the Salvation Army that also turned out to be a Godsend.

But it was merely a facade. Frank and I were still drinking like there was no tomorrow. Whatever concern I had back in 1980 was long gone. My reasoning was that if you lived my life, you'd drink too. Oh, the rationalizing of the alcoholic. It sounded good at the time but once again it was starting to wear thin. And besides, tomorrow would be the perfect day to quit. What I didn't anticipate was that when 1986 came along, my entire life would be turned upside down.

I was still on the street with Chief and when one of the K-9 cruisers was in the shop, Big Foot and I would ride together. That was always interesting because we were like a bickering married couple for eight hours. It was only because he was such a good cop that I put up with him. He might have said the same about me.

I had the opportunity to do some drug training with Chief that took me out of 3D for a little bit. The dogs become bored very quickly sniffing out drugs so we frequently changed out the hiding spots to try and keep them interested. We got to go on trains at Union Station, busses at the old Greyhound depot, the Kennedy Center and all over National Airport. Anywhere that would be a good place to hide narcotics.

The docents at the Kennedy Center were horrified to see our dogs climbing all around the seats in the Concert Hall. I have to admit I made a quick detour to check out the Presidential box, where a coaster and box of matches may have fallen in my pocket. That particular day was going well until I happened to enter a backstage elevator filled with ballet dancers. All of them put together wouldn't have weighed what I did. And that included the men.

At National Airport (no, it wasn't Reagan yet), the dogs were all over the moving conveyor belts holding luggage that had just come off a plane. Some of the airport employees were freaked out by the dogs and wouldn't come near us, so we had to leave and go to another area.

We were taken to a small building, way back in the middle of nowhere. One of the instructors told us that there were drugs hidden inside and to go in one at a time. When my turn came, I entered the poorly lit premises with Chief and observed a bunch of odd shaped containers. I directed Chief to sniff each one but he wasn't showing much interest. This wasn't good so when I saw that one of them was partially cracked, I hesitantly pushed the top aside and got the surprise of my life. All of these containers had caskets inside. With Dead Bodies! We were being punked for the amusement of the instructors and anyone else in the immediate vicinity. I was just glad to know there were no drugs hidden in the coffins that we may have missed.

146.

Every six weeks, all the K-9 handlers and their dogs had to go over to the Academy

for two days of retraining. It was a good way
for everyone to hone up on their skills and it
looked good in court if you were testifying in
a case. It was also fun to spend time with
handlers from other Police Districts and
Departments that you didn't see very often. As
in other specialized units, we were a pretty
tight knit group that covered each other's
backs. And for the most part, the Officials
had us covered too.

On March 14th of '86, I happened to
have retraining and it was also my thirty-
fifth birthday. When lunch time rolled around,
one of the instructors and a couple of
Officers took me out for a birthday lunch in
Arlington. The subject came up about whether I
had any interest in trying to become the first
female K-9 trainer. The thought had crossed my
mind many times but I had never voiced it out
loud. I felt I was certainly qualified and God
knows, I was starting to get burned out from
working the street. I hesitantly admitted my
interest and was pleasantly surprised at the
positive response I received. I knew I could
do a good job and it would be a great way to
spend the last years of my career on the
Department. Little did I know.....

There were no current openings though
so I had to bide my time and return to the
street. It seemed that when things were
relatively calm in my life, all hell was
breaking loose in Frank's.

One of our friends down the street
asked if he could ride along with Frank on an
evening shift. His name was Hani and he was a
Jordanian-American. Real nice guy whose wife
Mary Ann, happened to be the nurse that
delivered Michael at Fairfax Hospital.
Sometimes this could be a really small town.

The two of them went out together so Hani
could get a taste of what the life of a cop
was like. Frank was a Sergeant in 4D at the
time, so the likelihood of running into
trouble would probably be less. And that was
just like the Officer saying, "It sure is
quiet tonight."

They were doing well until Frank
responded for a fight in front of a Church in
Mt. Pleasant. When he arrived on the scene,
there was a free-for-all involving the Police
and several men. Frank grabbed the closest one
and the two of them began slugging it out.
Eventually, reinforcements arrived and
everyone was arrested and transported to the
Fourth District for processing. Hani certainly
got more than his share of excitement that
night. What nobody knew at the time was that
this was just the beginning of what would
include Internal Affairs, Trial Board and
constant threats to Hani about immediate
deportation. It turned out that Frank had
gotten into a fistfight and arrested one of
Marion Barry's best buds. Let the nightmare
begin.

147.

The man that Frank had the altercation
with immediately made a complaint of Police
brutality through the Mayor's office. It was
then turned over to Internal Affairs, who were
basically instructed to charge Frank and try
his case before a Police Trial Board.

Somewhere in the mix, Hani was
contacted by Internal Affairs for a statement.
He agreed with Frank and the other Officers
involved; that S-1 had attacked them and they
were only trying to effect an arrest using the

minimum amount of necessary force. I know. I know. That's a mouthful, but almost anyone in law enforcement can recite it verbatim. The Detectives at Internal Affairs were not pleased with his response and it was at this point things got really ugly.

Hani began getting phone calls at all hours threatening him with deportation if he didn't tell the truth. After these threats, he would run down to our house in near hysteria. He was paralyzed with fear even though he had become an American citizen several years before. What they were doing to this poor man was totally illegal but that didn't calm his fears.

Frank was freaking out too because he knew that even though he had done no wrong, the wrath of Marion Barry and his cohorts was going to bite him in the ass. This reminded me of the Sparkle incident years ago when Frank was a basket case for almost a year, until the Trial Board finally exonerated him. This was going to be a long, hard road for all of us. I did what I could to be supportive but I was about to become involved in my own shit. My Own Shit, Part 1, that is.

148.

Sometimes when another District was shorthanded, we would be called to assist them. One night I was dispatched to an office building in the 1900 block of I St NW, which was located in the Second District. Officer Donald Levering and his K-9 dog, Sarge, needed help in searching a building which was about six stories high. Officers on the scene found the point of entry and one of them thought they heard a noise coming from inside. When it was determined that all the custodial staff had already left for the night, we decided to put Sarge and Chief inside to take a look around.

Office buildings are a pain to search because there are so many nooks and crannies. Lots of locked rooms that nobody seemed to have access to. But off to the sixth floor we went. This way we could work methodically down to the ground level where Officers were waiting, in case the suspect attempted to escape.

Sarge and Chief knew each other because Don and I were competition buddies. He was my decoy in the attack work and I was his, so we were familiar with how each other's dog worked. We thoroughly searched each floor without finding anyone. It appeared that S-1 was long gone but there was still one more floor to check.

As we entered the second floor from the stairwell, both dogs immediately perked up. Don and I silently looked at each other, knowing that S-1 was hiding somewhere. It would just be a matter of time before the dogs found him.

At one point, we came to a receptionist's desk where both dogs were really starting to get excited. I walked around to the other side of the desk with Chief to see if anyone was hiding there.

Meanwhile, Sarge had just found the burglar hiding in a corner off to the left. I knew this was going to get real interesting when Sarge was sent to "politely" escort S-1 out of his hiding place and into custody.

Sarge was looking right at the guy and began to move in his direction. But for whatever reason he then turned toward me and made a flying leap over the receptionist's desk in a full on attack. AT ME!

I saw it coming and knew this was going to hurt. Really bad! I also knew I was going to have to feed him some part of my body because he was going to bite the first part of me he could get to. Being that I am right-handed, I quickly threw out my left arm and that's exactly where he got me. And yes, it hurt like hell! As soon as he bit me, he jumped away with a look that was kind of like, "Damn, wrong person. Sorry."

S-1 had given up by that time and was quickly put in handcuffs. Donald was totally horrified by Sarge's error but I was in too much pain to care about anything other than I needed to go to the hospital.

A bunch of stitches were involved and I was off work for several weeks. Later, several Officers asked me why I didn't just shoot Sarge to avoid being injured.

That would never have happened, especially after the Akita shootings in 1980. In this situation, it was just part of the job and I never held it against Sarge. I still have a big old scar on my left arm as a reminder of that night so many years ago.

149.

At this point, I was done with working the street and couldn't wait for the next K-9 trainer's position to come open. I've always compared a street cop to a professional athlete. When you're young and physically fit, you're able to chase and take on all the criminals that are doing their best to hurt and/or escape from you. The street is very seductive and the adrenaline rush is second to

none. I might even call it addictive. But once
you reach your thirties, as with the athlete,
you've lost a step or two and are physically
unable to keep up with all the Hucklebucks
(juveniles) who are just as fast and dangerous
as ever.

I found myself drinking even more and
becoming more cynical and hardened by the day.
My arm hurt from the dog bite and Frank was
still beside himself with the ongoing use of
force investigation and pending Trial Board.
Except for that brief period of light duty
during my pregnancy and Michael's birth, I had
been on the street since I was twenty-two. I
was now thirty-five and I was tired. Something
had to give. And boy, did it!

150.

June 9, 1986. A date that is burned
inside me forever.

I was at home getting dressed for the
midnight shift when my telephone rang. It was
Big Foot calling, which was highly unusual. He
told me he wouldn't be coming into work
because he had been fishing all day and was so
sunburned he could hardly move. I was kind of
disappointed because we would have been
working together since his cruiser was being
repaired. I knew he had to be really hurting
because he never used his sick leave.

I went on to 3D and in the K-9 office I
spent a few minutes talking to the 3 to 11
Officer, Cliff Wilson, who turned the cruiser
over to me.

The first thing a K-9 handler does when
they get on the street is head somewhere so
the dog can take care of business. Since 3D
had so few open spaces, there were very few

places to go, so we all went to the same location. It was a small parking lot with a couple of trees in the 1600 block of Crescent Pl NW.

I pulled out of the 3D parking garage and onto U St, toward 16th St NW. At 16th St, I started to turn left when a man ran into the intersection, wildly waving his arms in an attempt to stop me. I didn't have a choice so I halted right there, traffic be damned. He excitedly told me there was a crazy naked man that had just beaten him up and was making his way up 16th St, destroying everything in his path.

As this was going on, I had been monitoring on the radio a shooting and high speed chase over in the Second District. They had just chased the getaway car into the Kennedy Center parking garage. It was obviously a very tense and dangerous situation and everybody better stay off the air that wasn't involved.

Unless you got into something that trumped an armed robbery, shots fired and high speed chase. Highly unlikely but not impossible. Normally I would have asked for a unit to assist me but I decided to investigate first since the radio was so congested at the time.

I drove up to the building that the man had pointed out, 2120 16th St NW. It was an apartment building at the corner of 16th and Florida Ave, with a circular driveway that I pulled into.

As I came to a stop at the top of the driveway, I observed a young Black male standing by the front door. He was naked as a Jaybird and had ripped the the security phone receiver off the wall which he was banging as hard as he could against the glass front door.

I knew immediately I was going to be in way over my head if I didn't get some assistance. I put my hand on the radio mic and as I did, the young man dropped the phone and ran over to my open cruiser window. He had a wild look on his face and I think I said something like, "What in the hell is wrong with you?" I was hoping to buy enough time to radio for backup but it was simply too late for that.

A split second after I spoke to him, he dove through the open window of my cruiser, knocking me onto the passenger seat. I was completely taken by surprise but instinct took over and I was able to push him as hard as I could off of me.

Unfortunately and without hesitation, he attacked me again. But this time he decided to try and get my service revolver, which luckily was laying underneath me. During this round, he was making guttural, animal like noises as he systematically tore my uniform shirt from my body in an effort to undo my Sam Browne belt which held my holstered gun.

151.

I was able to push him off me again but by this time I was losing strength, since he outweighed me by about fifty pounds.

He came back in for the third time and I knew I was running out of options. His focus this time was not in ascertaining my weapon but in strangling me to death. As he put his hands around my throat, I did the only thing I could to end this nightmare. I pushed him with whatever remaining strength I had, and as I

did I was able to swing my right hand, that
now held my service revolver in his direction.

He never had another opportunity to
assault me because I fired two rounds at
almost pointblank range. I didn't actually
know if I had shot him or not until I looked
out my window. And there he was, sprawled out
on his back not moving.

I knew I had to advise the dispatcher
of my situation so I picked up the mic and
said, "593, emergency!" The Second District
was still caught up with their robbery but the
dispatcher, Officer Mike Beutel knew that it
had to be something serious if I broke in with
my call for help. He immediately turned his
attention to me so I was able to report that I
was involved in a shooting, the location,
request for an ambulance and additional
Officers. Donald heard my transmission and
drove over to my location as fast as he could
to see if he could assist with Chief. He
pulled up behind my cruiser and when I saw him
in the rear view mirror, I jumped out and ran
back to him.

I must have been in some kind of shock
because my first words to him were, "We're
still competing in Atlantic City and I have a
map with the directions. I'll go get it for
you." Before Donald could respond I walked
back to the cruiser, actually stepping over
the body to get the damn map to Atlantic City.
We were supposed to compete there four days
later and I guess this was the only way I
could cope with the horror that had just
occurred. Donald didn't try to reason with me.
He just got Chief out of my cruiser and took
care of him until I was able to go home. After
having been through this once before I knew it
was going to be a very long night.

152

It didn't take long for the cavalry to arrive. I remember watching Officers surrounding the area with yellow crime scene tape to keep out the crowd that was quickly forming, and wondering, "Where the hell did they get all that tape?"

I was standing in the middle of total chaos and really never felt so alone in my life. The front of my uniform shirt was ripped to shreds and even though I had body armor on underneath, I couldn't have felt more vulnerable. Whether it was true or not, it seemed like everyone was avoiding me. Maybe my total lack of outer emotion was keeping them away. I just didn't know.

The Technicians from the Mobile Crime lab came from downtown to process the scene since this event was a bit out of the ordinary. One of the Techs wanted to take a picture of me in my tattered uniform but at this point I felt like a freak show performer since everyone seemed to be staring directly at me. And by this time, the crowd outside the yellow tape had gotten pretty large. Plus, people inside the apartment building itself, were hanging out their windows to get a better look. I told the Technician I didn't have a problem with him taking my picture, but could we go inside the lobby so I could have a little friggin' privacy? He agreed and inside we went where he also swabbed my hands for gunshot residue. I wasn't sure why that was necessary, but I didn't say anything. My goal at the time was to get the hell out of there and away from the insanity. This was still before there was any kind of support offered

to the Officer who had just been involved in a
fatal shooting. We were still in the Suck It
Up era. Since I didn't know any better I
didn't expect, nor did I receive any show of
concern for my well-being. That's just the way
it was in 1986.

I was driven down to Police
Headquarters at 300 Indiana Ave NW, where the
Homicide Division was located so I could make
statements. It was a place I hadn't been in
since 1977 and never imagined I would be in
again. Especially for this reason.

I was placed in the Captain's office
where I waited for quite some time for anyone
to appear. As I sat there by myself, the
horrific event that had occurred earlier
played like an endless loop in my head.

After awhile, a Sergeant and Detective
came in and sat down. The Sergeant was
somebody I had worked with for several years
in 3D, named Al Mayo. He was as Black as they
came, to the point that everyone called him
the Brother Man from the Motherland. To his
face. I had never had any problems with him
but I wasn't real comfortable with him taking
my statement. It briefly crossed my mind to
ask to speak to an attorney but that would
have been viewed very unfavorably. As if I had
something to hide. What would be routine today
just wasn't done in 1986.

So, still half in shock I made a very
detailed statement about the shooting. Sgt.
Mayo's typing skills were deplorable so he
kept telling me to slow down or repeat myself
as he slowly hunted and pecked his way on an
old standard typewriter. Neither he nor the
Detective were very reassuring which also
added to the tension I was feeling. I sure
could have used a drink, but this time there

was no Rita Head there to bartend in the Ladies Room.

I spent the rest of the night in the Captain's office. When my statement was completed, I had to sign additional paperwork informing me my Police powers had been suspended and I was now on Administrative Leave pending the outcome of a Grand Jury. So long, Officer. Your Lieutenant wants you to return to 3D ASAP. It was now about 0700 hours and I was totally exhausted. But my truck with Chief in the back was parked in the 3D garage, so I had no choice but to return there before I went home.

As I entered the K-9 office there were several Officers waiting for me, to get the "inside scoop." Also, my Lieutenant, Alan Drier was there with the first look of compassion that I had seen all night. But that was short-lived when he told me that I was being ordered to respond to the Police and Fire clinic for some kind of evaluation. The clinic was on the other side of the city, it was the height of rush hour and there was no way I was driving over there that morning. I told Lt. Drier of this and he seemed to understand, but he said his hands were tied and that if I did not report there as ordered then disciplinary action would be taken against me. Really?!?! I had just shot and killed somebody seven hours before, I was up all night making statements without one ounce of support and the Department was threatening to discipline me if I didn't report to the clinic immediately. I told Lt. Drier to relay this message verbatim, "Kiss my ass. I'll come in and see you in a day or two. I'm going home." And I left.

153

I drove home in a daze and as soon as I arrived, I went right for the nearest bottle and got rip roaring drunk. I was so intoxicated that I never even made it to my bed. I fell on the bedroom floor, vaguely wondering why the ceiling was spinning before I passed out.

Four days later, I drove up to Atlantic City with Frank, Donald and the rest of the DC K-9 team to compete in the Region 6 Dog Trials. And I actually came in second place. It was as if nothing had happened mere days ago. I think I was so shut down I couldn't comprehend the magnitude of such a life changing event. Nobody was calling to see if I was okay, so I guess I must have been. Of course I was drinking more, but wouldn't anybody under these circumstances? Frank was somewhat supportive but I was keeping my feelings away from him too. Hell, I didn't even know what my feelings were. He was still immersed in his crap with the Department, so it was all he could do to get through that without trying to figure me out. We were both a complete mess.

The ground rules for being on Administrative Leave were that I could not leave my house from 0800 to 1630 hours, Monday through Friday. It was in case the Grand Jury needed me to come downtown during that time period to answer questions. This was still before cell phones, so if I did have to leave home I had to call the Desk Sgt. at 3D and give him a number where I could be reached. I was now a prisoner in my own home until God knew when. In 1977, the Grand Jury met five days after the Q St shooting and I was back on the street the day after. Looking back, that was a totally ludicrous decision on the Department's part, but once again nobody knew any better. Least of all me.

It was unknown when this Grand Jury would decide to review my case so I was basically left hanging until then. If anybody had told me it would take fifty-four WEEKS, I would have never believed it.

154.

My parenting skills were deteriorating because of my increased alcohol use. Luckily, Mama Ann was able to take care of Michael on a daily basis.

That Fourth of July, Donald had a big party at his home in Reston, Virginia. There were lots of cops, illegal fireworks and booze. That was my kind of party so Frank, Michael and I drove over there to be a part of the merriment.

Once we all got sufficiently lubricated, someone brought out the fireworks. I decided all the bottle rockets were mine so I grabbed them and began launching each one in every direction. I was doing fine until I started aiming them closer and closer to the crowd. At one point, my hand slipped and a bottle rocket struck Michael over his eye. He was of course, screaming and crying in pain and when he ran over to me I just brushed him away, telling him he was okay. Frank wasn't in any better shape to handle the situation, so one of the more sober Mothers took charge and did what we were unable to. Was that a wakeup call for either one of us? Nope, not yet.

I spent the rest of the summer hanging out at the community pool with my cooler readily at hand. Since I was there so much, I got to know the teenage lifeguards pretty well. When they discovered that I had alcohol in my cooler, I instantly became the "cool" Mom. Even more so, when I volunteered to buy them whatever they wanted from the ABC store. I mean, how pathetic was that? But I was in no condition to think rationally. I felt I was totally forgotten by the Department, other than one day I would receive a call that the Grand Jury was meeting to decide whether to indict me or not.

Since Chief and I had qualified in Atlantic City to compete in the National Dog Trials in October, I thought that the diversion of traveling to Baton Rouge, Louisiana was a great idea.

Apparently, there had never been an Officer on Administrative Leave that wanted to compete in the Dog Trials. After all, the competitors were required to wear their uniform, which included the badge and gun. None of which I had, since they had both been seized on that awful night. I was told that the Higher Ups in the Canine Association had a meeting and decided it wouldn't be fair to disallow me to compete. So I cobbled together a uniform by borrowing Frank's badge and my off duty weapon.

A team of five DC handlers and their dogs was put together and we spent the remainder of the summer and part of the Fall, practicing for The Big Show in Baton Rouge. This year, the Department wouldn't give us any money or cruisers, so Frank made it his mission to fly everyone down there as inexpensively as possible. The sticking point was that we refused to allow the dogs to be anywhere on the plane except by our sides, in the passenger compartment.

Frank made countless phone calls to find an airline that would accommodate us. Uncrated and unmuzzled. And the only airline among the bunch was Delta, which had to seek approval from its corporate office in Atlanta.

155.

The day finally came to fly to Baton Rouge and we all met in the concourse of Dulles airport. I wish I could deny it but there's photographic evidence that I arrived wearing pink short shorts. A "great" representative of the DC Metropolitan Police Department, don't ya think?

We were told to stay back while the plane was loaded and then we boarded the People Mover, which we had all to ourselves. We later found out that before our actual boarding, the Delta pilot informed the passengers that five fully trained DC Police K-9s were about to come onto the plane. He also advised everyone not to make any sudden moves or pet the dogs during the duration of the flight.

And then, there we were. Some of the dogs had their own seats and the others sat on the floor in front of us. One dog even got to sit in first class with his handler. The passengers loved us and many took movies with their video cameras. The flight attendants pretty much ignored the passengers so they could give us all their attention. Free drinks and free food for all (except the dogs, who we were afraid might get sick). And I must add, they all behaved perfectly.

Being that there were no nonstop flights to Baton Rouge, we had to first fly into Dallas. Upon landing, the copilot insisted on leading us to the only available trees for the dogs. Then when it was time to reboard, we went through the routine once again without incident.

Arriving at Baton Rouge, we picked up rental cars and drove toward the host hotel. Frank and I stopped at a grocery store and saw something we'd never seen before. Along with the beer and wine was Hard Liquor! In a friggin' grocery store! So we immediately traded our wimpy hand basket for the largest cart we could find. And we filled that Bad Boy up! This was going to be a great week! Yeah, right.

I think the competition began the next day so we had a little time to practice on the actual fields which were located in a suburb of Baton Rouge. I knew right away that I was off my game, but I thought maybe it was due to the long trip we had just been on. Everybody else seemed okay, so I kept my concerns to myself.

Qualifying for the National Dog Trails while on Administrative Leave after the shooting. I think the badge came from a Cracker Jack box.

Leaving for Baton Rouge at Dulles, representing the Department in my pink hot pants!!!

Competing in Baton Rouge with Chief in 1986

DC Police K-9 Team in Baton Rouge

Chief and I in Baton Rouge
I have no Police Powers, I'm waiting for a
Grand Jury to meet, and in 10 days I will be
in Rehab back in DC.

156.

I was certain I would never take any
trophies, which was alright with me. I just
didn't want to embarrass myself or the team.
The initial part of the competition involved
just the Officer and his/her dog. Then you
came to the attack phase where the decoy was
added to the mix. The mission of the decoy is
to do whatever possible to make the dog look
good. The decoy knows the dog almost as well
as its handler does. They know exactly where
the dog likes to go for the hit and they are
able to make any split second adjustments to
be sure the bite itself is full mouth and
without any hesitation.
It used to be that some decoys would
always fall on the ground, as if to show the
Judges that the dog was so powerful they were

able to knock somebody down. This looks pretty dramatic but then it seemed that all the decoys were taking a dive for the dog so the Judges told everyone to cut it out. There are times of course, that a dog is genuinely able to take down a decoy but the Judges have become savvy enough to be able to determine what is real and what is showboating.

Even though I hated running from the dogs, it really was an honor that Donald had enough faith in me that I was chosen to be his decoy for Sarge. Yes, the same Sarge that mauled me six months prior in the office building on I St. As far as I was concerned, that was ancient history. And this time I would be wearing a protective sleeve.

As a team, DC was in the middle of the pack of competitors. There were some Departments that did nothing but train their dogs all day, every day. They did absolutely no actual Police work with their K-9's which put everyone else at a disadvantage. Every dog on our team though was a working patrol dog and we had to fit training in when we could. It wasn't fair but that was the way it was.

There were several nights that Donald and I would be down on the National Mall at 0300 hours, doing obedience with Chief and Sarge. We'd also be monitoring the radio for calls which would require us to haul ass back to our respective Districts. Looking back, I wouldn't have had it any other way.

When it came time for me to run from Sarge in Baton Rouge, I was still off my game. I didn't do as well as I should have and I really kept Donald and Sarge from earning all the points they deserved. The rest of the team was very unhappy with me, and rightly so. We had worked so hard, for so long and I was letting everyone down. Pickling my brain with alcohol every minute I was off the field couldn't possibly be a factor, could it?

157

The week in Baton Rouge turned out to be a total drag. By the time we left, the rest of the team was barely speaking to me. I knew that when I returned home there had to be some kind of change. Frank was a nervous wreck about the impending Trial Board and I still hadn't received any word from the Grand Jury.

Shortly after I got home, I got a phone call from a woman who identified herself as Beverly Anderson. She told me she was working on her Master's degree at George Mason University and was doing research on female Police Officers who had been involved in fatal shootings. To this day, I don't know how she got my name and number, but I was very brusque and told her I was not interested in speaking with her.

A day or two later, she called again, making the same request. Ballsy broad, but I was having none of it.

But on her fourth attempt, for whatever reason I said yes. Was it to get her off my back, I don't remember. She lived in Springfield, Virginia so we set up a time for me to go over to her house.

On the appointed day, I drove to the address she gave me and when she answered the door, I was in for a surprise. The first thing I thought was, she looked like a friggin' Barbie doll. Perfect hair, perfect figure, and perfect make up. Reminded me of a 1986 version of June Cleaver. Really?! Like I'm going to open up to this lady? She invited me inside and for the next couple of hours, I spilled my guts like I never had done before.

As I was finishing, she asked me if there was anything else I would like to add. Before I could stop myself, the words, "I can't stop drinking" came out of my mouth. Damn, where did that come from?

158.

The next surprise was that she then informed me she worked at a substance abuse rehab in downtown DC, and could get me in immediately. I really didn't understand what she was telling me, but I drove home and told Frank I would be out of commission for the next twenty-eight days.

I was uncertain about what was going to happen there, but I knew it involved not drinking. So I did what every good alcoholic would do: I tried to drink as much as I could before that fateful day came around.

A lot of rehabs have real positive sounding names, but no, I had to go to Psychiatric Institute. Not only was I a drunk but I was also crazy. Great combination. The facility was located on the ninth floor of an office building on K St NW, near George Washington Hospital.

I felt like the biggest loser in the world. On visiting days Frank brought Michael and Chief, which was a mixed blessing. It was wonderful to see them but it just reinforced what a terrible person I was.

It wasn't long though before I realized I was in the right place. The information I was hearing was beginning to make sense and after awhile I became an avid student of the recovery process. The twenty-eight days flew by and when it was time to leave, I was scared and excited at the same time.

It was the week before Thanksgiving but as soon as I returned home, I hit the ground running. A wonderful woman named Ann, who had been at PI three months before, took me under her wing and introduced me to a support group that met every day. Since I was still on Administrative Leave, I had the luxury of attending meetings as often as I wanted.

Fall turned into winter and then spring, and still the Grand Jury hadn't met. Periodically, I would receive phone calls telling me they would be convening the next day. So I would get all psyched up but inevitably there would be a continuance. It caused such a roller coaster of emotions. The old me would have been drinking nonstop, but the women in my support group were so helpful and encouraging, I didn't want to let them down. Also, I thought I would get in trouble if I drank. In trouble with who, I had no idea. But I didn't take that drink.

The Police Department was totally out of touch with me. Nobody called to ask how I was doing. I was really out on my own, but I was doing the best I could.

159.

One year and two weeks after the shooting, I got a call that the Grand Jury was actually going to meet. For real!

I was pretty nervous but when the following day came, I did what any person with a potential indictment hanging over their head would do. I went to the Kings Ridge community pool and this time my cooler was filled with juice and soda.

About 3:30 pm, a lifeguard paged me over the loudspeaker that I had a phone call. Over the din of the splashing and kids yelling, I heard an Assistant US Attorney inform me that I had just been acquitted.

I had been waiting so long for this day and this decision, yet I just felt completely numb. Of course it was good news, but now what? Was the Department going to throw me back on the street like they did in 1977? I knew there was no way I could ever do that again but I had no idea what to expect.

Periodically, I had to make an appearance at the Police and Fire clinic in Southwest DC. I had to sit in the hallway, among all the armed Officers who took great pride in sharing the most violent and outrageous War stories among themselves. Normally, this would not have bothered me but I was still so traumatized, I begged the Officials at the clinic not to make me go there anymore. I'm sure they thought I was trying to get one over on them because the only answer I got was an emphatic No. A couple of times I had a total melt down from the stress, but the answer was always the same. Nobody still seemed to "get it."

160.

During all this endless waiting, I received a phone call from a Doctor at the Police and Fire clinic. He informed me he was making a recommendation to the DC Retirement Board that I retire on disability for Post-Traumatic Stress Disorder. I had never even heard of PTSD so I went to the library to find out what in the hell it was. After doing a bit of research I determined that yup, that's what

I had. Nobody told me anything about what to do about it, but that wasn't anything new. It kinda reminded me of a Doctor saying you have cancer and then turning around and leaving the room. What was I supposed to do with that information?

So I sat and waited for the Retirement Board to meet. I was told that there were only a certain number of disability slots available per year and that 1987 had already met its allotment. The next time the Board was going to meet would be in February of 1988, and my name and recommendation would be put before them then. Well, that was another eight months after the acquittal but there was nothing else I could do but continue to wait.

During this time, I started to get phone calls from another K-9 handler, Perry Rhames. He was supposed to be going into the next K-9 class to train a new dog but he got wind that I might be retiring. He decided that rather than go through the fifteen weeks of training, I should just give him my beloved Chief. I told him there was no way I was giving up my dog, but he was insistent and called me countless times. Each time he reminded me that Chief actually belonged to the Department and not me. Thanks for the reminder, Perry. I was so stressed out anyway, I didn't need this additional shit.

I got so fed up, that one day I drove over to the K-9 office by the Academy and confronted the Sergeant. He was normally a total jerk but I think my crazed look may have contributed to what he said so "eloquently."

"Goddamnit, you can keep the fucking dog. Sign these papers and get the hell out of here because I'm sick of hearing about it."

Some people get a gold watch when they retire. It looked like I was getting a Black German Shepherd, thank you very much.

161.

I received word on February 12th, 1988 that I was to report to the DC Retirement Board so they could decide what to do with me. Frank and I drove downtown to G St NW and were met outside the hearing room by the Police Clinic Doctor who would be testifying on my behalf. My presence was required in case the Board wanted to question me.

After sitting awhile in the waiting room, the Doctor came out and told me that my disability retirement had been approved but that the Board wanted to see me before I left. I couldn't imagine what they wanted as I cautiously entered the room, ready for anything.

One of the Board members told me that on behalf of the group, she wanted to wish me good luck and would I please go around the table and shake everyone's hand? Oh sure, whatever. And that's what I did as each person said a kind word or two. When I was able to make my way back to the waiting room, the Doctor told me he had never seen that happen before. Ohhh, I was just sooo special.

I was handed a piece of paper containing a list of all the Departmental agencies that had to sign off on me before I was officially retired. The first was Clothing and Equipment where I had to return all my uniforms and such. There was just so much of it, that over the years I had lost or misplaced some of it. That was duly noted by the Officer, who had probably never spent more than thirty seconds on the street. He was more than happy to remind me I would be billed for every missing or damaged article.

I also had to visit the Mobile Crime office for whatever reason, I didn't know. But it was on the list. The Sergeant there was someone I used to work for in 3D. A very nice man who always had his Officer's backs. We spoke for a few minutes and then he told me he had the evidence folder containing the autopsy photos of the man I shot and killed. I know to this day he meant no malice but he then asked me if I wanted to see them. I should have immediately declined but the old defenses took over and I replied, "Oh, sure."

His name had been Mustapha Muhammad Damulak but I had always referred to him as Omar. Still do, in fact. When the Sergeant opened the folder, I thought I was going to pass out. There he was lying on the Medical Examiner's table, cut wide open from stem to stern. The photographs were in color which added to the horror of what I was viewing. Outwardly, I guess I was able to pass myself off as okay. But inside, I could barely breathe. I was just praying I wouldn't keel over, and of course I didn't. I will admit though that even today, those photos still haunt me. At that point, I really had nothing to prove. I just didn't know it.

My last stop was to return to the Third District and report to Desk Sergeant Nicken's office. This was where I had to relinquish my badge for the final time. I quickly gave it to him and then got the hell out of there. No goodbyes, no nothing. It really was one of the lowest points in my life. I was thirty-six years old, with untreated PTSD and without a clue as to what I was supposed to do next.

To add insult to injury, I received a voicemail a couple of weeks later from an Officer who informed me that since I hadn't filled out forms X, Y and Z in a timely fashion, all my health benefits had been cancelled. Goodbye and have a nice day. This was information that was supposed to be given every retiring DC employee. But I guess I had slipped through the cracks, so once again I had to take up battle to have my benefits reinstated. Not easy, but I was able to get it done.

162.

Despite everything, I remained sober and Frank quit drinking too. But the strain on our marriage was almost at the breaking point. His incident with Marion Barry's buddy ended with him receiving a reprimand and fine. The Internal Affairs Detectives finally left Hani alone but their unrelenting threats irreparably damaged our friendship and we rarely saw him again.

After all those years, Frank was finally able to transfer, going from 4D to Court Liaison. This meant he could now work normal hours with weekends off. Working the street had certainly taken a toll on Frank, so the timing could not have been better. I do have to add that he and I may have had our differences but he was one hell of a street cop.

There were a few requirements I had to fulfill even though I was retired. I had to report to the Police and Fire clinic annually until I reached the age of fifty. I guess they wanted to take a look at their investment but it was pure torture for me. Same macho

Bullshit, same bloody War stories. Some things just never changed. After I recovered days later, I'd write a letter to the Retirement Board pleading with them to allow me to find an alternative that would satisfy them. But the answer was always a resounding No.

If I sought employment, I could only earn up to 80% of what I was receiving on disability. To show proof, I had to annually submit my tax returns until I turned fifty. If you didn't meet these two requirements, I guess they'd put your ass back on the street until eternity. After the age of fifty the decision apparently was that you were so far Over the Hill, there was no hope of getting anything else out of you.

The first two years of retirement, I mainly did nothing but take care of my recovery and try to figure out what I should do next. I spent a lot of time volunteering at Mike's elementary school and ended up giving them so many hours, that eventually I began substitute teaching.

I remember one day, while subbing a fourth grade class, I decided to forgo the teacher's lesson plan and teach the class how to conduct a proper traffic stop. I diagramed the correct way to position the Police cruiser behind the vehicle and how to safely approach the driver's side window. I had chairs set up in the front of the classroom and the students took turns being the cop and S-1.

For a long time afterwards, kids would stop me and report that they had observed a traffic stop and that the Officer was standing directly next to the driver, instead of slightly behind the window. Or he (she) had properly parked their cruiser in such a manner that it protected the Officer from oncoming traffic. I couldn't have been prouder.

163.

Even though I was functioning well on the outside, the untreated PTSD was still kicking my behind. Flashbacks of all the violence would rear its ugly little head and come out in different ways, all bad. Sometimes I would start shaking so badly I'd have to stop whatever I was doing and find a private place until it stopped. Panic attacks were not uncommon, especially in crowds. A sound or a smell could bring me right back to memories of the street. Another word that I didn't know until much later, was hypervigilance. And boy, did that apply to me. I was wearing myself out by constantly being on guard. Checking license plates, suspicious autos and people. Scanning the premises for anything out of the ordinary whenever I was out in public. Sometimes Mike would notice and remind me that I wasn't a cop anymore. But I couldn't stop and I didn't know what to do. I thought that going to sleep at night would give me a brief respite but the nightmares merely exasperated the situation and I was an exhausted wreck in the morning.

I finally did a little research and located a Doctor at Johns Hopkins Hospital in Baltimore who was allegedly an authority on PTSD. After driving up there and spending two hours with him, he declared I was a narcissist and didn't believe my story. I knew that I was not a narcissist but I felt so defeated at that point, I almost gave up completely.

I found a Doctor in Tysons Corner, who was very nice but told me up front that he had no training in PTSD.

I located another Doctor at Georgetown University Hospital who was really old and just wanted to talk about his Grandchildren.

Finally, nine years after the Omar shooting I contacted a female Psychologist, with no expectations other than this would be another disappointment. Little did I know that this would be the beginning of me reclaiming my life.

164.

The work was difficult but the alternative was worse. Fortunately, I was almost nine years away from my last drink so I was able to jump full force into my next step of recovery. Treatment of PTSD was still relatively new but with the help of Dr. Sue Connor and LCSW Nancy Wachtenheim, I was slowly able to regain my life. Even though Frank and I had both stopped drinking, our marriage was not salvageable and we ending up divorcing when Michael was six.

Other than the breakup of my marriage, one of my biggest regrets was that I was never able to become the first female K-9 trainer in the Department. But it just wasn't meant to be and today I'm okay with that.

Besides substitute teaching I delivered flowers, was a school Clinic Aide, school bus driver, and worked at two retirement communities. I enjoyed each job for different reasons and met some amazing people who helped show me that there was more to life than being a cop.

Michael grew up to be a fine young man, currently married with a young daughter, Emily, and one on the way. In 2006, while in the Army Reserve, he was sent to fight in Iraq for a year which was a true test of my recovery. But I'm convinced that I can get through anything without turning to a drink or drug.

Another big test was when he became a Police Officer with the Metro Transit Police Department in Washington DC. I know the apple didn't fall far from the tree but of all the careers he could have chosen, he had to become a friggin' cop.

On his fourth day, he was stabbed in the hand by an irate teenager in Anacostia which is one of the roughest areas in the District. After some stitches at the same hospital where I had received mine so many years before, he went back on the street and is now in Motors, which means he is a motorcycle Officer.

It's kind of a double edged sword because on the one hand, I know exactly what he's going through. But on the other hand, I know exactly what he's going through. At least he doesn't work anywhere near the Third District.

Today, I mostly enjoy hearing the "War stories," and occasionally he even asks me my opinion about something that happened on the street. Back in the day, we were allowed to do our job without a lot of interference and for the most part we had the support of our community and Officials. No, we didn't have the equipment and technology available to law enforcement today but we did the best we could with what we had. Even though they've been in Police cars for years now, I'm still amazed to see computers in the front seating area. Something I could have only dreamed about. And take home cruisers! Those of us in K-9 were promised for years we would be assigned one, but it never happened while I was still there. We received Tech Pay, which meant a few extra bucks were thrown our way to help offset the wear and tear on our POVs (privately owned vehicles).

Frank went on to remarry but died in 2011 of congestive heart failure. His old partner, R.C. White, did indeed rise through the ranks and as of this writing is currently the Police Chief in Denver, Colorado. It meant a lot to us when he flew back East to speak at Frank's funeral in Falls Church, Virginia. I sometimes look back today and ask what, if anything I would change. I'm certainly sorry that I was forced to take two human lives but of everything I was involved in, there is one event that I still have trouble speaking about. And that is having to shoot those two dogs. The whole situation could have been avoided if that man had stepped in, at least try and separate his dogs. Hell, I took a hit from Sarge. He could have done the same but he didn't.

Everything that occurred during my career changed me as a person. And many of these changes were good. I've certainly made many mistakes, but for the most part I'm not afraid to do the hard work that will ultimately pay off in the end. I haven't had a drink since 1986 and have always been active in my recovery, since I can now give back what was so freely given to me. Therapy also helped and my PTSD has been under control now for many years.

When I hit my fifties, I decided to get several tattoos and actually have my Police badge inked over my heart. In 2004, I bought a Harley Davidson Road King and joined the Blue Knights, a law enforcement motorcycle club. I also had to have the super-fast Chevy Camaro that the Po Po loved to stop for excessive speed (thank goodness for FOP license plates). After many years, I even started attending the local K-9 competitions that I had been a part of so long ago. Some of the handlers even asked me for advice, which just made my day.

Recently, I bought an old Chevy camper van and have driven across the country twice with my beloved dogs, Rudy and Calvin. So many people didn't understand why I would want to do that, but why wouldn't I? I'm going to keep doing what I'm doing as long as I am able. Yes, I was young, dumb and thin at twenty-two. But it was a roller coaster ride I wouldn't have missed for the world. I have experienced life in ways that many people have not. Or probably would want to.

I still critique traffic stops, scan my bank for bad guys before I enter, check inspection stickers and license plates and sit facing the front door in restaurants. But now I just laugh about it because I'll be doing this till the day I die. My life today is filled with a lot more good memories than regrets. And that's just the way it should be.

39777847R00189

Made in the USA
Middletown, DE
25 January 2017